ESSEX BOYS

ESSEX BOYS

A TERRIFYING EXPOSÉ OF THE BRITISH DRUGS SCENE

BERNARD O'MAHONEY

MAINSTREAM
PUBLISHING

EDINBURGH AND LONDON

First published in Great Britain in 2000 by
MAINSTREAM PUBLISHING COMPANY (EDINBURGH) LTD
7 Albany Street
Edinburgh EH1 3UG

ISBN 1 84018 285 7

Reprinted 2001, 2003, 2004, 2005

Some of the material in this book was originally published
under the title So This Is Ecstasy?

A catalogue record for this book is available
from the British Library

Typeset in Stone Print
Printed and bound in Great Britain by Cox & Wyman Ltd

Chapter *One*

8 JULY 1986. THE PRISON WARDER UNLOCKED THE DOOR, AND I stepped onto the street. 'See you soon, O'Mahoney. Next time bring a friend,' he said. I turned to answer but the main gate of Stafford Prison slammed behind me.

I'd just finished six months of a twelve-month sentence for wounding with intent. It was no big deal. I'd cut a man with a bottle following an argument in a pub in Staffordshire. I was in my mother's home town and arguing with a friend about village gossip, where people were badmouthing me and my friends. Another man kept getting involved, which made it doubly annoying. I kept telling him to go away, but he persisted in interfering. Eventually I was so angry I hit him across the forehead with a bottle.

Prison didn't agree with me at all. It's not so much the Victorian environment, it's the company you are forced to keep. I was sick of petty rules, petty screws and wannabe movie star gangsters.

It was good to be out. It was two years since I had been free in England. I'd gone to South Africa following the bottling incident, as I'd previously been convicted of the same offence and I knew I would go to prison. I was arrested when I tried to make my way back into the country. But that was history now, and I was thinking all the philosophical shit you have to believe in: a fresh start; new beginnings; no more trouble. Futile, but essential to raise your hopes.

My first port of call was the mandatory appointment with one of my probation officers in Basildon, Essex. When I was convicted, she had been appointed to give me supervision and guidance. She certainly had her work cut out. She had spent twenty-three years of a sheltered life in school and college earning qualifications. But she had skipped the practical side of her subject. The first time we met I explained politely that she couldn't begin to assist me, or understand the world I inhabited. Without much argument, she agreed.

Instead of paying me regular visits in prison, as per regulations, she used to have a day out of the office shopping, and I used to write to her saying what a good and fruitful visit we had enjoyed together. That way she would not have to bother me and she could enjoy an all-expenses-paid day out on the town with her mum.

On the train journey south, I was considering my prospects. I had never been to Basildon before. I had met my girlfriend, Debra, in Johannesburg. She was in South Africa working as a rep for a British hairdressing company and I was out there distancing myself from the constabulary. She lived in Basildon and had helped me secure parole by allowing me to use her address.

There was no romance between us in South Africa. Debra and I were just very good friends. Our first embrace had been in the police cells in Dover where she'd come to meet me as I re-entered the UK. Unfortunately, two detectives had also decided to welcome me home. They took me back to Staffordshire that day and the following morning I was in Crown Court having pleaded guilty to bottling the man in the pub.

Debra had been very loyal to me, visiting me in every dustbin the Home Office had sent me to. We were not Richard and Judy, but we were very happy.

Because of my reluctance to conform, I had been in six prisons in six months. First was Shrewsbury, then Birmingham, which was an allocation place. After that I went to Ranby in Nottinghamshire. It was full of low-intelligence criminals: shoplifters and petty crooks. I was accused of trying to escape from there, which wasn't true. I had only been there six or seven hours when I was put in an isolation unit. Then I was moved to Lincoln, which was full of northern prison officers who thought they were on this earth to persecute the prisoners. I asked to be moved closer to my home town, and they said they'd never move me under any circumstances.

But I worked out a way round that. They have a box for mail, but a lot of cons put notes in there about other prisoners. Another guy and I devised a plan where we would put notes in this box about me, saying O'Mahoney's got a works (a syringe), so a prison officer would search my cell for heroin every morning. We went even further, saying O'Mahoney's selling bad gear and we're going to kill him. The plan worked. The governor decided he didn't want drugs in his prison, and we were moved to Stafford via Birmingham.

My first sight of Basildon new town was Laindon Station and the Alcatraz Estate, so called because of the warren of alleyways and Legoland-type flats it was made up of. I was to ring Debra from the station, but as she said she only lived five minutes away, I thought I would surprise her. Armed with her address I set off. The only person I surprised was myself.

I spent an hour walking round identical streets, hopelessly lost, before I finally found her home. I was very pleased to see Debra. Unfortunately, the Home Office do not allow for such feelings. I had to report to my probation officer within one hour of reaching the town. I've had several probation officers in my life, so I know the ritual. Sit down, smile. 'How are you? How are you feeling? Do you regret the crime? Do you think you'll be in trouble again? Congratulations, Mr O'Mahoney, you've just won your freedom. See you again next month. Goodbye.'

Coming out of prison is a shock to the system. Employers don't want to know you, and the fact that you've been inside carries some stigma. But eventually Debra and I did settle down to what most would consider to be a normal life.

Debra had her own hairdressing business, and I used to commute to London every day to work as a heavy goods vehicle driver. The hours were very, very long. I'd leave my house at quarter to five in the morning and return at seven in the evening. But it kept our heads above water. I didn't really mix with anyone from Basildon. My friends were in south London, where I'd lived before going on the run to South Africa.

In June 1987 Debra and I had our first child, Vinney. We both wanted children, and Vinney brought us a lot of happiness. We lived a pretty uneventful life, really. Vinney took up most of our time, but he was a labour of love rather than a chore.

Debra and I had never got married, but because of society's rather outdated views on children born out of wedlock, I had adopted her surname.

In 1988 this simple exercise of changing my name brought rather surprising results. I had heard of young children and deceased persons being summoned for jury service due to clerical errors, but an ex-prisoner with at least five different reasons for being disqualified did seem rather bizarre. Nevertheless, the thought of me, a habitual criminal, sitting in judgement on others was intriguing. The desire to see for myself what went on on the other side was the major factor in my deciding to go.

I was asked if I had any convictions, and my denial was accepted without any checks being made. Once inside the jury's waiting room, I sat for the entire morning with approximately fifty other potential jurors, the vast majority of them obviously middle-class. The main topic of conversation revolved around bringing back the birch and the need to reinstate national service. A group of middle-aged ladies at an adjoining table talked as if they were already on the point of passing sentence on the as yet unseen defendant. They agreed on suitable punishments for burglars, rapists (quite unprintable), car thieves and vandals. They were not quite so ready to discuss the question of innocence or guilt.

It struck me that by extracting jurors from a group of people of 'good character', we were in fact denying the accused person the chance of a fair trial. Judging by the blinkered views of those I was mixing with at Chelmsford Crown Court, anyone charged with a crime must carry a degree of guilt.

The second thing I learned was that judges' directions are ignored. Jurors *do* discuss their cases with other people, and they *are* influenced by other people's views. In this room of fifty or more people the majority were discussing the cases they were on with jurors from other cases. It was during these conversations that I learned just how easily I could influence these people. Because we did not know each other, nobody wanted to say the wrong thing to upset the other person. For the vast majority of them, it was the first time they had been part of such a sinister and exciting world. They kept their mouths shut and their ears open. They wanted to absorb knowledge from the more experienced and not expose their innocence.

I sat on two rather minor cases. One was a fraud case where a man had relieved a company of some money. The second was a family dispute which had escalated into minor warfare.

After hearing all the evidence, the jurors are ushered into a room and locked in. They select a foreman and then they are supposed to discuss the case and come to an agreed verdict. On both occasions, none of us had met before, other than to exchange pleasantries. We all sat round a big table, and there was nervous sniggering and an uneasy silence. No one wanted to begin talking. I took the initiative and suggested that they elect a foreman.

I knew straight away who they were going to elect. It was an elderly gentleman wearing a regimental badge on his blazer. It signalled doom for the accused man who was sitting in the cells below waiting for us to decide his fate. They started off going down the track of guilt. I learned in the waiting room outside that to be outspoken is to be heard. I attacked the evidence with vigour and before too long I had everyone in the room in agreement.

I've always believed that law and justice are two separate things. Law is man-made, and justice is natural. In the family dispute case a teenager had assaulted an elderly gentleman who lived next door. The gentleman's sons had gathered and gone round to the teenager's house and assaulted the boy and his brothers. They were guilty in law, but it was justice to me. The man in the fraud case had fallen on hard times, and had acquired a bit of money – not a lot – from a very large national company for his family, which to me was fair enough. In the end both cases were found not guilty.

People may say that my actions are the very reason that persons with convictions shouldn't sit on a jury, but I'd argue that most of these cases should not have come to court in the first place, and if there were more people with knowledge of life involved in the judicial system many such trials wouldn't take place. Criminals do not set crime figures, the law does. Fifteen years ago, if a boy stole apples from a farmer's field and he was chased by the farmer with a stick, there would be no action. It's an everyday occurrence of no significance. Today the youth would be charged with theft and probably trespass, while the farmer would be charged with carrying an offensive weapon, using threatening words and behaviour and possibly assault. This is why crime figures are spiralling out of control, not because young people are any worse. I know from personal experience that if you treat an impressionable young juvenile like a criminal, you will create a criminal.

In October 1988 I read a newspaper article about a ten-year-old boy named James Fallon. He'd been the victim of a horrific accident in Johannesburg. James was riding his bicycle when he was struck by a car driven by a 17-year-old schoolboy who had no licence. The vehicle dragged James 30 metres along the road. There was virtually no hope that he would live. He was unconscious with serious internal injuries and a crushed leg. He also suffered severe spinal injuries and 'died' twice. Top surgeons from all over South Africa managed to save his life with a seven-hour operation which received worldwide publicity. It was the first time such an operation had been carried out in the country, and only the fourth time anywhere in the world. James could not talk, breathe or swallow without the aid of a life-support system, though. His mother had been brought up in the same street as me in the Midlands. I read that James needed a computer similar to those used by jet fighter pilots which would allow him to communicate by eye movement. As his mother was from my home town, I decided I would try to help them raise this money and I figured that the best way to do this would be to stage a charity auction. I set about writing to more than 150 celebrities asking them to send me something which they had signed or was somehow connected to them. Phil Collins, U2, Tina

Turner, The Rolling Stones, The Who, Liverpool FC, Manchester United, Arsenal and countless other people and organisations responded. Probably the most surprising response I got was from Ronnie and Reggie Kray. Reggie rang my house and said he had heard about James and my efforts through somebody who worked for Dire Straits and that he and his family were touched by James's plight and wished to help me.

It seemed pointless trying to raise money for a boy from the Midlands in the south of England, particularly as he was in a South African hospital – this was the height of the anti-apartheid period and feelings were running high against South Africa – so I decided to stage the event at a hotel on the outskirts of Birmingham.

I booked the hotel and travelled to Birmingham with my brothers, Michael and Paul, and we began to try and sell tickets for it. However, my reputation went before me and the locals didn't show much enthusiasm, not because they didn't have feelings for James, but because they considered a criminal assisting another human somehow a bit suspect.

I thought their actions were far worse than any act I had committed. While travelling from pub to pub in our efforts to sell tickets, we encountered a group of young men hanging about in the street acting loutishly. One of these boys, Stuart Darley, shouted an obscenity at me. I stopped, turned round and asked him what he had said. He denied saying anything. I turned and began to walk again with my brothers. He repeated his shout and I turned round again. He had had his chance. I walked up to him and hit him in the face. He started saying: 'Don't hit me, please don't hit me, I haven't done anything.'

His friend ran to a nearby telephone box and tried to call the police. I ran over to stop him. Meanwhile, Stuart Darley began to get brave again. He started shouting further obscenities. I walked over and I hit him again.

Vulnerable people walking the streets may have to endure this behaviour, but I certainly wasn't going to. The following day, Paul and I returned to our homes (Paul lived in south London and

Michael remained in Birmingham). At about midday I received a phone call and I was told that the police were looking for us. Throughout my youth I had experienced quite a volatile relationship with the local police, and I wasn't too concerned. I certainly wasn't going to jump into my car and go and hand myself in.

I rang James Fallon's grandmother and explained that I would not be able to attend the event because of personal problems. It had been advertised in the local papers and pubs, it was all organised, so there was no real reason for me to go.

I wasn't surprised to learn later that only twenty people attended. I had half-expected it. The locals had let James down badly. They had ignored his needs in an attempt to get at me.

Debra was still running her hairdressing business, and I was still commuting to London driving heavy goods vehicles. We moved out of the flat on the Alcatraz estate to a three-bedroomed house nearer to Basildon town centre. In November 1989, our second child was born: Karis, a girl. I had no sisters and I'd never imagined myself having a daughter. Debra and I were overjoyed.

Without me realising it, my efforts on behalf of James began to put a strain on my family life. I'd been trying to assist James for over a year and I had become so immersed in it that I forgot about my own family. It wasn't intentional but with me, it's all or nothing – that's my nature.

I travelled to Broadmoor Hospital in Berkshire on 16 November 1989 for my first meeting with Ronnie Kray. He wanted to discuss with me ways of raising money for James Fallon. I was quite surprised when I first met Ronnie. He was a small man, and good manners personified. He and I got on very well. We sat in a visiting room, which was very much like a hospital day room, and drank can after can of Kaliber alcohol-free lager. Ronnie was genuinely concerned about James Fallon. He told me he considered himself lucky. He had his health, he had his strength. He had his new wife, Kate. He said he could smoke and drink and wasn't complaining about his lot. 'Anybody with feelings would be concerned about what happened to James,' he said. 'It's one of the most terrible cases I've heard of in my life.' After that, I started to visit Ronnie on a regular basis, sometimes twice a day.

Ronnie was on the same ward as the Yorkshire Ripper, and sometimes I would see him in the same visiting room at an adjacent table. Ronnie despised him. He considered it an insult that Peter Sutcliffe had been given a 25-year recommendation after butchering 13 women and attempting to murder a further seven, while he had been given a 30-year recommendation after shooting a fellow criminal. 'It is as if,' he would say, 'the law considers me a worse man than him.'

After toying with various ideas, Ronnie, his brother Reggie and I decided to stage a charity boxing show for James Fallon in the south of England. The twins said that I shouldn't concern myself with the events in Birmingham as they would ask their friends and the numerous people who supported them to rally round and support it. Again I threw myself wholeheartedly into preparing for a fundraising event for James Fallon.

The police in Birmingham, meanwhile, were still trying to track me and my older brother down. They had arrested my brother Michael and he was on police bail.

In January 1990 I was in Peckham, south London, with my friends Colin and Ray. Colin was on the run from the army over a compassionate leave application. During the winter of 1987, a very good friend of ours, Adrian Boreham, from Battersea, was killed in a road accident while serving with the British Army in West Germany. He was 19 years old. Colin had gone AWOL because they refused him permission to attend his friend's funeral as he was not immediate family. Colin had gone to the funeral anyway.

We were having a drink in the Heaton Arms, Peckham Rye, near where Ray lived. At about 10.30 Ray said he was going home, and asked Colin, who lived in Stratford, east London, how he was getting back. Colin replied, 'I'm going to get the tube to Stratford.'

Unbeknown to us, a group of very large men, probably in their forties, were standing nearby listening to our conversation.

Apparently Millwall FC, the local team, and their arch Docklands rivals, West Ham United, had been playing at the Den in New Cross that day and I can only assume that when Colin said he was returning to Stratford, these people thought we were West Ham supporters.

Ray went home first and Colin and I left the pub at closing time.

I was walking in front of Colin when I heard a loud thud. I turned around and saw four or five men, the forty-year-olds, with baseball bats. Colin was lying flat out on the ground. He had been hit in the face with the baseball bat. His jaw and his cheekbone were broken. His teeth hadn't been knocked out: they had been pushed flat underneath and above his tongue.

I ran to help him and they knocked me unconscious. The police were told by a witness that I was laid on my back and my knees were smashed by the bats, and that my assailants were shouting: 'Cripple the bastard, cripple him!'

When I came round I was in King's College Hospital. I had stitches in my head and both my knees were swollen to twice their normal size. I had no money on me. Whether this had been stolen or whether it had been lost *en route* to the hospital, I really didn't know. My first reaction when I woke up was to tell the nurses I was going home. They thought this rather amusing: I could barely sit up or move because of my injuries. But I still got out of bed and managed to reach the street.

All my clothes were covered in blood. It was about eight o'clock in the morning and I scrambled onto a bus full of commuters. I said to the driver, 'I've just come out of hospital. I've got no money on me. I've got to get to a tube,' and I just sat down. He didn't say anything to me.

I managed to get onto the tube network and eventually on a train to Basildon. This was about a quarter to nine. I must have looked like a lunatic sitting there, covered in blood, disorientated because of the injuries to my head. I reached Upminster, two stops from Basildon, thinking I was home and dry, when suddenly a ticket inspector appeared. He demanded a ticket. I said to him: 'Look, mate, I've had a bad fucking day. Leave me alone. I'm not in the mood. Go away.' To my surprise, he did.

Since that assault I've had an operation on my knees and I underwent physiotherapy every week for almost two years. I still suffer from arthritis and other related problems. I went back to the pub on a number of occasions with my friends to seek revenge, but I've never found who was responsible.

During the preparations for the boxing show for James Fallon, I was contacted by a man called James Campbell, who had been appointed by the Kray twins to assist me in promoting the show. He in turn had appointed a partner, a man called David Brazier, whom Campbell worked for in a taxi office in Chigwell, Essex. I didn't particularly see the need for persons to be named as promoters etc, and was not happy with the situation. But I was grateful for the twins' assistance and let matters be.

Reggie Kray sent me a list of phone numbers and addresses of all his friends and anyone he thought could assist me or attend. These were people from the criminal world: Charlie Richardson, Frankie Fraser, Tony Lambrianou, whom I had met on various visits with Ronnie Kray, John Masterson and the Scotsman Jimmy Boyle. Celebrities included Barbara Windsor, Bob Hoskins, Roger Daltrey, Jon Bon Jovi (who had been in contact with Ronnie) and Gary and Martin Kemp who were at that time making the film *The Krays*. Another person on the list was a man named Keith Bonsor. He, the letter said, was the manager of a local nightclub in Basildon called Raquels, and Reggie suggested I go and see if he might attend and also sell tickets in the nightclub.

I went to see Keith Bonsor one Wednesday afternoon, 21 March 1990, two days before the event, which was to be held at the Prince Regent Hotel in Woodford, Essex. Keith said he couldn't go, but would pass on my phone number to people he thought would be interested.

Debra and I were encountering financial problems because of our new house. Like all parents we wanted to give our children everything, so I was looking for further employment. Reg suggested

15

I ask Bonsor while I was there if he had any door work available, which I could do on Friday evenings and the weekends for additional income. Bonsor told me that they employed a security company and that David Vine, head of that company, was responsible for the hiring and firing of all the doormen. Vine would be in on Friday and Saturday evenings. If I was to turn up at an adjacent bar, Strings – The Piano Bar, any Friday or Saturday evening, I would be able to speak to him personally, and he would be able to help me.

That same Wednesday evening, I had a meeting with James Campbell and David Brazier at a pub in Epping. When we'd finished discussing Friday's event, I rang Debra to tell her I was on my way home. She told me that James Fallon had lost his fight for life that day. I really felt sorry for the boy and his family. He had put up a terrific battle, and so had they.

I went back to Campbell and Brazier and told them that James had died. Their reaction was, well, what should we do with the money? I felt sick. I told them that James's family had incurred huge debts during their ordeal, as there was no national health service in South Africa, and all monies from the event would go to the family.

I know Reg and Ronnie were deeply moved and upset by the news of James's death. It was reported at the time that Reg wept. It certainly wouldn't surprise me, because when he talked to me on the phone, he was really choked up. On the night of the event, a telephone was connected to the public address system and the two hundred diners, who had each paid £40 to attend, fell silent as Reggie Kray paid a moving tribute to James – he'd been granted special permission to telephone the hotel from Lewes Prison.

It was a sight to see so many criminal heavyweights standing sombre, paying tribute to ten-year-old James Fallon. Charlie Kray attended, as did Ronnie's new wife Kate, Joey Pyle, former Page 3 model Flannagan, Chris Lambrianou and his brother Tony, who had both been convicted with the Krays for the murder of Jack the Hat, and various other people who did not want to publicise their presence as they were normally exiled in Spain, but had risked attending at the express wishes of Reg.

Glenn Murphy and Ray Winstone also attended. It was at this event that I met Geoff Allen, who is said in various books and newspaper articles to be the man they call the Godfather of the Krays. Geoff was 70 but had the mind and heart of a young man. He was jailed at Norwich for seven years in 1976 for masterminding a £300,000 insurance swindle after a historic building named Briggatt Mill was burned down. It was also believed in police circles that Geoff was the man behind the Great Train Robbery. Geoff told me it was to his house in Suffolk that Ronnie and Reggie went to lie low after murdering Jack the Hat.

The event raised a reported £15,000. At the end of the evening when I went to collect this money, however, I could not find Campbell or Brazier. The hotel and other expenses had been paid, but there didn't seem to be any balance forthcoming. Despite my efforts I was unable to contact either of the men that evening.

During the following days, calls from Ronnie and Reggie were fast and furious. They demanded that the money be handed over to the family. I was in total agreement, but I could not find the men. Promise after promise followed meeting after meeting, but the money never did materialise. To this day it remains a mystery as to where it went.

The promoters insisted that it was swallowed up by expenses. I find that hard to believe. I thought it rather ironic when I read one year later, on 22 December 1991, in the *Sunday People*, that David Brazier had taken the dying for a ride when he pocketed the proceeds of a charity football match.

I told the twins at the time that I wanted to seek some sort of retribution, but Reg was adamant that it be forgotten, because the Krays had always been associated with charitable funds, and, understandably, they didn't want to be associated with a rip-off. I rang the Fallon family and told them I would be unable to attend the service being held in this country for James as I still had problems with the local police force who were looking for me for the earlier assault. The truth of the matter was, I was too embarrassed to show my face.

The following weekend Debra and I asked her mother if she would babysit for us. We were going to the cinema in Basildon to see the film *Ghost*. At the end of the film Debra and I had to wait until everyone else had left the cinema because she was in tears over the film. She was still quite tearful when we had walked the 500 yards or so to the entrance of Raquels where I was due to go and see David Vine. It's ironic, looking back now, that my arrival at Raquels was shrouded in sadness. My departure would be in much the same vein.

Chapter *Two*

THE BAR WAS FAIRLY QUIET WHEN I WENT IN. ON A SMALL STAGE there was a white grand piano, a memorial to the man who tried to bring culture to Basildon. He'd called the place Strings – The Piano Bar.

Although it was done out like a fancy cocktail bar, the clientele were mainly middle-aged heavy drinkers and peroxide blonde Essex girls. The pianist had been replaced by a DJ who had put his record decks on the piano lid and wrapped flashing rope lights around the legs. I asked the barmaid where I could find Dave Vine. After undergoing the 'who wants to know?' formalities, I was finally introduced to him.

Dave was about six foot tall, balding, and very powerfully built. He told me he had a partner, Micky Pierce, and they ran a couple of clubs and most pubs in the Basildon area. He offered me £40 a night and told me I could start on Friday. We shook hands. I wasn't surprised to be offered the job straight away; Reggie's recommendation helped, as did the fact that doormen know doormen, by the way they look and act. I'd done this job before. You speak the same language, you're all on the same level.

Wearing a dinner suit and a bow-tie and being surrounded by drunks is quite an unpleasant experience, so I was pleased to learn on my first night that I would be working at the top bar rather than the front door. But it wasn't long before I discovered that this was where most of the heavy drinkers gathered and where most of the trouble took place.

Vine introduced me to my fellow doormen. There was no unity

among them. Most of them there were like me, just working for a bit of extra money. They were not a gang or a firm. I wasn't impressed. I said hello, and went straight to work.

About two hours into the night a pot-man, the guy who collects the empty glasses, came over to me and said somebody was causing trouble on the dance floor. He pointed to probably the largest man in the club. He was gripping another man by his neck and was threatening him. I went over and said: 'Leave it out, mate, or you'll have to go.'

'It's all right, I know the score, I'm a doorman,' he replied.

I said: 'It's not all right, and if you are a doorman and you do know the score, then you will leave it out. If you wish to sort it out, you'll have to sort it out outside.'

He let go of the man, and started walking down the stairs with me following him. We went down one flight of stairs and he stopped at the cloakroom and began to talk to a woman, maybe his wife or girlfriend. I was insistent: 'I'm sorry, you've got to leave.'

'Who the fuck are you, anyway?' the man shouted. 'No fucking northerner tells me what to do.'

I grabbed him in a headlock and tried to force him down the stairs. He struggled and I began to punch him in the face. We both rolled down the stairs and at the bottom, as I was fighting with him, his girlfriend hit me across the nose with a champagne glass, took off her high-heeled shoe and started to hit me across the head with it. It was laughable, really, but we continued fighting on the stairs.

He was a big man, so it was difficult to fight him and defend myself from the blows from his girlfriend at the same time. I somehow managed to keep going until eventually we were fighting in the foyer where five or six of the other doormen were. I remember thinking: 'Why aren't they helping me?'

I saw that Micky Pierce, Dave Vine's partner, was laughing. I couldn't work it out at all. Eventually the doormen split us up and the man went out of the door of his own free will. I was livid: 'What the fuck do you think you're doing? Do you work on your own here or what?' Pierce calmly explained to me that the man I'd thrown out was a doorman who worked with us, but it was his night off.

It wasn't the best impression I've made on my first day at a new job, but it was to secure my reputation. It was an impression people retained about me throughout my time at Raquels.

Raquels was a very violent club. I expected to be involved in at least two fights each night I worked. However, it wasn't all gloom. One evening, Keith Bonsor had booked a fire-eater to do a stage show. The fire-eater turned up drunk and was quite unsteady on his feet. During the show he tipped flammable fluid in his mouth and blew out a large cloud of fire over a naked flame. But because he was drunk, when he swigged back the fluid, he'd poured it down his chest and his arm, and set himself alight. He fell off the stage backwards, into the curtains behind the stage, and the curtains caught fire. The doormen were despatched to put him and the curtains out. It was a funny moment.

Things were going okay for me and Debra now I had extra income, so I decided to get the matter with Stuart Darley sorted out rather than wait for the police to catch up with me and arrest me when it may not have been convenient.

My brother and I travelled to the Midlands and gave ourselves up. Over a period we went through the rigmarole of attending numerous Magistrates Courts waiting to be committed to Crown Court. Eventually we were told we had to appear at Stafford Crown Court for trial. No date was fixed, however. When you're sent to a Crown Court, you are not given a date; you are told usually two or three weeks prior to the trial that you're being put on a waiting list. Judges and the police don't know how long a trial's going to last, because a defendant could change his plea or a witness might fail to attend or whatever. It could be over in a day, for example, so you are told to ring your legal representatives each evening to find out if you're in court the next morning.

One evening I was in Newcastle driving a heavy goods vehicle and I rang my legal representative. I was told I had to attend Stafford Crown Court at ten o' clock the following morning. I said

I'd be unable to reach Stafford by then, because of the legal restrictions on the hours you can drive such lorries, but that I would be there not long afterwards. My brother Michael was with me at the time.

We set off as soon as we could and made our way to Stafford. On the way there we rang the court telling them where we were and our expected time of arrival. However, when we did arrive at 11.30 we were told that a warrant had been issued for our arrest and the case was being put off until a later date.

Two weeks later the trial started. We were all charged for not answering our bail. This matter related to the one and a half hours that we were late on the first day. For this heinous offence we were each fined £50. We all pleaded not guilty to the charge of assaulting Stuart Darley. The police suggested that we had tried to intimidate witnesses prior to the trial and intimidate Darley himself. The prosecution were throwing plenty of mud at us, but it was hard for them to make it stick because we all decided to exercise our right not to enter the witness box. However, our trump defence card was Stuart Darley himself. We knew the type he was, and we knew when he entered the witness box, he would do all our work for us.

True to form, Darley was rude, sarcastic and brazen. He insulted our counsel and we could see the straight people on the jury were not impressed. They returned very quickly with a not guilty verdict. The law failed and justice prevailed.

I was still visiting Ronnie Kray on a regular basis. On one occasion Ronnie told me that he was quite upset by a new house rule brought in at Broadmoor. He said they were now banned from smoking in the day room and were forced to go to a room set aside especially for smoking. Ronnie was a chain smoker, and this caused him a lot of distress. What made me laugh was that he was ranting and raving at me, saying it was a fucking liberty that he had to sit in a smoke-filled room with a load of nutters and he couldn't sit where he wanted to and smoke in peace.

Ronnie asked me to write to Broadmoor and say that I had met prison officers in a nearby pub. I was to say that they were outraged at the unhappiness that this was causing inmates and they were concerned it was going to cause incidents. I wrote the letter from a friend's address and used a false name in the hope that I could help Ronnie.

On my next visit to Broadmoor the manager called me into an office on my way out. I had made a silly mistake. He showed me the letter I had written to Ronnie and he showed me the letter I had written to the hospital. Both were in my handwriting. From that time onwards, because I would not reveal the names of the prison officers who allegedly told me about this matter, I was banned from visiting Ronnie. I thought it was quite amusing that I had been banned from Broadmoor Hospital.

Once I had settled in at Raquels it became quite clear to me that things were not running the way they should be. It was as if a handful of local hardmen were running the club, and not the doormen. Local men with reputations would fight in the club and the following evening they would be allowed in – because, as the other doormen said, 'It's not worth the trouble.'

The doormen thought that if they barred one of these local hardmen who kept causing trouble, they might meet him in the street, or the man might call round to their house and they would end up the victims of an assault. I was of the opinion that if someone wanted trouble, they could fucking have trouble. And if they came into the club they behaved themselves or they wouldn't be allowed back in. Simple as that.

Dave Vine and I became quite good friends. I was moved from the top bar down to work on the front door with him. We were able to fiddle a bit of door money by letting customers in and pocketing the cash ourselves. Some Saturday nights we would make an extra £200 each. Christmas Eve and New Year's Eve were always sold out and they were ticket-only events. We decided to print our own tickets for each night at Raquels and another local disco. We asked Debra's brother Keith to sell these tickets outside the venues on Christmas Eve and New Year's Eve.

We sold approximately 200 of these fakes, but unfortunately the other club had already sold out its quota of tickets. When the extra 200 people tried to get in, the place was crammed shoulder-to-shoulder and there were disturbances when it was discovered they'd bought forged tickets. The ones who were turned away were so irate at having their Christmas Eve night out ruined, they came in search of Keith. Eventually we had to hide him in the toilet upstairs in the club.

I could never understand why Dave allowed local people to take liberties with him. He certainly was no fool. But it was as if he couldn't be bothered with the trouble – hardly the attitude for a doorman.

In January 1992 things started to come to a head. Dave did security with Micky Pierce at a local pub called the Bullseye. An 18-year-old local man named Shaun Dunbar had been asked to leave by the manageress, and he had refused. The manageress rang Dave Vine and asked him to come down to throw him out. Dave rang round all the doormen and we went down there. There was a scuffle. A man named Tim Whidlake hit Dunbar and broke his jaw. The following evening Tim and another doorman, Ronnie Downes, were working in the Bullseye. Some local men who had taken exception to what had happened to Dunbar went into the pub and attacked them with machetes. Tim escaped unhurt but Ronnie suffered severe injuries to his hands trying to protect himself. Once more we were all called out to attend the incident. I was of the opinion that we should have gone after those responsible and sorted it out there and then. But Dave Vine suggested that we leave it till later. I really felt it was the wrong way to handle things.

The next evening a man named Les Murphy came into Raquels. Vine said that he was one of those responsible for the attack on the doormen in the Bullseye. I said it should be sorted out, but he told me to leave it. A doorman friend of Ronnie Downes was in Raquels and told Tim that because he was the intended victim and Ronnie had ended up injured, it was Tim who should confront Les Murphy.

Tim went over to Les and said: 'You've got to leave.'

'The only cunt who's leaving here is you,' said Murphy, and picked up an ashtray.

Somebody – I don't know who – squirted cleaning fluid, industrial ammonia, at Les Murphy which hit him in the eye, and he fell against the bar. He was then hit over the head with a water jug and kicked and beaten. He had head injuries and, we later learned, was blinded in one eye. If Les had any idea that he was going to be subjected to this kind of attack, I don't think he would have come into the club in the first place. It seemed that Dave Vine's way of solving things wasn't working. He was being too soft and no one had any respect for him. It was becoming clear to me that combating violence with violence was the only way to gain control of the club.

Vine's partner Micky Pierce quit directly after the Les Murphy incident. He had had enough of trouble on the doors, and went to work on his father's farm. Vine was relying too much on him and as a result lost more and more control.

Further unrelated incidents followed. A man who refused to be searched returned to Raquels and petrol-bombed the front doors. Jason Riley, a local man and friend of ours, put a gun to someone's head on the dancefloor. Jason was barred by the management when the customer complained. Because he was a friend, I actually told the manager that Jason had been to a fancy-dress party and had come to the club dressed as a German and the firearm was an imitation. But the manager was not fooled. He said the customer was going to go to the police and it was in everyone's interest that Jason be barred – for the time being, anyway.

The following week Jason came to the club and asked if he could come in. As I said, we were Jason's friends and the gun he had pulled on this person was in fact owned by the Raquels door staff. Jason had ordered it, but, although it remained in his possession, he had not paid for it. We explained the situation to him regarding the management and suggested he go over to Time, another local disco, for a couple of weeks until things had died down. Jason agreed and left with his friend Simon Wally.

Jason and Simon were in Time when a girl accused Jason of pinching her backside. He said it wasn't him, but she said she was going to tell a man who was with her. The man came over and hit Jason. The two began fighting with his attacker and the doormen became involved. Jason was ejected from the club and was livid because he had done nothing.

He told the doorman and his attacker that he would be back. It's a threat people who work on the door hear at least once a week. Few take notice of it, but everybody should.

Jason jumped into a taxi and told the driver to take him home. Simon was still with him and was trying to calm him down, but Jason was out of control. He told the taxi to wait outside and he went into his house.

When Jason got back into the cab, he had a gun in his pocket, and he kept saying that he was going to 'shoot the bastards'. All the time Simon was telling him to calm down. Jason shouldn't have said what he did in front of the cab driver, and he should have listened to Simon.

But he went back to Time, got out of the cab, walked up to the front doors and fired into the reception area at the people who had assaulted him. They were still talking to the bouncers there. He was incensed that they hadn't been kicked out. One man was hit in the ankle and the other put his hand up to protect himself. The bullet entered his wrist and came out through his elbow.

I got a phone call at Raquels and was told what had happened. Because the door staff owned the gun with which he had committed the crime and because Jason was a friend, I thought we should help. Dave Vine and I went over to Time to see what we could learn. Everybody was saying that it was Jason Riley who had shot the two people.

I rang Jason's girlfriend and told her to tell him to stay wherever he was and we would be in touch. When Raquels closed that night, Dave Vine and I met Simon Wally and Jason's girlfriend outside a pub not far from Jason's house. I told Simon that he should go to Jason and meet me round the corner at an agreed time. I would take him to my brother's flat in south London. On the way we could dispose of the gun and wait to see what happened when the dust settled. He would then be in a far better position to give himself up and get the matter resolved.

We were the only people who knew where he was. Dave said he had to go home and he left us. I went to the agreed meeting place to pick Jason up, but he didn't show. Nobody knows how the police knew where to find him, but armed officers stormed the house where he was hiding and he was arrested.

Jason's friends believed it was Dave Vine who had told the police where he was. It may have been just chance. Nobody will ever know. In this world where there's always doubt, the rumours never decrease, they always increase. People will always try and discredit you when it's in their interests to do so. Jason was sentenced to twelve years for two attempted murders.

Dave Vine had been working at Epping Forest Country Club, which is frequented by various celebrities. He asked me if I would do his Wednesday nights up there as he had other commitments, and I agreed.

It was while working at Epping that I first met Dave Done from Romford. Dave was a fanatical bodybuilder. We got on very well and not long after he came to work with me and Dave Vine at Raquels.

On Sundays at Epping, they started playing rave and house music, and I was asked to work then as well. They were very busy. All club people who had worked Friday and Saturday used to go to Epping socially, as it was their night off, so I very soon got to know many people in clubland throughout London.

One of the people I met, and became quite friendly with, was Tony Tucker. Tucker was in his mid-30s and a mountain of a man. He ran a very big and well-respected door firm. He was strange in many ways. He spoke to few people and was quite abrupt. He had a very dry sense of humour. He was aggressive to those who tried to enter his circle without invitation.

I learned some years later that it was in August 1992 while I was working at Epping that the police had begun watching me. My way of dealing with problems, compared to the way Dave Vine handled them at Raquels and elsewhere, had begun to earn me something of a reputation in Basildon, and this had brought interest from the police.

Geoff Allen, the old gentleman I had met at the James Fallon boxing show, had become a good friend. I would meet Geoff occasionally in the village of Lavenham in Suffolk.

Dave Vine had told me about a scam which was going down in the City: people working in a bank would put dodgy cheques or a sum of dirty money into your account, and for this service, they would get 25 per cent, the manager of the bank would also get 25 per cent, and you would get the other 50 per cent.

It sounded too good to be true. The catch, apparently, was that the bank manager insisted on the money being paid into a healthy bank account as they were talking about amounts in excess of £100,000, and an average account, of course, wouldn't be able to contain such amounts without it arousing suspicion.

Vine suggested I ask my friend Geoff if he would be interested. I didn't want to involve him in something which might have resulted in him spending his last years in prison, but I did mention it to him, and he did express an interest. He suggested that those involved meet at his home.

Dave Vine, a man named Tony Bones, and two other men who allegedly worked in the bank travelled to Geoff's house and we had a meeting. Geoff was very wise. He said he would not commit himself to anything unless he spoke to the bank manager involved. Bones, Vine and the other two were not so wise. It transpired that the two were not bank employees, but cleaners. Their rather sad attempt at defrauding the bank from within failed miserably, and the person they had talked into putting the cheques into his account was promptly arrested and charged.

I was annoyed that Vine and Bones had tried to get my friend Geoff into such a stupid thing. They insisted that they had been told in good faith that it was a good earner and it was the two cleaners who were responsible. I saw this as the turning point in my friendship with Vine.

On 9 September 1992 Vine left Raquels and was on his way home when he was stopped by the police and it was found that the car he was driving was ringed (a stolen car with false number plates). Further searches at his home revealed 25 ecstasy tablets and a knife. He was never convicted of possessing an offensive weapon, driving a stolen car or being in possession of class A drugs. I suspect he told the police that he had confiscated the ecstasy tablets from somebody at the club, he had bought the car in good faith and that the knife was not kept for any sinister purpose. However, this event certainly caused Dave a lot of problems among those in clubland.

Many people suggested that he had not been prosecuted because he was a police informer, particularly in view of what had happened to Jason Riley four months previously. That's the way things are when you fall out of favour.

Raquels continued to be a hotbed of trouble, not only from the customers, but seemingly from everybody even loosely associated with it. Opposite the main doors of the club there was a small market shop, brick built and a permanent fixture. A man sold fancy goods there. He complained to the club that when revellers were leaving Raquels, they were breaking his windows and he wanted shutters put up on his windows at the club's expense, otherwise he would object to their licence. The area manager agreed that the club would pay for these shutters. I thought it was a right liberty that this man could just come along and demand money on a whim and the club agree to pay it. However, it was their choice.

The following Sunday night Dave Vine, Tim Whidlake and I were driving home from working at Epping. We stopped near the shop at a burger van to buy a cup of tea, and then we went home. I lived not far from the nightclub at the time, and I heard sirens heading towards the town. I learned the next day that the shop had been burned to the ground. The man never did get his shutters.

On Christmas Eve 1992, my friend Geoff Allen died. His wife

Annie rang and told me. I was very upset. Geoff was a real gentleman. I attended Geoff's funeral with Dave Vine. Charlie Kray attended, as did Bill Wyman of The Rolling Stones, a good friend of Geoff and his family.

When a person who makes such an impression dies, I find it hard to believe that they have gone. Annie and I were having a drink at their house after the funeral. I said to her, 'Geoff's probably upstairs having a good laugh now. It's probably another insurance fiddle.' We laughed, but it was a very sad occasion.

Paul Trehern, a local doorman in Basildon who used to work with us, was getting married and he phoned to tell us that he was having a stag night and he and perhaps 30 other doormen from various clubs would be coming into Raquels for a drink. It was to be expected that they'd be rowdy, but they were doormen like us. Paul had worked with us on a number of occasions, and he had had the courtesy to ring us days before the event to inform us that he and his friends would be coming to the club.

I told Vine that he should go and see Paul and explain to him that there would only be four or five of us working and it would be inconceivable for us to control 30 door staff; we would expect Paul to supervise his own friends, and if he could they would be most welcome to come into the club. However, Dave discussed it with the management, and together they decided that Paul Trehern and his friends would not be allowed in. I thought it was ridiculous.

When the night came around, Paul and his friends turned up and were quite rightly disgusted to learn that they were not allowed in the club. Paul ended up grappling on the floor with Dave Vine and, despite his objections, they still all entered the club and drank at the bar. Apart from the trouble with Dave Vine getting in, they weren't a bit of bother at all. I was quite embarrassed to be working with doormen who turned other doormen away for no reason whatsoever, particularly guys who had worked with us.

The following night Dave Vine didn't come into work. He knew I had the serious hump with him. Dave Godding, a good friend of his, and a man named Joe had trouble in the Piano Bar. Joe had hit a guy and dislocated his arm. Godding insisted that an ambulance be called. I refused, because if you rang an ambulance, the police would also turn up. He went behind my back and called them. He also said he was going to ring Dave. I went berserk. I shouted at him and I told him what I thought of Dave. He got nervous and left the premises at about 1 a.m.

The following day I received a phone call from the manager, Ralph Paris. Ralph asked me to come in and see him during the day. He told me that Dave Vine had resigned that morning. He thought he could no longer work with me. I was in total agreement. Prior to my arrival at the club people had taken liberties all the time. By using excessive violence to combat violence, I had reduced the amount of trouble, and people were thinking twice about starting anything in the club.

It's easy to say with hindsight now that I should have realised that excess would eventually have been met with excess.

Chapter *Three*

NOW THAT I HAD CONTROL OF RAQUELS, I WASN'T SURE THAT I really wanted it. The door was still made up of Basildon men, and they still feared local guys with reputations. They had earned them in the playground, and they were going to take them to their graves. The only way to regain control of the club was to bring in outsiders. But, for now, the local doormen were all I had and I would have to make do. To be honest, I was nervous about my position, but the game's all about front. I couldn't walk away.

My first problem was going to be getting invoices as Raquels would only pay cheques to a limited company. I approached Dave Vine's old partner Micky Pierce to see if he knew anybody who could front the door for me. He suggested a man I had met several times, Peter Clarke, a local Mr Fixit, who agreed to supply the invoices in return for one or two of his doormen being given work.

I was rather concerned that he was involved with a rival door firm run by a man called Charlie Jones. Jones was very interested in taking over the Raquels door. While Vine was in charge he had approached the manager on several occasions. But for the time being it was all that was available to me.

Word soon got round Basildon that Vine had given up the door and I had taken over. I was preparing myself to be tested. I knew trouble was going to come, but I wasn't sure from whom, or in what form. Somebody was bound to try and make a name for themselves, that was certain.

To this day, I have been unable to find out who was behind one particular incident. A man named Israeli Frank, a well-known villain, came to see me one evening and asked if I knew anybody who could get hold of some bullets. I asked him what calibre. He said he needed some nine millimetres, and I agreed to give him some. It's not uncommon to do something like this – it's almost like giving someone a sample. I hadn't paid for the ones I had myself – there were only six, and people wouldn't charge for that quantity.

The following Friday Israeli Frank came to see me and we went into the back fire exit out of view from people and the noise of the disco. We spoke about things in general, and the conversation got round to why he needed the bullets, which I'd handed over to him. He told me that he'd been approached by a doorman in Basildon; someone had come on the scene recently and taken over a club and he was being paid to shoot him.

He had been given the gun and was waiting for the bullets. Since there are only three or four nightclubs in Basildon, it seemed quite obvious that I was the intended victim. Frank, of course, was at that stage unaware it was me.

When I said this to Frank, he gave the bullets back to me, but would not disclose who his employer was. I've never been able to get to the bottom of this, but I have my suspicions as to who was behind it: Dave Vine.

Micky Pierce visited me at the club on several occasions and told me that Vine had been badmouthing me to other people. Vine was now working at Time and had brought in a new partner. On a couple of occasions, when Pierce had told me that Vine had been badmouthing me, I'd gone over to Time looking for him and threatened his doormen.

The new partner, whom I had met while I was at Epping and always got on with, called me the following day, and we met and resolved the matter. He told me that what Pierce was saying was untrue. Pierce, he said, was trying to cause trouble between me and Vine so I would be arrested and lose the door at Raquels so he and his sleeping partner Jones could take over the club. I had been completely taken in by Micky Pierce, and with hindsight, that was probably foolish.

(It's worth mentioning here that a door registration scheme operates in Basildon and it's a condition of nightclubs and all licensed premises that they employ registered doormen. The police can object to your registration or your licence, if you like, if you're convicted of an offence. If you lose your door registration licence, the club obviously has to get rid of you.)

It was around this time that the farm Pierce lived on near Basildon was raided by the police following a surveillance operation and a tip-off. Police uncovered a firearm and various pieces of equipment they said had been used in the manufacture of amphetamine sulphate. They said it was a speed factory. Pierce automatically blamed Vine.

David Done, the fanatical bodybuilder, was at this time my closest friend. He had a serious problem with steroids. I used to warn him about the excessive doses he was taking. His problems with steroids led to problems with money. He was even resorting to being a pizza delivery boy to help finance his drug-taking. He wouldn't listen to reason and his addiction began to affect his judgement.

One Monday morning, Dave Done rang me up and told me that he had been sacked from Epping Country Club for allegedly selling drugs. I knew this was false. Dave did not sell drugs. I told him that if he was out then all the doormen should be out, myself included. I said I'd go with him and see the head doorman, Joe.

I asked Joe who had said that Dave was dealing. He said that the club had received a telephone call. I got quite annoyed and said that if the person who alleged Dave was a dealer didn't do it openly, then he shouldn't be believed. Eventually Joe agreed that Dave could have his job back, and we both went home. However, that evening I received a phone call from Vine (it was a split door up there: the club employed Joe, but he farmed out half of his work to Vine, who employed me, and supplied invoices for Joe) and I was told that I had been sacked in Dave Done's place. No reason was given. I was later told that Vine was behind these phone calls to the club because he wanted me and Dave Done out of Epping.

What particularly annoyed me was that now I had been sacked, Dave Done refused to stand by me. He said that he needed the money, and the fact that I'd lost my job was unfortunate, but there was nothing he could do. I was really angry about Dave's double standards.

Within a couple of days Dave Done left Raquels and went to work at the Ministry of Sound in south-east London. He suggested that I should work with him there on the odd nights when extra work arose. I agreed. Unknown to me, at that time there was a lot of doorman's politics connected to the Ministry of Sound. A notorious East End villain and doorman, Rod, had just been asked to give up the door by the management because he was under police surveillance. Two very well-known south London brothers had taken over. Everybody was expecting an all-out war. I was acquainted with Rod, but Dave Done was a friend of his, so I was surprised when he asked me to go and work with him for the two south London brothers, Paul and Tim. I told him that it would be insulting to his friend and we should stay out of it. However, he told me he had discussed it with his friend and that it was okay, so I agreed to work with him.

On my first night there, we were standing on the door and there was a discussion about the problem between Rod, Paul and Tim. Dave Done started siding with those loyal to Paul and Tim. 'You shouldn't get involved, Dave, Rod's your friend,' I said. Dave ignored me – he obviously needed the work.

A couple of days later I learned that Dave had lied to me. When he'd approached Rod about working at the Ministry of Sound, Rod had told him he'd rather Dave didn't work for Paul and Tim. When Dave explained that he needed the money, Rod said he'd pay him his wages – £100 a night – not to work there. Dave was taking the money from both of them. I wanted nothing more to do with it, and we fell out.

I was still seeing a fair bit of Tony Tucker, the man I had met socially at Epping Country Club. He was also a friend of Rod's. Tucker asked me what had gone on between me and Dave Done. I told Tucker and he subsequently told Rod about the incidents when Done was in the company of people badmouthing him. Dave denied it and slagged me off, so when he rang me, I taped the conversation to prove he had been badmouthing Rod and the things he'd said about me in return were untrue.

Around the same time, an article appeared in the *News of the World* about two of the Ministry of Sound doormen, Mark Rothermel and a South African named Chris Raal. Rothermel had left before I started work at the club but Raal was working during my time there. He was in this country on the run from the South African police after it was alleged that he had shot dead a nightclub manager. I had never met Rothermel, and up until reading this article hadn't even heard of him. The Ministry of Sound had at that time won one of its many awards and the article was making a big deal about men with violent pasts working there.

In November 1989 Mark Rothermel was sentenced to six years for assisting in the disposal of a body. Mark had been working at Hollywoods in Romford, one of Tony Tucker's doors, with another man, Pierre St Ange. Pierre had been having an affair with Pamela, the ex-wife of a DJ named Bernie Burns. Eventually Pierre, another bodybuilder, who was six foot four, moved in with Pamela in Ilford. But Burns kept calling round pestering and sexually harassing her.

Pierre thought he was a 'little runt', and decided to teach him a lesson by slapping him around. Bernie Burns was cornered in the Ilford flat, where he was beaten up and throttled by a mystery assailant, helped by Pierre. Initially Pierre had told police that it was Mark Rothermel who had strangled Bernie Burns. He later retracted this in court.

The body was wrapped in a red blanket, put in the boot of a car and taken to a quiet copse in Longspring Wood near Chelmsford, Essex. It was there that Mark, who was nicknamed the Colonel because of the way he planned things with military precision, took an axe to the body. He hacked off Burns's head and both of his hands so that it would be difficult to identify the body. Mark is reported to have told a friend: 'The hands came off easily, but the head was more of a problem because of the veins in the neck.'

Burns was buried in a shallow woodland grave. His head and hands have never been recovered. Police found Burns's body after a tip-off and collared Rothermel at the same time. He was hiding up to his neck in a pond near the grave. A police helicopter pilot spotted his head as the chopper skimmed across the tops of trees, and armed detectives moved in. Rothermel was ordered out of the pond at gunpoint.

Mark was found not guilty of murder and not guilty of manslaughter, but he received six years for disposing of the body. Pierre was found not guilty of murder but sentenced to ten years for manslaughter.

It wasn't the only time a member of the Burns family had been a victim of violent death. In July 1984 Bernie's father Peter was killed when former soldier James Melloy thrust a four-foot metal stake through his eye. The 60-year-old railway guard died ten days later in hospital.

Dave Done was still working at the Ministry of Sound. At first people blamed Rod for the newspaper article. In order to win favour, Done told people that it was me. It must have been easy to believe. I made no secret of the fact that I had many newspaper contacts which I had made during my days working on the James Fallon fundraising events. It was Ronnie and Reggie Kray who had shown me the importance and usefulness of a relationship with the press.

It was a childish and dangerous thing for Dave to say; Mark Rothermel and Chris Raal were certainly no fools. But if Dave Done was trying to cause me trouble, he couldn't have picked two better people to cause it for me.

I was unaware of what he said. And the next time I worked at the Ministry of Sound you could have cut the atmosphere with a knife. It soon became clear that it wasn't the atmosphere that people wanted to cut. I went out to the front door and said: 'What the fuck's going on, Dunny?' He said nothing, although I could tell by his manner that whatever was going on, he was behind it. I went inside and spoke to South African Chris. He seemed okay, but I could tell that something was brewing. There was an air of menace, but I wasn't going to run anywhere. I hadn't done anything. I stayed until the end and left.

On Sunday evenings there was a house and garage night on a boat permanently moored at the Embankment. The following Sunday I went to the boat and had a drink with David Courtney, whom I'd met on the club circuit. Again I noticed the atmosphere was odd – so much so that when I sat with Courtney everyone around us began to move away, a sure sign that something was going to happen. I asked Courtney what was going down, and he said there was nothing the matter.

As I was leaving the boat, I saw Courtney arguing with a tall man with a ponytail who had a knife with a green handle in his hand. Courtney was telling him: 'Not here, not here.' It was quite obvious what they were talking about. I went over to Courtney and said: 'What the fuck's he doing with a knife?' He denied the man was carrying one. I knew it was bollocks. As we left the boat, Courtney asked me if I would give a friend of his a lift to a party. I thought that if something was going to happen, it was going to happen at the boat, so I agreed.

The person who got into my car was in his twenties. He said he was from Coventry. He didn't look up to much. He said the party was in a house in north London. It sounds corny, but you can actually sense fear, or the coming of violence. The atmosphere in the car was very, very tense. He was asking me about Dave Done and if I knew South African Chris. He asked too many questions, because the penny had dropped straight away with me. I kept a First World War bayonet down the side of my seat in the car. The first wrong move this guy made, he was going to get it.

The so-called party was in a house on a main road heading towards the A1. He kept saying to me: 'This looks like it, this looks like it.' By pure coincidence, every place that looked like it happened to be a dark, unlit, uninhabited area. He told me the number of the house the party was meant to be at and we were unable to find it. He kept saying, 'Pull over here and I'll knock a door.' Each time I ignored him and pulled into a brightly lit garage forecourt or similar spot. As we were driving up the dual carriageway I noticed two cars following us. Dave Courtney was driving one of them, and the tall man with the ponytail was in the other.

I wasn't thick. It was an amateurish attempt to corner me. My confidence grew when I realised the type of people I was dealing with. These pantomime gangsters had been watching too many Jimmy Cagney movies. If they wanted to do something to me, they had had their chance on the boat. I stopped the car, grabbed my passenger, shoved him onto the street and slammed the door shut. As I drove away, I noticed he had left a lock-knife on the seat.

The following day, I rang Tony Tucker, because he knew all these people and Rothermel and Raal had worked for him. I told him what had gone on. I said there was only one way to sort it out: ring Rod, ring Rothermel, ring South African Chris and arrange a meeting.

A meeting is not a democratic discussion. Each person says their piece, and whoever is not believed does not usually get to leave the room under his own steam. Despite being disadvantaged, as I was from the Midlands and these people already knew each other, I was still keen to let the meeting go ahead. Later that day Tucker rang me and said the meeting was on for the following morning at a portacabin in Essex. The next day I was told it was called off because they had been unable to get hold of David Done. Another meeting was arranged. This time they had been able to reach him, but he said he did not want to go to any meeting. The matter, I was told, was then closed. Dave had an excuse for his actions: his drug problem. The rules could be changed when it suited him. I doubt if I would have enjoyed the same privilege.

I found it hard to contain my anger. People had been plotting to stab me for no reason, and now I was told to forget it. I reluctantly agreed. I didn't want any more enemies – I had enough in Basildon. The standard of doormen being provided by Peter Clarke was deteriorating rapidly. It was as if he was supplying me with people not up to the job on purpose in the hope that we could come unstuck against the locals who were testing us.

The only effect it did have was that every time there was an incident, the violence to counteract what had occurred became more and more excessive. The legacy of the last door firm was over, and I wasn't going to make the same mistakes as Vine. More and more people were getting seriously hurt. Knives and other weapons were being used. On the surface revellers were beginning to see a decrease in violence, but behind the scenes those who wished to cause trouble were paying dearly.

In one incident a local man came to the front door and became abusive because I insisted that he be searched before he entered the club. He went away and returned with a baseball bat. Maurice Golding, a doorman from Bristol who worked for me, was hit across the head and the man ran away. We all chased him and the manager, Ian Blackwell, followed, trying to calm me down. We caught the man approximately 500 yards away from Raquels outside the local bingo hall.

The doorman who caught him began to hit him, but I told him to stop. The man was cut twice with a sheath knife, once in the face, and once in his upper thigh. The manager was outraged. I told him that if he had chased Maurice with the bat and Maurice had fallen over, what would he have done with the baseball bat? It was only right that he got a bit of his own medicine.

In another incident a man from Leeds was refused entry because he was drunk. He produced a knife and began waving it and shouting obscenities. I told him to put the knife down. But he kept shouting: 'Do you want some? Do you want some?'

'It's up to you which way this goes,' I said. 'Put the knife down.'

He refused. He was slashed and received serious injuries to the left-hand side of his face.

Again I justified this by asking what would have happened if I had walked towards him without a knife and he was still brandishing his? I've always said they dictate the way things go. If they put their hands up, I'll put my hands up. If they pull out a weapon, I'll pull out a weapon. It's entirely their choice. Violence is a messy business.

It wasn't all one-way traffic. On Friday, 4 April 1993, I'd been to the Ministry of Sound on a social visit. When I left in the early hours of the morning four or five youths followed me up the Borough High Street and I sensed there was going to be trouble. I turned around and stopped, and one of them asked if I had a problem. I said no, and he hit me on the side of the face. We began fighting and ended up being bundled into a shop doorway. I had one of them by the head, and was hitting him. With the force of us fighting and me being shoved backwards, the window of the shop broke and an alarm went off. I felt what seemed like a hard punch in my stomach and the youths ran away. When I looked down blood was pouring from my stomach. I had been stabbed. I found it hard to stop the flow, but I applied pressure to the wound with a cloth, and some-how drove home.

I lost a lot of blood and tried to dress the wound myself. However, four days later I was admitted to Basildon Hospital. I had an infection, and the wound was nearly two inches deep and was causing me quite a lot of problems. I later discovered that my attackers had been in the Ministry of Sound selling drugs which had been confiscated. They had decided to wait outside for a doorman to leave. They assumed that I worked there as I was dressed in the uniform – black trousers, white shirt and a black bomber jacket – so they attacked me. I never found out who they were. It's one of those things.

One afternoon I received a phone call from Rod Chapman, the assistant manager at Raquels. He told me that my partners had been in to have a meeting with the manager of the club about security and there were a few points he wished to discuss with me. I was totally confused; I didn't have a partner. I went down to the club and asked who 'my partners' were. I was told that Peter Clarke and Charlie Jones had been having a meeting with the manager.

I asked Clarke what was going on, and he told me that the management had asked them to go in for a meeting about the levels of violence being used in the club, because he wasn't happy with it and there were a couple of doormen who worked for me that they wanted to get rid of. I went mad. I told them that it was my door, nothing to do with him, and that Jones should stay out of the club. I would choose the doormen I wanted to work with me, I insisted, and I wouldn't be told what to do by anybody, particularly Jones. If he wanted to take the door from me, he should come and try man to man and not do things behind my back.

That night Clarke sent three of the saddest doormen I have ever seen in my life. I told them all to go home. I rang Peter Clarke and told him I didn't want any doormen from him or Charlie Jones, his partner (whom I wasn't meant to know about). In fact, any agreement we had was then terminated. That Friday night, another doorman and I worked at Raquels on our own.

I had arranged to go to Epping Country Club that week with Steven Richards, Noel Palmer and David Thomkins. They were from the Bristol area. I had met them in the Ministry of Sound, and on Sundays they used to come to Epping. This particular Sunday, I was to introduce them to Tony Tucker as he was looking for dealers for his clubs. At the same time I thought I would use the opportunity to discuss a deal concerning Raquels with Tony.

I'll always remember introducing Steve and Noel to Tony. He wanted to know if they had any drugs with them. I asked them if they could sort Tony out. They said they had and asked Tony for £40. Tony started to laugh and said to me: 'Tell them to hand over what I asked for, or I'll take the fucking lot.' It was typical of Tony. He wasn't in the habit of paying for things.

That same evening I told Tucker about the problems I was having, and said I needed the back-up of a strong firm. I told him I would run the door and he could reap whatever benefits there were from providing invoices and any other 'commodities' – drugs, protection, debts and so on. I would not bother him with the day-to-day running of the club. The only time I would call on him was if I had a severe problem and I needed back-up. In return he would make money each week from the club. We shook hands, and on 4 September 1993 Tony Tucker and I began our partnership at Raquels.

Chapter *Four*

LESS THAN TWO WEEKS AFTER OUR PARTNERSHIP BEGAN, I MADE the front page of the local papers for all the wrong reasons. On 15 September I was outside the club near a burger van when a man made a few silly remarks about the Raquels door staff. I told him to shut up, but he wouldn't, so I hit him. He was knocked out when his head hit the pavement. His friends had difficulty bringing him round. They called an ambulance and the police showed up.

At the hospital, Dave Case, the injured man, told police he wished to press charges. The police appealed for witnesses on the front of the local paper, saying it was an unprovoked attack by a man approximately 40 years old, heavily built, with a Birmingham accent. I was outraged. I was only 33 at the time.

Within a day or so I was arrested. The police found the number of calls they had received giving my name quite amusing; it seemed I was the only heavily built man in Basildon with a Birmingham accent. I told the police it was self-defence and I had been attacked first, and backed this up by providing numerous witnesses from the club. Case was spotted in a pub in Basildon by a mutual friend, and he suddenly remembered that it was entirely his fault and the case against me was dropped.

The agreement with Tucker brought new faces onto the scene in Basildon. Men who worked for him and were looking for a change would come and work for me at Raquels. Troublemakers began to go to other clubs and the violence in Raquels began to die a death. Local hardmen who did remain as customers became more friendly and wanted to get on with our firm.

A man called Jason Vella was at that time making a name for himself in Basildon. He had a firm who were causing chaos across the south-east. He used to come to Raquels, and we got on quite well.

Vella was short but stocky. He was in his early twenties, but had a fearsome reputation. He was considered more of a nutter than a hardman. People who crossed him wouldn't get an opportunity to fight him: they would be cut, shot or stabbed. I always thought Vella was all right. He certainly wasn't loud. He was quiet and he never put himself about. His victims entered the business through their own choice. If he had let them go unpunished, he would have become a victim himself. That's the way things were in the world we inhabited.

Another hardman was Jason Draper, who was also in his twenties. Few messed with him in the Basildon area. He too became quite friendly with me and the other doormen.

Tony Tucker told me he was having his birthday party at the Prince of Wales in South Ockendon, and he invited me and all the other doormen from Raquels. He asked me to bring along Steve and Noel from Epping so that there would be a supply of drugs for him and his guests. The party was a real success. Doormen from everywhere were there. Most were out of their faces on cocaine, Special K or ecstasy or a cocktail of all three and more. Tucker was in a really good mood.

In the early hours of the morning I was sitting on the floor of a room with Steve and Noel and my wife Debra. A man in his early twenties pushed open the door, which hit me. I looked at him, waiting for him to apologise, and he asked me what the matter was. I said to him: 'You've just knocked the fucking door into me.' He said: 'Well, you're a doorman, aren't you?' It was a stupid thing to say, because it was obviously intended to cause trouble. I got up and walked towards the man. He walked out to the kitchen and I followed him. Friends of Tucker's also followed us, but before the fight could start, we were separated.

I later learned he was Tucker's closest friend, Craig Rolfe. He was possessive of his friendship with Tucker. I told him that out of respect for Tucker he shouldn't cause trouble at his birthday party. He seemed all right afterwards, but he still had an attitude. It was Tucker who told me a few days later, when I was explaining what had gone on, why Rolfe had this chip on his shoulder.

On Christmas Eve 1968, a man was found murdered in a van in a layby on the A13 between Stanford-Le-Hope and Vange in Basildon. The dead man had been found slumped in the seat of a grey Austin van. He was Brian Rolfe, a market trader from Basildon. At the postmortem later that day the cause of death was determined as a fractured skull. In less than 24 hours the case had been solved. On Boxing Day a 19-year-old motor fitter, John Kennedy from Basildon, was charged with the murder together with 23-year-old Lorraine Rolfe, the wife of the murdered man.

When she was charged, it is reported that Lorraine said: 'I never touched him, honest, on my baby's life.' Lorraine was at that time the mother of three children and was expecting a fourth – Craig. Kennedy and Rolfe were lovers. When the case came to trial at Maidstone in March 1969 the prosecution alleged that Lorraine and Kennedy murdered Brian Rolfe and tried to fake a roadside robbery.

Both pleaded not guilty to the murder charges and Lorraine not guilty to making false statements. The prosecution alleged the murder was committed so the accused could simultaneously get rid of Rolfe and acquire his money. It was said that Rolfe was hit over the head in the early hours of Christmas Eve in the bedroom of his Linford Drive home with a ten-pin bowling skittle which weighed nearly four pounds. His skull was crushed like an eggshell. Kennedy was found guilty of murder, and jailed for life. He was also given a concurrent sentence of seven years for breaking and entering Rolfe's home and stealing £597.10/-. Lorraine Rolfe was found not guilty of murder, but sent to prison for 18 months for making false statements to impede Kennedy's arrest. It was while serving this sentence in Holloway Prison that Lorraine gave birth to Craig. Little wonder he had a chip on his shoulder and he'd chosen a life of crime.

Rolfe and I never really did see eye to eye after that first meeting. Our views clashed on most things. However, my association with Tony Tucker was business, Rolfe's was personal, so like and dislike didn't really come into it. Rolfe had a fairly serious cocaine problem, and hanging around with Tucker helped, because there was a constant supply at a discount price, if not for free.

Merging with anyone in business is always potentially hazardous, but particularly so if you're involved in our line of work. When I had taken over Raquels from Dave Vine I had, in the eyes of those concerned, become top of that particular heap. When I merged with Tucker, who ran a much larger door firm, however, my position was automatically questioned. Long-standing members of his firm resented me. It's sad but true – men are like children. They felt threatened in some way by a newcomer. The fact that I was also introducing people like the drug dealers Steve and Noel into the situation caused further resentment. Tucker's doormen had their own people they were earning from. I didn't know they had dealers, and thought I was being helpful.

Shortly after Tucker's birthday party, Steve and Noel and their runners, who included Dave Thomkins, began work at Club UK in Wandsworth, where Tony Tucker ran the security. (Their position had been discussed at Tucker's birthday party.) For the exclusive rights to sell drugs in there, they paid Tucker £1,000 per weekend. On average their return for Friday and Saturday nights was £12,000.

Christmas 1993, and the firm celebrated in style. My brother Michael and his wife Carol came to a party we were attending at the Café de Paris in the West End. It was one of the most exclusive clubs at the time. There were queues of people outside, which we ignored as a matter of course. These events where the firm got together were extraordinary. Nobody connected to us paid to get in anywhere. Nobody paid for drugs. Huge bags of cocaine, Special K and ecstasy were made available to the firm and their associates. You look around the dark room, you're surrounded by 40 or more friends, all faces (well-known figures). Everyone else in the place knows it, too.

The music's so loud it lifts you; you're all one – you have total control. Those in the firm created an atmosphere which demanded respect from other villains. Straight people hardly noticed. On the surface, everyone was friendly, but there was this feeling of power and evil. Tucker felt it, too. Often he would look across the club and smile knowingly. Looking back, we revelled in the atmosphere we created wherever we went.

It was a memorable Christmas. After the party we went back to Steve and Noel's flat at Denmark Court in Surrey Quays, an exclusive development in the Docklands area. Strewn across the floor, spilling out of a carrier bag, lay more than £20,000, the proceeds of that weekend. The dealers had so much money about them, they didn't know how to spend it or where to put it.

Around that time in London, there was a little firm going around the clubs who used to look out for the dealers, follow them home and rob them of their proceeds. It was quite a lucrative operation because the victims couldn't go to the police. Steve and Noel had been victims of this firm while dealing in the Ministry of Sound. A man had knocked on the door while Steve was in the house alone. When Steve had answered, the man had pushed his way in with an accomplice, tied Steve up and threatened him with a knife, but Steve would not say where the money was. The man cut Steve several times in the mouth, demanding to know where it was hidden. Eventually, fearing for his life, Steve handed over £4,000 and the robbers left.

Steve and Noel feared another attack, and on occasion they would pay me to protect them. During their career in the drug world, they were to call on me many times for assistance.

On Sunday, 23 January, Debra and I and some other friends were at the Gass club in central London when we heard that a friend of mine and well-known villain, Michael McCarthy, had been shot in Basildon. Mick was sitting having breakfast with his wife at his father-in-law's café, Rebels. They heard a woman screaming and a door bang open. The gunman entered and it was reported that he said, 'I'm going to kill you, McCarthy.' As Mick stood up, he shot him in the back. The gunman then stood over Mick, put the gun to his head and fired it again. Beverley, Mick's wife, wrestled with the gunman, and pleaded with him not to shoot any more. She caught her finger in the buttonhole of his coat, and couldn't get away. It is reported he swung around and pointed the gun at her forehead at close range. She said: 'I don't know whether the gun went off or not. He went to pull the trigger. I saw that.' Other customers grabbed the gunman and bundled him out of the door.

Mick, incredibly, survived the attack. However, he's paralysed for life from the waist down. To this day nobody has been convicted of the attack.

I had known Mick for some time. He often came to Raquels, and his children attended the same school as mine. A lot of people were not surprised by what happened, but I thought it was a tragedy none the less. It was a sign of the times, a prophecy of things to come.

Guns had always been set aside for special occasions, but more and more often they were being used to sort out trivial arguments. Drugs, too, were becoming more prevalent, bringing in huge rewards for villains. The more money there was, the more violence there was. The more violence there was, the more guns were being used. The stakes were being upped all the time. Every Tom, Dick and Harry was strolling round Essex with a gun, although McCarthy's shooting wasn't drugs-related, but due to another feud.

Business at Raquels was not booming, so the powers-that-be decided a change was needed. Out went the grand piano and in came framed gold discs, electric guitars, trumpets, American football jerseys, American football helmets and baseball bats (purely for decor). They turned it into an American-style bar, and called it the Buzz Bar. It had the desired effect and attracted more people.

Along with the good came the bad. Raquels is situated in Basildon town centre, next door to a butcher's in the middle of a market. In that market square is the Bullseye pub, the place where Vine's doormen had been attacked by the men wielding machetes.

The regulars were known as 'the Bullseye'. They had a reputation for violence. When the Buzz Bar opened they began drinking there. The most well-known member of their gang was Jason Draper.

Draper, as I said before, could be quite friendly when he was just with one or two of his friends. However, when the Bullseye firm was together, his minions seemed to play up for him. I thought everybody deserved a chance, so I let them drink in there until they outstayed their welcome.

In January 1994 there was a bomb scare on the Southend-to-Fenchurch St British Rail line. All trains were prevented from leaving Basildon station. Passengers were not allowed to go into the station and so in a short period of time there was a large group of people hanging around the town centre. Rather than wait in the street on a cold winter's night, they headed to the Buzz Bar for a drink. As soon as I went into work, I told the manager, 'You should get some more doormen down here, there is going to be trouble.'

There was a group of about ten men from Romford and seven or eight men from the Bullseye. By half past eight the Buzz Bar was completely packed. One of the men from the Bullseye came up to me and said, 'Look, Bernie, we don't want to cause trouble in here, but one of those geezers from Romford is giving it to us.' I said, 'What do you mean, "giving it"?' He said, 'Every time he walks past, he knocks into us, and it's going to go off in here in a minute.'

I said, 'I don't want any grief in here, so if you want, I'll ask them to leave, and do what you want outside. I don't want it to happen in here.' I went downstairs to get a tea from the burger van and I was followed outside by one of the Bullseye firm. He said it was going to go off and a fat man had been mouthing off saying he was going to use some CS gas. He didn't want to fall out with me and was advising me that the fat man was definitely going to use it. As I was walking upstairs I could hear the sound of smashing glass and people screaming. I ran up the stairs and there was a huge fight in progress. The Bullseye firm were hammering the men from Romford. The fat man had let off the CS gas and people were running and screaming everywhere. I was trying to pull people apart, but the fight spilled out onto the stairs. Several men were bleeding heavily. I managed to get the men from the Bullseye out of the doors and lock the men from Romford in the Buzz Bar. One of the Romford guys hit me and I began fighting with him.

Suddenly the doors burst open. The Bullseye lot came back in and the fight continued. Some of the men from Romford had escaped into the street but they were being attacked there also. Eventually I managed to get both parties outside as the police were pulling up. I saw one man lying on the ground. Blood was gushing from a wound in his head. I ran over to him and saw that it was a very serious injury. There was a gaping wound around his eye. I couldn't tell whether he'd been stabbed above his eye or glassed. I put him in the recovery position and wrapped my coat around his head to try to stop the flow.

The police pulled up, jumped out and grabbed me. I said: 'I'm a doorman, I'm trying to help him.' An ambulance arrived and took the man to hospital. Through police enquiries I later learned the man had lost his eye and suffered severe injury to his face. He had been repeatedly glassed. I wasn't very happy with the people from the Bullseye, as they should have sorted their problem with these people outside. They had brought police attention to me.

In the following few days I learned that the man who'd been blinded was a friend of Mark Rothermel's. Tony Tucker, for whom Mark used to work, rang me and told me this. He asked me who Jason Draper was and where he could be found. I had a photograph of Draper and me together which had been taken at a social night out at Epping Country Club. The firm's business came before friendship. Tucker said he would need to know what Draper looked like and so asked me to take the photo over to his house in Chafford Hundred.

When I got there Tucker was suggesting ways of mounting a revenge attack on Draper and his friends from the Bullseye. All the plans were pretty gruesome. While we were talking, Craig Rolfe arrived and saw the photograph. He asked Tucker why he had a photograph of Jason Draper. It turned out Rolfe knew him, as he had been brought up in Basildon. When Tucker told him, Rolfe was furious. He was arguing that Draper was all right and nothing should be done about the attack on the man from Romford.

Again I was in confrontation with Rolfe. I said to Tucker: 'If this man is a friend of Mark's, then it's up to Mark to decide what is to be done. If Mark wants to do something about it, I'm going to help him.' Tucker said he'd ring me later, and I left.

Tucker rang me that night and told me to ignore Rolfe. He said if Mark was going to do something about it, then we would back him. To my surprise it was the man who had lost his eye who came to Draper's rescue. He said that he didn't want any retaliation. I think he had had enough of violence. The firm from the Bullseye stayed away for a few weeks. I think they were expecting a comeback, but because the injured party had declined, none was forthcoming.

On 11 February the Bullseye gang turned up at Raquels. I told them to fuck off. A fight started on the door and they backed off. They smashed pallets up and produced weapons from their cars which were parked nearby. They threw bottles and bricks at the doors, so I closed them. They then charged the doors, trying to smash them with an axe and iron bars. They doused the doors in petrol and tried to burn them. I opened the doors and we ran at them.

Draper, the man they looked up to, wasn't with them, so they didn't have that much heart. They dropped their weapons and ran. We gave chase. We caught two or three of them. One of the men who was beaten stopped breathing. The police arrived and went to his assistance, and an ambulance was called. I was arrested and kept in the police station until 5.40 the following morning.

It was self-defence, and I had the usual coach-load of witnesses from the club to verify the fact. No charges were ever brought. The man lived to tell the tale and both sides were happy.

Violence I can deal with, but intrigue has never been my forte. Micky Pierce, Dave Vine's old partner, was still on the scene, lurking in the background. He came to me and asked me to assist him with the charges he was facing in relation to the gun found on his farm and the equipment used to manufacture amphetamine. I said I would help.

On 21 February I went to his solicitors in London and made a statement. I told the solicitor I worked occasionally for Micky Pierce on a casual basis, repossessing cars, vans and commercial vehicles. I said at the end of January 1993 I was asked to repossess an Iveco box van from a yard at the Amstrad factory in Shoeburyness. I said Micky had phoned me the previous evening to ask if I was available for a day's work because he would be busy on the farm all day and would be unable to do it himself. I was to go to the yard at Amstrad's and pick up the van for one of the finance companies Pierce had a contract with. I was then to take the van to Pierce's house, remove all the items from the vehicle except the spare wheel, the jack and the wheel brace and place any excess items in a shed at the rear of Pierce's property. I said I did this.

The excess items were two boxes which I described as resembling tea chests. These contained glassware, a radio and a multi-coloured folding deckchair. I said there was nobody at Pierce's property. I then completed my instructions by taking the empty vehicle to Micky's father's farm a little further up the road. I said this was standard procedure regarding all the vehicles I was involved in repossessing.

When Micky Pierce's case came to court the charges relating to the drugs were dropped and he was fined £1,000 for possessing the firearm. I thought I had done him a good turn. He, unknown to me at the time, was not grateful at all, and together with others was plotting my downfall.

Tony Tucker and I took over security at the Towngate Theatre in Basildon where pop concerts were held. It was hardly a lucrative contract, but it was work and additional money. One evening I was told that there were doormen already there. To my surprise a security company from Kent had taken over our contract, which was a verbal one, without me or Tucker being notified. I asked the Towngate Theatre manager what was going on, and he said that these people were cheaper than us and he had therefore hired them. I explained to him that things didn't work like that, and they would not remain there.

A few days later another doorman from Raquels and I went over to the Towngate Theatre to have a drink. There was a disturbance, and the security ran off and telephoned the police. Large numbers of officers turned up and insisted that the other doormen and I, who were in there having a quiet drink, should leave at once.

As a result of that disagreement, I was visited at Raquels by the licensing police in Basildon, who weren't keen on me anyway. They told me that they would revoke my licence if this behaviour persisted. They suggested that if I had a grievance with the way things were being run concerning doormen, I should approach the council, who ran the door registration scheme, and not take matters into my own hands.

They were also concerned about doormen working for me who were not registered. They said anyone with a conviction in recent years should be excluded from working. They told me I had to register all of my doormen. If they were concerned about people having convictions for fisticuffs who were working with me, I thought I'd better not mention that Mark Rothermel had also begun working occasionally at Raquels.

They weren't all dark days. We had good times too. Tony Tucker used to lead Nigel Benn, the boxer, into the ring at all of his fights and on occasion we would be invited to parties in honour of Nigel and his friends. After one of his fights a party was held at the Park nightclub in Kensington High Street. Everyone was there. We really had a good time. Tucker was in his element – out of his head, shitfaced on coke and Special K, one of his favourite cocktails.

All sorts of people attended these parties. I became very friendly with Dave Lea who now lives in Hollywood. He started out working as Sam Fox's bodyguard. He was the British kickboxing champion and used his skills to further his career as a stuntman. He worked on the *Batman* films, *Hook* and *Tango & Cash*. Dave also trained Sylvester Stallone and many other Hollywood names. When he was in England he stayed at his sister's in Basildon, and we often went out together. As a favour, he had gone with me to collect my son from school with his Batman outfit on. The other six- or seven-year-old boys could not believe it. They thought my son really knew Batman. The people we knew were like that – they would do anything for you.

In March 1994, a 20-year-old, Kevin Jones, died in Club UK. Shortly after the death, the police, who had Steve and Noel under surveillance, found 1,500 ecstasy pills in a stolen car from Bristol in an underground carpark at the back of their flat. Steve and Noel were arrested, as was Noel's girlfriend, an Asian princess named Yasmin. At the same time Dave Thomkins was arrested at his home in Bath.

Thomkins was bailed. He rang me and told me what had happened. I organised a 'proper' solicitor for Steve and Noel and we attended their court hearing at Tower Bridge Magistrates Court in London. Yasmin turned up for the hearing, as did Steve's girlfriend, a stunning Swedish girl. Both girls had initially been arrested but were put on police bail and had to return to the police station at a later date.

Our first problem was going to be getting Steve and Noel out on bail, which was set at £10,000 each. Thomkins and I met Yasmin the following day and she gave us £20,000 in cash. We took this to Leman St Police Station in the City, plonked it on the counter and asked for our friends to be released. The officer at the desk was unsure what to do. Dave and I were kept waiting for several hours while enquiries were made as to what the procedure should be. We were taken into a room and asked about our identities and where the money had come from and so on. We said a family friend had loaned the money, but the police officer said he was going to refuse it. Bail would be granted only if it could be shown that the money was in an account prior to their arrest. After making several frantic phone calls, we found someone who was able to do the necessary and the following morning they were released on bail.

At the first trial, the jury could not reach a verdict. At the final trial Steve and Noel were acquitted and returned to their native Bath. (No charges were ever brought against Yasmin, Steve's girlfriend or Dave Thomkins.) Tucker was shouting and screaming about their arrests. He claimed they'd been grassed up because of the young man dying in the nightclub. It seemed obvious to me that people involved in this trade only have a limited time. To be successful you have to tell as many people as possible what you are doing. It's no good standing in a nightclub with 500 ecstasy pills in your pocket and keeping the fact to yourself. The more people you tell, the more pills you sell, but at the same time the chance of you being arrested rises dramatically. Tucker was concerned that they were going to grass on him for taking rent, but there was no danger of that, and I reassured him of the fact.

Back in Basildon I was asked to attend a meeting with David Britt and Dawn French, two environmental health officers who ran the door registration scheme for Basildon Council. The manager of Raquels, Ian Blackwell, was also asked to be there. At the meeting the subject of the Towngate Theatre incident arose. I told the council they were getting involved in something they knew little about. People couldn't just turn up from another town and undercut you and take over your door and expect nothing to happen. They argued that competition was good. They obviously didn't understand. I got rather angry and Britt mentioned that they had received reports that I had been taking protection money from a pub in Basildon called the Castlemayne. I told him this was nonsense. I had taken money from the pub, but it was for a favour I'd done the manager. Some hooligans had been causing problems in there, and I had spoken to them and told them to stay out. Britt told me that Basildon was not Chicago. His implication was clear.

'Maybe it's not Chicago,' I thought, 'but there are people in the town who wish it was.' Events in Basildon were becoming far more violent.

Chapter *Five*

AS THE NOTORIETY OF THE FIRM GREW, SO TOO DID THE NUMBER of people who wanted to be known as our associates. The presence of the firm in pubs or clubs in the area prompted respect, and I have to admit it was a good feeling.

Because of the firm's reputation for sorting out problems and people, we were now doing a lot more than running the door at weekends. Additional work was forthcoming. Protection, punishment beatings and debt recovery were all added to the firm's CV. It wasn't just local work, either. Cries for help came from as far afield as Sunderland, Manchester, Bristol and the Midlands. The work was diverse. Some of it was legal, some of it gratuitous, some of it downright illegal. It seemed that anybody who had a grievance wanted to use our violent firm to get their revenge on whoever had slighted them.

Peter Singh, an Asian from Basildon, paid me and another doorman to protect his brother who had been threatened in a family feud. His brother had entered an arranged marriage and after a couple of years he wanted a divorce. The girl's family took it as a great insult and they had threatened his life. At the divorce proceedings in Southend County Court, there was pushing, shoving and shouting, and threats were issued. The judge removed me and my friend from the court after the girl's family said they'd been threatened. Eventually Peter's brother got his divorce.

A man from Leicester named Martin Davies contacted us and asked us to recover a series of debts which had accumulated following the collapse of his video hire shop chain. I travelled to

Leicestershire with two other men and soon discovered most of the debts were useless. The people involved had lost heavily in the business also, and they had no money to repay the outstanding debt. One of the men who owed money was a taxi driver named Danny Marlow. I went to his house, knocked on the door and a woman, whom I assumed was his wife, answered. She told me he wasn't in and she had no way of contacting him. Through a neighbour I learned which cab office he worked at and went to see him there. The controller was persuaded to contact Danny on his radio. He told him to come back to the cab office but Danny refused. I gave the controller my number, and Danny rang me. We had a row and I threatened him. He said he was going to contact the police.

Some time later, at about 11 o'clock one evening, Danny was outside his home and he was struck by a speeding car. He had received a phone call at his local pub, the Bell, at 10.30 p.m. He left about ten minutes later.

A witness heard two men talking. The voices got louder, then he heard a high-revving car and Danny's pool cue case clatter to the ground. Danny died on his way to hospital. Forty minutes later, a stolen Ford Granada was found burnt out nine miles away.

The police interviewed me, Martin Davies and the other two men. They were convinced that Marlow had died for the £800 he owed. That may have been the case. It was certainly nothing to do with our firm. We would hardly kill anyone for a share of £800. We were annoyed that Davies had revealed our identities during questioning by the police, and decided that we should be compensated. We fined Davies £3,000, a grand for each member of the firm whose name he had given. He paid up, and we have not heard from or seen him since.

These people were not from our world, and were considered easy pickings. We were contacted about a man named Jackson in Southend, for example. He had borrowed £60,000 to invest. The business venture had gone horribly wrong and the man who was holding his money had disappeared to Geneva. We descended on Jackson. He was very middle-class: nice house, nice wife, nice job.

He didn't like our kind of people around, so after a bit of intimidation he agreed to pay us £3,000 expenses to fly to Geneva to try and apprehend the man who was holding his money. We took Jackson's cash but never went as far as the end of Southend Pier.

A week later we returned to his house and told him we had been unsuccessful and needed to go on further trips. I think he smelled a rat, because eventually he had an injunction put on us preventing us from approaching him.

We devised a set of rules for straight people requiring our services for debt recovery. When someone came to us with a debt we used to tell them that there was no fee for our services until the money had been recovered. Then we would require a third of everything we had collected. Most of these people had been through solicitors or the courts and paid huge fees for little or no result, and so the deal we offered seemed quite good. After all, they had nothing to lose – or so they thought. The other clause in the agreement was that once we were on the debt it remained ours and they couldn't employ other people to chase it. Also, once we'd agreed to take it on, we would remain with it until the money was recovered; the person who employed us couldn't change his mind, or if he did, he had to pay us a third of the debt as our fee. It all seemed fair, and everyone agreed.

What we used to do, however, was intimidate the person owing the money, or cause a scene at his home so he would call the police. The police, not knowing who we were, would go to the person the money was owed to and tell them that if there were any more problems, they would be prosecuted. So the person who was owed money would get in touch with us and ask us to pull out because the police had threatened to prosecute. We would remind them of the clause that if they called it off, they would have to pay us a third. Fearing prosecution from the police on one side, and violence from us on the other, they had no choice but to pay.

The illegal side of our operation was far less complex. We did a job for one man who'd been hounded by a motorist in a flashy car. The guy used to do wheel spins in his street and play loud music from his car stereo; the man was at his wits' end. He said the driver was using his street as a race track. He feared for his children. He couldn't get any peace and quiet because of the music. He paid us £500 to sort it out. The car which was causing the problem was the guy's pride and joy. We were told he was putting it in for a respray and contacted the garage to find out when he was picking it up. On the day the man collected his newly resprayed car, he was followed and when he parked it outside his home and went inside, it was petrol-bombed, burnt out, absolutely gutted. We were told the aggrieved man danced in his front room as he watched the car burn.

The firm were also employed as minders on drug deals. The fee would depend on the size of the parcel. When the two parties met to do the deal, a member of the firm was present just to make sure one side didn't have the other over. They weren't required to say or do anything unless something didn't go according to plan.

When things didn't go to plan, we were often called in to make matters right. A man named Kevin Gray came to see us. He was a drug courier who worked for a firm from West Ham in the east end of London. Kevin had been sent to Sunderland with a parcel of £16,000-worth of ecstasy which he was going to trade with a firm of Geordies run by two brothers, Billy and John Carruthers. When Kevin got to Sunderland he was taken to a house and the brothers told him that they didn't have the money with them because they feared the police were watching them. They told Kevin to give them the parcel and said they would go and fetch the money.

Rather foolishly Kevin handed it over. Once a person becomes a courier and is given a parcel, it is his responsibility. If it goes missing, he has to pay. Billy Carruthers stayed with Kevin and his brother went off with the parcel.

Half an hour later his brother came running back into the house, appearing flustered. He told everyone to get out of the house, and everybody ran. Kevin couldn't find anyone. When he went back to the house some hours later, a girl was there. She told him that John Carruthers had been going to another house with the parcel and the police had stopped him. He had jumped out of his car, run down the railway embankment and thrown the parcel away. She told Kevin that John assumed that the police had picked up the parcel.

Kevin couldn't do anything because he was alone, and so headed back down to London. I was surprised that he swallowed the story. Normally you would ask people to produce paperwork to prove that the police have been involved. I was even more surprised he'd handed over the parcel. It was quite obvious the Geordies had had him over. The firm from West Ham was now onto Kevin. He owed them £16,000 and they wanted to know what he was going to do about it.

I felt the only way to get his money back would be if we kidnapped one of the Carruthers brothers and brought him down to London. We could then contact the other brother, and tell him that when we got the parcel back he would get his brother back.

We armed ourselves and headed up north to have it out with the Geordies. Billy and John weren't new to this game. They had upped and left long before we arrived. We did manage to get hold of an associate of theirs known as Alan. He was either very brave, or really didn't know the whereabouts of his friends. From the beating he received, I believe he didn't know where they were. He was pushed to the floor, stamped on and kicked repeatedly. If he did know, he would have told us.

Already £16,000 in debt, the courier could not afford the cost of us remaining in Sunderland searching for people who had obviously left, so he cut his losses and we returned south. To recover the money he was forced to sell his car and run drugs around the country for no payment. The Geordies had a result that time. But blagging (robbing) shipments of drugs is not the kind of thing you last very long doing.

A new manager, Mark Combes, took over Raquels and there was soon an agreement that the way forward was to have house and garage nights rather than three hours of chart music and five slow dances at the end of the night, which had been the format up until his arrival.

To the revellers, Raquels was now trouble-free. Most of the violence was behind the scenes, away from the premises. The noticeable change brought offers from promoters who wanted to hire out the club. The rave scene had no place for violence; all the kids now were into this peace and happiness thing. Mark Combes was approached by a promotions team from Southend who were very professional and very successful. They were currently hiring out a club in the Southend area which didn't hold enough people to satisfy the demand. They were looking for larger premises and had heard about the improvements at Raquels.

An agreement was reached and a date was set for them to begin. The following day Mark Murray, a drug dealer, and his partner Bob Smith, whom I had not previously met, came into the Buzz Bar and asked to speak to me. They told me that they sold most of the gear in the clubs around the Basildon and Southend area and they had heard that the promotions team from Southend were coming into Raquels. They asked if they could strike up a deal whereby they would be allowed to sell their drugs exclusively in our club.

I called Tony Tucker and he told me to let them start. The fee depended on the amount of drugs they sold per night. If it became busy, that fee would be reviewed. Both parties agreed to see how it went. It was going to be the door staff's job to ensure there was no trouble from other dealers and also that an early warning was given about any police presence.

I wasn't concerned about men like Jason Vella. He often used to come into the club and I'd become friendly with him. But Murray, not being a violent man, had heard, like everyone else, what Vella was up to in the Essex area. He was concerned that Vella was going to muscle in and put his operation out of business. Although only 23 at the time, Vella was a notorious man on the Essex drugs scene. He specialised in kidnapping, torturing and humiliating his opponents. One man had a broomstick inserted into his backside and Vella took pictures of him. These were then circulated to show what would happen to people who crossed him.

Another man, Mark Skeets, sent Vella's girlfriend a Christmas card. Vella decided that he was taking a liberty. He invited Skeets out for a drink to lure him into a trap. Skeets was tied up and beaten. Vella then chopped off Skeets's hair and shaved his eyebrows off. Again photographs were taken to humiliate him. He was jabbed with knives and burned with cigarettes. The soles of his feet were also burned. He was forced to take the hallucinogenic drug acid, and snort 12 lines of cocaine. He was completely drugged out of his brains. Coupled with the assaults, the effects must have been terrifying.

Another man, Dean Power, was trapped in a similar way. He was whipped with a metal coat hanger and flogged with a bamboo stick. In a second attack some time later, Power was jabbed with a roasting fork and beaten with lumps of wood. His crime? He had tried to restrain Vella in a pub argument over money. His head was also kicked, his feet and arms were stamped on. He was totally disfigured. Power told people Vella was like the devil, he was possessed. Although the police were well aware of Vella's activities, nobody would give evidence against him.

The police were called to many incidents. One man was admitted to hospital with burns to the back of his hands from a hot iron. He wouldn't talk. Another had been shot at close range with a handgun. He wouldn't talk either. One house had the door kicked in. The people inside were sprayed with CS gas and the TV was blown out by a sawn-off shotgun. They refused to complain.

A man named Reggie Nunn owed Vella £7,000. He had been sent to Scotland as a courier and he had spent some of the profits on what he called expenses. Vella lured him to his home in Basildon to discuss the debt. When Nunn couldn't explain to Vella's satisfaction what had happened, he was beaten and kicked. Then a sword was produced and Vella stabbed him. Afterwards Vella started shouting at Nunn. 'There's blood on my settee, stop whimpering like a little boy. You know it's not going to end here, Reg.' Vella gave him a few more slaps and swipes and went out of the room. Reggie overheard Vella saying he would be kept overnight and finished off in the morning. In panic he jumped through the upstairs window, falling nearly 20 feet to the ground. He staggered to a neighbour's door, begging for help, and they called the police. There was no need. At that time, 40 officers from Essex had been assigned to an investigation against Vella, known as operation Max, and his flat was under surveillance. Police video cameras had caught Nunn jumping from the window and staggering to the neighbour's house. It was the end of the road for Vella and his firm. Shortly afterwards they were all arrested and remanded in custody to await trial for various offences ranging from drug dealing to serious assault. But to secure a conviction, three men had to be provided with new identities after giving evidence – an expensive business.

In the same month that Vella's world collapsed, a new outlet for drug users in Basildon opened up, and the firm started its ascendancy. Its activities would make Vella's seem user-friendly.

On Friday, 25 July 1994, Raquels opened its doors for the first house and garage night promoted by the team from Southend. It was absolutely packed, because this type of event was rare in a violent town like Basildon, where peroxide blondes, cheap drinks and drunken nights were more commonplace. We kept all those types out, and for those not involved in the politics it really was an enjoyable night. There was no trouble among the customers and the atmosphere in there was fantastic. It's hard to describe. You could feel the music, it was so loud. You could see little because of the darkness and dry ice, but already there was a feeling of unity among the revellers.

I had begun to experience a new feeling myself which at first I dismissed. In the firm you had a sense of security. On your home ground, you felt safe. Everyone in that particular jungle knew who to avoid. It was when we moved to seemingly greener pastures working in northern England, the Midlands or Bristol that the problems for me started. Danger was everywhere, yet you couldn't see it – there was just a feeling that something was going to happen. It is then that paranoia creeps in, and for me it struck deep. I became suspicious of everybody.

If a car pulled up outside the club, I was expecting somebody to get out and launch some sort of attack upon us. Groups of men in the club probably talking about everyday business aroused suspicion in me. The pressures of my environment were beginning to affect me. I wouldn't leave the house unless I was armed. Even during the day, if I went to fetch a newspaper or post a letter in the town I took a sheath knife with me. My car had weapons hidden in the boot and under the dashboard on the driver's side. There could be anything from a knife to a gun, depending on where I was going and what I was up to. I even kept a gun in my bedroom and there was a baseball bat and squirt (ammonia) in the cupboard by the front door. I considered every possibility. If they kicked the door in and I was upstairs in bed the weapons by the door were useless. Therefore I had to have a weapon in my bedroom. If I was getting something out of the boot of my car and they came, the weapon in the dashboard was useless, therefore I had to have one in the boot. I tried to convince myself of the stupidity of it all, but paranoia had taken a grip of me.

With the crowds and the house music came a demand for ecstasy. Raquels was hit by an avalanche of drugs. Local men were quickly recruited by Murray. Dealers were everywhere in the club. The demand was being met.

I had now recruited what I considered to be an ideal door. I had doormen who were not bullies. They were friendly and could mix with the people who were entering the club and they were not seen as intimidating. Yet if someone wanted trouble, they would fucking get it, and they would regret it. None of the men was from the Basildon area; they came from south and east London. They weren't impressed by the local hardmen's reputations. They took people how they found them. They dealt with them accordingly.

Without exception, everybody accepted it. On the face of it the police now had a peaceful club and they could divert their attention elsewhere. The occasional victim was of our own kind and so of little concern to them. Previously we had endured twice-weekly visits from the constabulary, but we rarely saw them now, and on the odd occasion we did, it was only as they drove past to buy tea from the burger van.

We now had a club full to capacity with peaceful people. The customers were getting what they wanted, and the firm had got what it wanted.

In that same July of 1994 an explosive ingredient was added to what was, under the surface, becoming an increasingly unstable and volatile situation.

Pat Tate was released from prison after serving four years of a six-year sentence. In December 1988 Tate had robbed a restaurant in Basildon. He had been in a Happy Eater with his girlfriend and had got into a dispute with the staff about his bill. He decided to help himself to the takings.

When he was arrested he was found to be in possession of a small amount of cocaine, which was for his personal use. Billericay magistrates decided that Tate would see in the new year within the confines of Chelmsford Prison.

Tate, however, had made other plans. He jumped over the side of the dock and made for the door. Six police officers joined the jailer and jumped onto his back, but he broke free and ran off. One WPC received a black eye and another police officer was kicked in the face as they tried to block his escape. He ploughed his way out of the court to a waiting motorcycle. Roadblocks which were immediately set up failed to trap him. His escape was so speedy, the police couldn't say what type of motorcycle it was, or whether he was alone or travelled as a passenger.

Several days later, Tate surfaced in Spain. He remained there for a year, but he made the mistake of crossing over into Gibraltar where he was arrested by the British authorities.

Everybody in Basildon had a good word for Tate, but he had begun using harder drugs in prison and this caused a marked change in his character. I call prisons hate factories, because all they produce is people full of hatred. Tate came out of prison that way. He wanted the world to know he was out and he was not happy about the way he had been treated.

Tucker warmed to men like him. He was six foot two, very broad, 18 stone and no fool. He also had a glamorous bit of history. His fight with the police in court and escape on a motorbike were talking points in criminal circles. He was soon recruited by the firm.

Tate's arrival was met with resentment by some members. Chris Wheatley had returned from America some time before Tate's release. Tucker had latched on to him, giving him control of one of his clubs in Southend, and he became a close friend. However, when Tate came out, Tucker dropped Chris as if he didn't exist. Chris is one of only a few of my former associates that I have any time for. I do not think he deserved the treatment he received from Tucker; he turned on him for no reason, and the firm followed suit. Tate took his place.

Others who had no reason to dislike Tate felt their position in the firm was being threatened. Few felt comfortable about his appointment because he had an explosive temper. Tucker, on the other hand, was loving every minute of it. He loved to pitch people against one another.

On one occasion a doorman from Chelmsford mentioned in conversation that he thought one of his colleagues was a police informant. Tucker rang the guy and arranged a meeting outside McDonald's in Chelmsford. Then he told the other man that if he thought someone was a grass, he should confront him and not talk about him behind his back. He was allowed to arm himself with a machete and was then taken to the meeting at McDonald's. Fearing he was going to lose face, he accused his colleague of being a grass in front of Tucker. The man denied it, of course.

'He's just called you a fucking grass,' said Tucker. 'What are you going to do about it? I'd fucking hit him if he said that to me.'

The so-called grass threw a half-hearted punch and the other man slashed his arm with the machete before he fled. You didn't get a P45 in our firm.

Pat Tate brought with him ideas of grandeur. He had made lots of useful contacts in prison whom he thought we could work with or exploit. Prison is the university of crime, and such meetings are inevitable. Dealing with the unknown is a dangerous business, however. I was all for looking after what was already there rather than expanding into unknown territory. Tucker and Tate felt everyone was there for the taking. They began to talk about lorries bringing in drugs from the continent and small aircraft dropping shipments in the fields around Essex. However many times I told them it was risky, they wouldn't listen. Being king on your home ground is one thing, but going on an international crusade with the disregard they had for other people was a recipe for disaster.

Since the arrest of Steve and Noel and the death of Kevin Jones, Tucker had employed various dealers in Club UK. None was up to the job, really. In August 1994 a 19-year-old man from Essex came close to death at Club UK after a mixture of cocaine, speed and ecstasy brought on a fit. It attracted more bad publicity for the club, so Tucker decided to withdraw all dealers from the premises for six to eight weeks. He rang me and asked how Mark Murray and his dealers were performing in Raquels. I told him they were discreet and no problem.

Tucker asked me to take Murray over to his house in Chafford Hundred for a meeting. He told Murray that he wanted him to take over the sale of drugs in Club UK. Murray would have to buy all his drugs from Tucker and pay £1,200 rent each weekend. But in return, Tucker told him, he could earn in excess of £12,000.

Murray stuck out his hand without hesitation. The deal was done. He was to start in six to eight weeks' time when the publicity over the kid who collapsed and nearly died had abated. For introducing him to Tucker, Murray said he would pay me £500 a week once he had started. I would have no further involvement. It was, he said, a drink as a favour. It had been quite a lucrative ten-minute meeting.

Chapter *Six*

IT'S SAD BUT TRUE THAT THERE ARE PEOPLE IN ALL WALKS OF LIFE who take a favour as a sign of weakness. Jason Draper was regarded as a fearless hardman in Basildon. He had temporarily paralysed a man, Tony Aldridge, by attacking him with a machete and causing him brain damage. He had used a girl to drink with Aldridge and then lure him out of the pub by asking him to take her to a taxi rank. He was then attacked. As I wrote earlier, I had welcomed Draper and his cronies into Raquels, but there had been trouble on occasion. It had now reached the stage where I would let Jason in with his girlfriend but not with his firm.

One Friday night there was a significant disturbance at the top bar and the DJ called for security. When I got there, Draper was beating a man. I tried to separate them and Draper got upset, saying the man had assaulted his girlfriend. I knew this was nonsense and I told him to calm down. The manager came and I told Draper he would have to leave. He was getting very irate, saying he had done nothing. I told him to just go, and if he had a problem to see me the following day. He was still stroppy, but eventually he left.

I had a feeling that this would not be the end of the story. People with reputations don't like being put out, because they lose face. The following evening Draper came back to Raquels and asked if he could come in. I told him he was not allowed. He said he wanted to speak to me in private. We went outside and again he began getting angry, saying he had done nothing wrong, but I insisted that he would have to stay away for a few weeks.

Maurice, from Bristol, came outside and asked me if everything was all right. Draper took exception to this, and said: 'If it wasn't, what would you do about it?' Maurice laughed at Draper and said if he had a problem with him, they should sort it out. Draper started shouting. Maurice said, 'If you want to have a go, come on then.' He then started to walk towards Draper, who backed off, getting more and more angry, shouting obscenities, offering violence and saying he would be back. I said to him: 'What's the point of going away if you're going to come back? If you're going to do something, let's do it now.' He walked away, still shouting.

Ten minutes later, he returned. He said he was sorry. He had just got upset. I said to him again: 'Come back in a week or so and we'll sort it out. The manager won't let you into the club under any circumstances, so all this is pointless. When the dust settles, things may be different.'

The following weekend, Draper came into the Buzz Bar. He was quite a nice bloke, really, when he didn't have his cronies around him. We had a drink together and I explained that he couldn't come into Raquels. He agreed that I was right. He said he was going for a drink the following day in the Bull pub in Pitsea, and invited me to join him to show that there were no hard feelings. When the pub closed, Draper, his girlfriend, Debra and I went to a nightclub called Gass in the west end. We had a very good evening. Draper was apologetic about the trouble in the club and he agreed that he wouldn't come back for a few weeks until things had settled down.

It was all left on friendly terms. I was making the same mistakes Vine had made. I should have fucked him up when he put his first foot wrong. I considered him a friend. I know now you don't have friends when it comes to this business.

During the week I got a telephone call from Steve and Noel, the dealers from Bath. They were with Dave Thomkins, one of their friends who dealt in the clubs in London for them. They told me they were having trouble with some doormen from Bristol who, seeing them driving round in BMWs and knowing they had a flat in London, wanted to get in on the act. I told them I would make some phone calls and sort it out. I rang the doormen and told them to leave it out with Steve, Noel and Dave, otherwise they would have trouble. I gave the doormen the impression that the trio were working for a much more powerful firm and they should be left alone. We knew where the Bristol doormen worked, we knew their names, yet they didn't know a thing about us. We could attack them at our leisure and I let them know that fact. The doormen argued that Steve, Noel and Dave were the cause of the trouble, but they said it wasn't worth falling out over, and the matter would come to an end.

The next morning, I got a frantic phone call from Noel. He said that he had been driving through Bath in his BMW when two men had flagged him down. He was dragged from the car and told that they were taking it and keeping it. He said he wanted his car back, but he was scared of the men who had taken it. I told him and Steve that if we were going down to Bath to recover a car, we would have to go firm-handed as we did not know what we were up against until we got there. I asked them how many men we'd need, and they said if I could get ten down there, they would pay us all £300 each.

I asked for a contact number for the man who had taken the car and I said I'd be down that evening.

The man holding the car was Billy Gillings. He had a reputation in the area as a hardman. He had just come out of jail for robbing a security van. I rang Billy, and asked him if he had Steve and Noel's car. He got all shirty at first, and so I told him to calm down and listen. I pointed out to him that I knew where he lived, and he didn't even know my name. I was coming to Bath to recover the car. I had no particular loyalty to Steve and Noel, and therefore we should come to an agreement. 'Falling out over a BMW is hardly worth it,' I said. Billy agreed. I told him for recovering the car I was going to be paid £1,000, and if he met me at Bath railway station and gave me the car, I would give him half the money. He would be able to return to his friends and tell them that we had chased him, assaulted him and taken the car back. We'd both be £500 better off and everyone would be happy.

I rang Steve and Noel and told them there were ten of us going down to Bath in two cars. They were to stay out of the way until we called them. I drove to Bath on my own and met Billy as arranged. I told him the plot and that I would meet him there again in an hour's time, but first he would have to give me the car. He agreed. I phoned Steve and Noel and drove to meet them. I said there had been a bit of trouble with Billy, and the other people with me had driven out of Bath. I added that I was to meet them afterwards because they feared the police would be looking for them. I gave Steve and Noel their car, and they gave me the £3,000.

Dave Thomkins, who had arrived with them, was going mad. He said another man, Steve Woods, had burgled his house and stolen a load of stuff – televisions, videos, etc – and covered his children's bedroom floor and walls with excrement. He was under the impression that we were to do Steve Woods as well for this money. He claimed that Woods and Gillings were in on it together. Gillings had the car. Woods, he alleged, had done the burglary, and gave the goods to Gillings to fence. I told them it was the first I had heard of it. I said if he wanted, we would resolve that matter for him also. But he was adamant he wanted it sorted that night. 'Suit yourself,' I said. I shook hands with Steve and Noel, jumped into a cab, and went to meet Billy.

I gave Billy his £500 and kept the £2,500 for myself. Later that night I got a call from Dave Thomkins. He told me he couldn't stand the thought of knowing Steve Woods had robbed his house and got away with it. I told him that Woods hadn't got away with it. He said: 'Too right he hasn't, I've just fucking shot him.'

He explained what he had done. After leaving me, he was in a rage. He had gone home and picked up a shotgun. He went to Woods's house and put on a balaclava before knocking on the door. Woods's girlfriend answered the door. Dave pushed her aside. Woods was in the hallway. It must have been a terrifying sight for him to see a man in a balaclava with a shotgun. Dave fired and hit Woods in the upper thigh. He then ran over to Woods, who had collapsed on the floor, put the gun to his head and shouted: 'I want my fucking television back.' Woods's girlfriend was screaming.

Dave levelled the gun at her head and told her to shut up. Then he made his escape. I couldn't stop laughing. I told him that this kind of behaviour was a bit over the top over a 14-inch television. He obviously did not think so. This was becoming the norm for more and more people in these firms. It was all front. Dave obviously wanted people to know you couldn't take liberties with him.

Now Dave had calmed down, he didn't have a clue as to what he was going to do. It wasn't really my problem, but he was associated with us, and you have to help your own. I suggested he hide the weapon, jump in a car and meet me in Basildon as soon as possible. I didn't know if Woods still had Dave's television or not. It didn't really matter. I thought Dave Thomkins was in luck. According to the tabloids, everyone who is sent to prison these days is given their own television anyway.

I could have done without Dave's problem at that particular time. The police in Basildon, although maintaining their distance, were keeping a very watchful eye on my activities. But Dave was in trouble and I felt obliged to help. I wouldn't be able to keep him at my house because the police often watched those who came and went. I rang Pat, the landlady at a pub called the Owl And Pussycat in Basildon. I had sorted out a bit of trouble for her when she ran a pub in Southend. I asked her if she would put my friend up for the night. She asked me what the problem was. It was no good lying. I told her Dave had shot somebody. At first she was reluctant to help, which is understandable; she had never even met the man, and he had just attempted to murder somebody. The thought of spending the night alone with him must have been quite unnerving. However, in the end, she agreed.

I met Dave in Basildon in the early hours of the morning. I took him to Pat's pub, where he spent the night. We would decide what we were going to do in the morning, when he had a clearer head.

The following day we contacted people in Bath to try and find out Steve Woods's condition. We heard that Dave had blasted a large hole in Woods's upper thigh. It was unlikely that he would ever be able to walk properly again. His life was not in danger, but we learned the police were treating the attack as attempted murder. We arranged for people to pick up the gun and dispose of it and then for Dave to go and stay with some friends in Liverpool for a few days.

Around the same time, Jason Vella and his firm went on trial for numerous offences. All were drug- or violence-related. One of the defendants, Wally Birch, was released halfway through the proceedings by the judge, because there was no evidence against him. Wally turned up at Raquels with all his supporters to celebrate. Unfortunately, his party included Jason Draper who had agreed only five days earlier that he would stay out of Raquels for a few weeks. He came to the door saying that this was an exception. He was celebrating Wally's release, would I let him in? I said no.

He got all stroppy and offered to fight me. I walked out into the street and the doormen were calling me back, telling me to leave it, he was not worth it. He continued to call me out, so I pulled out my sheath knife. He backed away, rather wisely, and I turned around and walked back into the club. If somebody wanted to fight, they wanted to fight. At my age I wasn't going to chase him around the town. I went upstairs and told a doorman named Liam to stand by the fire exit and ensure that nobody went in or out, because in previous weeks people had opened the fire exits to let their mates in without paying. Liam wasn't what I considered to be a proper doorman. He was one of a minority you have to employ when running a door. They are not up to much, these people, when it comes to handling trouble. You just use them for guarding fire exits, collecting tickets and other menial jobs such as searching, which the proper doormen don't really do. He was one of those people who thought it a glamorous world, and he was useful to me. He was under-age, so I fixed him up with a false birth certificate and he applied to the police and the council with it to get his registration.

I was standing at the bar talking to Wally Birch. Wally was upset about the way he had been dragged into the Vella trial. He said he had popped around to Vella's home in Basildon to buy a car. When he arrived Reggie Nunn – the guy who escaped by jumping out of the window – was in dispute with Vella. Vella was stabbing Nunn with a sword and so Wally, not wanting to get involved, had left. The police captured him on their video and he had been roped in. He was adamant he was innocent of any wrongdoing.

Vella's was not a firm anyone wished to be associated with at that particular time. The police had the serious hump with them because of their activities and anyone found guilty at their trial was going to be severely dealt with.

When the trial was concluded, Vella and five other gang members were found guilty. Vella's second-in-command, Simon Renaldi, who was 23, was sentenced to six years and eight months' imprisonment, after he was convicted of false imprisonment and of conspiring to supply ecstasy, speed and cannabis. Scott Hunt, 22, was sentenced to five years for conspiring to supply ecstasy. He was also given nine months' consecutive for possessing a revolver and four bullets. James Skeets, 21, was sentenced to two years after being convicted of conspiring to supply cannabis. Tony Barker, 31, was jailed for three years for conspiring to supply amphetamine sulphate. Anthony Dann, 25, was sentenced to three years for grievous bodily harm with intent on Reggie Nunn. Vella himself was convicted on four conspiracy charges to supply ecstasy, amphetamine sulphate and cannabis, causing grievous bodily harm with intent to Reg Nunn and actual bodily harm on Alan Bailey. He pleaded guilty to falsely imprisoning Mark Skeets and causing him actual bodily harm, falsely imprisoning Dean Power on two occasions and causing grievous bodily harm the first time and actual bodily harm the second.

Judge Alan Simpson branded Vella the Tsar of south-east Essex. He said: 'You've imposed your will on those who argued with you with torture and terror.' He sentenced Jason to 17 years' imprisonment. Jason turned to the judge and said: 'Fuck you.' He turned to the police officer who led the investigation and said: 'Fuck you, too.' Vella remained his old self to the end.

As I was talking to Wally at the bar, I felt a sharp blow to the side of my head. I spun round. Jason Draper was standing there. He hit me again. I pulled out my sheath knife and Draper backed off. He said: 'You wouldn't use that on a friend, would you?' I threw it on the floor and said: 'I don't need it for a cunt like you.' I saw his hand come up. He was wearing a knuckleduster. It struck me on the side of the face and I grabbed him. The fight dissolved into a wrestling match because the bar was so packed with people. I can remember thinking: 'I should have stuck the knife in him. The bastard used a weapon on me.' Eventually he stepped back and disappeared through the fire exit. I couldn't work out how he had got in, and I wasn't going to leave the matter there.

I asked the doormen how he got in and they told me his girlfriend had gone past Liam the doorman, down the stairs, and opened the fire exit. He'd come in and he had walked back past Liam. Liam was too scared to say or do anything. The following day I got hold of Liam when he came into work. We went into the toilets to talk. I asked him if it was true about him turning a blind eye and he admitted it was.

I headbutted him and he fell to the floor. I hit him a few more times and told him to get out. He was bleeding from the mouth and nose. But he still asked about his wages. I told him that the £200 he was owed wasn't going to be paid. He was being fined that amount for what he did. He left the club, and I have never seen him since.

I was really annoyed because even if he was frightened of Draper, he could at least have alerted me rather than stand there and pretend that he had not seen him. This was a typical problem with the door registration scheme. You're forced to take on soft people and it causes all sorts of trouble.

The following day the whole town was poised for battle. Rumours and speculation were rife. Everyone knew I would not let what had happened go. The only way to maintain an effective door was to be seen to take action. Messages were coming from Draper's side that he was going to kill me. I chose to say nothing and bide my time.

On the Saturday night two police officers came to see me and the manager at Raquels. They told me that they had received numerous calls about the incident on Friday, and they'd heard that something pretty serious was going to happen. I told them that it had all been sorted out, but they refused to believe me. I was told I wasn't to work for a week until things had calmed down. The police couldn't prevent me from working, but they could make it difficult for the manager. Not only was I told not to work, I was advised to go away for the week. I reluctantly agreed, because I did not want police attention focusing on the club. A couple of days later Draper and I had our homes spun (searched). Although I had weapons hidden there, including firearms, nothing was found. I stayed away for a couple of days, but a little voice in my head was telling me that people would think I had run from trouble. I returned to Basildon and to work on the Wednesday. The whole town was buzzing, waiting for one side to do something. Everyone seemed to think it was Draper who would follow through.

Meanwhile, Dave Thomkins rang from Liverpool. He told me he had outstayed his welcome and he had nowhere else to go. I said I had a friend in Edinburgh who would put him up, but Dave wanted to come back to Basildon. I sorted it out with the landlady at the pub and he returned.

Peter Clarke, the man I had gone into partnership with when I first took over Raquels from David Vine, said he had a gun I could use if I needed it. I thought it might prove useful for me, as an unregistered gun cannot be traced back to anyone. The way things were going, I could see I might have to use it. I assumed Clarke had heard about my problems with Draper.

He told me Micky Pierce had said I could have the gun as I had done him a favour by being a witness in his case. I should have been suspicious at the time, but I believed it was a genuine offer of help. I took the gun, because I knew in my heart Draper would have to be sorted properly.

For a week or so, nothing happened. And then, on 29 August, which was a bank holiday, I was returning from London with Dave Thomkins when I received a call on my mobile phone informing me that Draper and three of his firm had been in Pat's pub, the Owl and Pussycat. I was told they had a gun and were looking for me.

Because it was a bank holiday I thought it would be difficult to raise people. It was around lunchtime and I assumed most people would already have gone out for the day. Whatever, if someone was looking for me, I was going to find them first.

As I was driving towards Basildon, I saw Tucker in front in his black Porsche. I drove up next to him and beeped my horn. All he did was bang his steering wheel and accelerate away. I sped after him and he pulled off the main road and onto a roundabout. He stopped and was punching the wheel, going berserk. It wasn't hard to work out he wasn't in a good mood. He had fallen out with somebody and he didn't want to talk, so I reckoned he wouldn't be making himself available that day. When I arrived in Basildon, I rang around and managed to muster 14 members of the firm who agreed to help me resolve the problem with Draper.

I rang Pat to see if Draper was still in the pub. She told me he was on his way to the Bull. I knew the assistant manager of that pub, so I rang him and asked him if Draper was in there. He said he hadn't arrived. I didn't want to cause trouble in the pub, because I knew the people who ran it, and I also knew it was a busy family pub, so I advised him not to let Draper in when he arrived. The assistant manager said he would tell Johnny Jones, the manager. I rang 15 minutes later, and again asked if Draper had arrived. The assistant manager said he hadn't. When I carried on ringing back at regular intervals, I found the phone had been taken off the hook. We all drove to the Bull and parked in a side road.

I had the gun with me, and also a machete. It was clear in my mind what I had to do. It was pointless beating Draper up, as he would just bide his time and attack me at a later date. I thought the only way to end this problem was to cripple him or kill him. In the state of mind I was in at that time, I wasn't particularly bothered which one it was to be.

All the other members of the firm were armed with coshes, truncheons, industrial ammonia, knuckledusters and knives. Two of my closest friends knew I had the gun. One of them had already told me that he would murder Draper for me. The week before, we had driven around Draper's various haunts looking for a suitable place to shoot him. My other friend said that he would walk into the pub now and shoot Draper in the back of the head as he stood at the bar.

I said that it was my problem, and that I was going to sort it out. I have no doubt whatsoever that both would have done what they said they were prepared to do.

As Dave Thomkins was not known locally, I asked him if he would go into the pub, walk up to Draper, squirt him in the eyes with ammonia and then push him through a set of double doors into the street outside where he'd be beaten and then left. I told the other members of the firm that once he'd been beaten, I wanted them to walk away as there was something to do that I did not want them involved in. I had decided that I was going to shoot Draper through the head.

Dave walked up to the pub with a large bottle of industrial ammonia hidden in his jacket. Luck wasn't on our side. As it was a bank holiday there was security on the door (who weren't there normally), it was full of families and you had to have a ticket to get in. Dave came back and explained the problem. I said to everyone that I wasn't going into a pub tooled up when it was full of women and children. But they insisted it had to be sorted now.

I knew they were right. We walked up to the door and pushed past the doormen. Draper was standing right in front of us at the bar. He was having a drink with three or four members of his firm. They all jumped over the bar and ran. Draper stood his ground. I pulled out the machete, and Draper said: 'What are you doing with that, mate?' I said, 'Fucking mate,' and went to hit him with it. Dave squirted him with the ammonia and the publican started shouting. Draper ran blind through the pub and we chased him. Unfortunately the ammonia also hit several innocent bystanders. People were screaming and running everywhere.

I really wanted it to end. I had to catch him. I couldn't let it go now. We chased him out into the beer garden. People there started screaming and running. The doormen were trying to prevent us from catching him. We got him for a brief moment. He was hit across the head with a large wooden truncheon. The doormen were grabbing me because I had the machete, which made it difficult to get to him. Draper broke free and ran again through the crowds. There was blood coming from the top of his head. He ran behind the bar.

I ran to the bar, leant across it, and hit him twice with the machete: once across the head and once across the back. But I couldn't get him properly. The manager ran towards me with a lump of wood. During the distraction, Draper hid in the cellar. The pub was in chaos. It was time to leave.

We got into our cars and went our separate ways. I dropped the gun off at a house in Grays. I was annoyed things hadn't gone to plan, but it was too late to think about that now. I had to make myself scarce. I had arranged to meet Debra and the children in Chelmsford, some 15 miles away. They hadn't a clue what I was up to. I drove there, swapped my car with Debra's, and we went to spend the weekend in Holland. It was the only place I could think of within reach that the police in Essex would not look for me. We drove the 30 or 40 miles to Harwich, but we had missed the ferry so we had to spend the night in a hotel. I made a few phone calls, and sure enough, the police were asking where I was.

The next morning we caught the ferry to Holland and spent the day there. I knew Draper wouldn't go to the police. It was more likely they were investigating the disturbance. The following day, I returned to England and went into work that night. The police came to see me and asked about the trouble. They had heard that Draper had been looking for me and they also heard what had happened at the Bull. I was quite frank with them. I said if someone was looking for me, they were eventually going to run out of pubs where they could expect to find me. And if they couldn't find me, they would turn up on my doorstep. I wasn't going to sit in my house and wait for a gang of men to turn up in case my children were there. Therefore if someone was looking for me, I'd go and find them. The police said Draper hadn't made a complaint. I didn't expect him to, he was not that sort of man. They said, as policemen, they had to tell me that that sort of behaviour wouldn't be tolerated, and if a complaint could be substantiated I would be charged. However, man to man, they didn't blame me.

The incident had a big impact in Basildon because no one had ever messed with Draper before. People were terrified of him. It changed the way people viewed us. The trouble-makers wouldn't come near the club after that.

Trade was very good at Raquels. Every firm of trouble-makers was now out of the situation. Our tough tactics were working. To celebrate our success, the promoters held a party at the Cumberland Hotel in Southend and we were all invited. It was an excellent do. Tucker and Tate were there. Tucker said Murray would be unable to start dealing in Club UK for some time because there had been a 'development' there. He did not elaborate. We discussed the problem of Draper. He was attracting too much police attention at Raquels, attention we didn't want.

Tucker suggested abducting him and giving him a good hiding. I tried to explain that you couldn't do that with Draper, as he would only come back and cause further trouble. I was all for shooting him, but Tucker and Tate said that would only attract more police attention. They were adamant that whatever happened, it had to be done discreetly because they didn't want anything to upset the sale of drugs in clubs or to affect their distribution. Any police involvement had to be minimal. Tucker said the best way to take him out of the situation would be to give him a contaminated tablet of ecstasy. We had friends who were friends of Draper, and people often gave him free ecstasy in nightclubs, so it wouldn't be difficult for someone to slip him a free pill as a favour. Shortly afterwards he would collapse. Nobody would get too excited about it. Tucker said it was the ideal way to dispose of somebody. Everyone was in agreement. Tucker said he would sort out the pill and we set about recruiting somebody to supply it to him. Before the plan could be put into operation, though, Draper was arrested and imprisoned for driving while disqualified. Our chance had been taken away, but the idea remained appealing. Disposing of a drug user with drugs was never going to cause much fuss or arouse suspicion. The idea was put on the back burner for future use.

Chapter *Seven*

DAVE THOMKINS'S PROBLEM DOWN IN BATH HAD TO BE SORTED out, but it wasn't going to be easy because of the nature of the offence. Trying to persuade a man who had been shot that the person who had done it was not all that bad and didn't deserve to go to prison was going to take more than tact.

Steve Woods, the victim of the shooting, had a bit of form himself, so he knew the score. It meant our task was not impossible. I rang Billy Gillings, the man who had done the deal with me concerning Steve and Noel's car. I asked him if he would mediate and arrange a meeting between me and Woods. Woods could bring anyone he wished if it made him feel safer.

Woods had just spent a month in hospital. Billy went to see him and he agreed to meet me at Leigh Delamere motorway services near Bristol. Woods insisted that his brother, who was nicknamed Noddy, should accompany him. A date was set and I went to the meeting on my own. We all sat down at one of the cafeteria tables. Noddy Woods started getting a bit lippy about Dave Thomkins, so I told him in no uncertain terms that we didn't have to sit there and discuss it. I was offering him and his brother a way out. I said: 'If you persist with your lip, you'll get taken out of the game like your brother. I suggest you go and get some tea for us both, while I discuss this with Steve.' It was important to let him know who was in charge.

I told them both that we didn't normally do deals with people who inform on one of our number to the police, but because he had suffered over a rather trivial matter, we were making an exception.

We were prepared to offer him £20,000 not to make a statement against Dave Thomkins. Woods said he had already made a statement, so I said he would be paid the money if he retracted it. Woods wanted half up-front, and half on completion. 'Bollocks,' I told him. 'Our word is our bond. Do your part of the deal, and you'll get your dough.'

He agreed and we went our separate ways. I didn't have any intention of giving him a penny. As soon as he retracted his statement, he was going to be told to fuck off.

A member of the firm – Mark – and I went to the next meeting. Billy Gillings and Steve Woods met us outside Bristol. Billy came over to our car and I asked him if Woods had retracted his statement. Billy said he wouldn't unless he got half of the money up-front.

I said to Billy: 'Put Woods in your car and take him down the road. Then tell him to get out. Drive away, and don't look back.' Billy asked why. I told him that Woods was going to be shot. Gillings said he didn't want any part of it. I said: 'Okay, tell Woods to get in our car, because we want to discuss payment with him.' Billy agreed, but he kept repeating he wanted no part of it.

Woods came over. I said: 'There's no problem, get in the car.' We drove to a deserted lane, a gun was produced and Woods was told to get out of the car because we didn't want any of his 'shit or blood' messing up our vehicle. Woods was told to lie down on a grass bank. The gun was put to his head. He was terrified. He had not yet got over the trauma of being shot six weeks previously. His whole body was shaking, and he was weeping. He was told that the firm did not pay grasses: 'Now you are going to die.'

'I don't want any money, I just don't want any trouble,' he said.

'First you break into our friend's house and rub shit over the walls, and now you come and demand £20,000,' he was told. 'It doesn't work like that.'

'I'll retract my statement, and that will be the end of it,' he whimpered.

He was told that if he didn't, people would come back. The

talking was over. Woods went away, and within three hours he had retracted his statement.

We returned to Basildon and Dave contacted a solicitor. The solicitor said he would check to see if Woods had really done what he said, and if he had, he would arrange for Dave to give himself up the following day. The solicitor thought Woods had retracted it by his own free will. The following day, I took Dave to Barking station in east London and we said our goodbyes. He travelled to Bath where he gave himself up.

What we hadn't counted on was Steve Woods's wife. She had not retracted her statement, so Dave was charged with attempted murder, threats to kill and possessing a firearm with the intention of endangering life. He was remanded in custody to await trial. Obviously a lot of our conversation around that time was about Dave. Some liked him, some didn't. Once he was out of the situation, I was told that he had been talking behind my back about me. It was a hammer blow, really. I had done all I could to help him, and yet he had been slagging me off to promote himself. I wasn't happy at all, but our world was overflowing with such people.

I contacted Steve Woods via a third party. He was told that as Thomkins's cover had been lifted, Woods and his friends could do as they wished. I travelled to Horfield prison in Bristol, where Dave was being held on remand. I was with two friends of his who were going to see him. I said I wanted to go and see him first. I would only be five minutes. They could wait outside. I went into the visiting room and Dave reached out to shake my hand. He said: 'All right, mate.' I said: 'You're no fucking mate of mine. You've been slagging me off.'

A prison visiting room isn't the best place to settle your differences. At that moment, I didn't really care. I went for Dave. The prison officers saw what was happening, and Dave backed off to where they were. I walked out of the prison. I have not seen him since. It is a shame, because I considered him a good friend. Why he did what he did to me I will never know. He was later sentenced to ten years' imprisonment for shooting Steve Woods.

I still kept in contact with the Kray brothers. Reggie used to ring me on a regular basis, and I used to go and see him a couple of times each month at Maidstone Prison in Kent.

Drugs had infected every part of the underworld like a cancer. The unlikeliest of men had become involved. Everyone had some connection, whether it was as enforcers for the dealers, importers or wholesale stockists. Even car dealers were used to clean drug money. Reggie, who epitomised the old school, began using drugs and looking at the money that could be made in deals. He had started using ecstasy, cocaine and cannabis. Reg was always asking what was going on in the clubs. He asked me if I could arrange a meeting with Tucker. He said he knew some people, one person in particular, from Hull whom he thought we could do business with. I said I would speak to Tucker and arrange it.

Tucker said he had no interest in Reggie Kray's plans. He respected the Krays for what they were, but now, he said, Reggie was a has-been. Pat Tate had met far more useful people during his time inside. The firm was moving into the import market. Tucker said we wouldn't be needing the likes of Reggie Kray. However, he did say he would meet him out of interest, but as far as business went, Kray was to be excluded.

For Reggie's birthday, the firm were going to send him in a parcel of ecstasy and cocaine to celebrate. I'd always taken bottles of Napoleon brandy for Reggie when I visited. It was quite easy getting things into Maidstone, but they were tightening up. Sometimes Reggie could hardly stand, he was so drunk. I can remember one visit, his face was blood red and his speech was slurred. He kept asking me if the screws could notice anything. It was obvious to everybody in the visiting room that Reggie was steaming. He kept saying, 'I'm going to go to the toilet.' He stood up and staggered to the door. I couldn't stop laughing. Every last person in that room must have known that he was drunk. However, he had been in jail longer than most of the prison officers had been alive. He had never caused them problems, so they tended to turn a blind eye.

I was surprised that Reg wanted to get involved with drugs. I had always associated him with straight villainy. Not only did he want to get involved in the large deals, working as a middleman, he wanted to help putting on raves around the country. He put me in touch with Bryn Jones, who said he could hire out aircraft hangars in various parts of Wales. However, when we discussed money, he was talking '50-50' this and '50-50' that. I don't think he appreciated the way things work. By the time we had paid for security, DJs (who are very expensive), Reggie's drink and the cost of promoting the events, there wouldn't be a great deal left anyway. In the end I told Reg that we were not interested. The dealers he had put us in touch with were also amateurish. They talked big, but nothing seemed to materialise. They were wannabes going through the motions.

Being in the Krays' circle could be very tedious. They had more plastic action men around them than most high street toy shops. Their real friends call this army the fan club. Two of the biggest fools Reggie ever embraced were Lyndsey and Leighton Frayne, who came from Wales. They marketed themselves as Kray twin lookalikes. I suppose they could have carried it off for a little while, but their biggest failing was their accent. Instead of a Cockney growl, they spoke with a deep Welsh twang straight from the valleys.

After visiting Reg, they started wearing double-breasted suits, with their hair slicked back like their hero. They walked, talked and scowled just like the twins did in their heyday. They even visited the grave of Violet Kray, the twins' mother, and placed flowers there. They went to the Blind Beggar, where Ronnie murdered George Cornell. Finally they formed their own gang. Among their recruits was a 15-stone heavy who claimed to be a former SAS man. He would stuff a sawn-off double-barrelled shotgun under his jacket, and always carried a knife, which he called Big Bertha. Among their many harebrained schemes, they even planned to kidnap the footballer Paul Gascoigne.

The brothers were finally arrested after a robbery in their home town of Newbridge. They had planned to use the loot to finance their new crime empire in London. But the raid on the Halifax Building Society was badly bungled and they made off with less than ten grand. An accomplice, Steve Cook, was sentenced to six and a half years after he was apprehended trying to make his getaway on a bus. At their trial, the Fraynes were sentenced to eight years each.

The national press ridiculed them. One headline said: 'The Krays? We called them Pinky and Perky.' The Fraynes finally did succeed in correctly aping their heroes. They both ended up serving long prison sentences.

Our association with Reggie Kray was put on hold after the *News of the World* published an exposé on the drugs being smuggled into Maidstone. They titled the article 'Reg "E" Kray'. They claimed Reggie had become addicted to ecstasy in jail. Underworld cronies smuggled him in a regular supply at visiting times. They said he had become a haggard shadow of his former self. Reggie was reported as saying: 'They're fucking marvellous. When I'm out of my head I ring up all of my old enemies and ask them how they are.' I don't know if it was true, but it sounded about right.

I had always kept my business affairs secret from Debra, but my paranoia couldn't be hidden. She was becoming concerned about my behaviour and urged me to go and see a doctor about it. The thought of seeing a shrink horrified me. I couldn't take the suggestion seriously. But I knew I did have a problem. I now carried both a knife and a gun everywhere. My behaviour was not normal. The feelings I was experiencing scared me and I thought I'd end up killing somebody.

One evening I came home from work and thought I was being followed, so I parked my car three or four streets away, and made my way home through the alleyways. The following morning when I awoke I looked out of the window and thought my car had been stolen. For half an hour I ranted and raved, waiting for a taxi to take me to the police station to report the theft. I suddenly remembered where I had parked it.

On another occasion I imagined that a man who lived two streets away was following me. One evening coming in from work, I stabbed all the tyres on his car because I had a meeting the following day and I was convinced he was going to tail me. Debra thought I had finally flipped.

We were due to go out one morning when I noticed a van opposite my house with blacked-out windows. I closed the curtains in all the rooms, and told Debra we could not leave, as I was sure it was the type of van used to photograph people secretly. We stayed in the whole day. Debra was not amused. The following day the van was still there. I had even called the police and told them they were wasting their time as I knew they were watching me. They denied knowing anything about it. I later found out it was owned by a plumber who lived across the road.

Looking back, I can't believe what a state I was in. I just knew something, somewhere, was going to give. I saw danger in everything. Unless you have experienced paranoia, you cannot begin to believe how horrifying an illness it is. It begins with fear and escalates into violence.

The whole firm was afflicted by it to some degree. Tucker, Tate and Rolfe would never, ever, open the curtains in their homes. They remained closed all the time as they thought this would prevent police surveillance teams from keeping a watchful eye on their activities within. We would never use our home phones for the firm's business. There were designated public phone boxes which were used to circumvent the possibility of the police studying itemised bills which could link us to people from other firms. If you were on business, or thought you were being followed, it was common practice to drive around all roundabouts two or three times to shake off your pursuer.

If a person had been involved in something and he had difficulty getting home, we would get him to swap clothes with somebody who looked nothing like him. That way, if he was arrested, any description given to the police would not match the suspect. For example, one night there was a fight in Raquels and a doorman, Joe, bashed one of those fighting. The victim went to the police and gave Joe's name and a description of him. When the police came and arrested him he was wearing completely different clothing to that given in the description by the victim. It was impossible for any case to be mounted against him. The victim said he'd been assaulted by a man named Joe wearing jeans and a T-shirt. An hour or so later, when he was arrested, Joe was wearing trousers, a shirt with a collar and a smart jacket. The victim could not explain this, and no charges were made.

The paranoia was not all unfounded. The police were taking a lot of interest in me and other members of the firm. It was common knowledge that drugs were sold in Raquels, and that violence was used to maintain the peace among the revellers in the club. I had been stopped and my car searched on several occasions.

I didn't deal drugs, so there were none to find. I protected those in the trade, but people assumed I was involved in dealing and so these stops and searches became more frequent, which was inconvenient, but kept me on my toes.

One evening on the way into work I received a call from Micky Pierce, Dave Vine's ex-partner. He told me he needed a driver to take an articulated lorry loaded with stolen coffee beans to a warehouse in Liverpool. He had tried everyone, but nobody was available. He asked me if I would do it as a favour. Without giving it much thought, I said I would. I drove to his home and together we went to Manor Park in east London to pick up a lorry to pull the trailer up to Liverpool. It was a D-registered M.A.N., a right old banger. I was told that the truck belonged to Terry Edwards, brother of the infamous Buster Edwards, the Great Train Robber.

The coffee beans were in a 40-foot container which had been stolen some time earlier. The trailer had been parked on the farm for so long it had sunk into the mud, and we had great difficulty in getting it onto the road. I finally set off for Liverpool at about 10 p.m. I was to meet four or five men at a bonded warehouse at five o'clock the following morning. I've never held a licence to drive an articulated lorry, but it wasn't too difficult. There was no traffic about and, once on the motorway, it was just a case of pointing it in the right direction and putting my foot down.

When I reached the National Exhibition Centre turn-off in Birmingham, my problems began. Within seconds the temperature gauge had gone from normal to red, and the lorry ground to a halt. I wasn't happy. I was sitting with a sure prison sentence, unable to go anywhere. However, I thought I would try and sort it out rather than abandon ship. I waited about 20 minutes on the side of the motorway. I was panicking. I thought that every car that approached was a police car.

Buster had not planned this with the precision of earlier escapades. Eventually the engine had cooled sufficiently for me to start it again, drive it up the slip road and off the motorway. I tried ringing the people in London who owned the lorry, but I couldn't get hold of them. I thought I would sit it out until dawn broke and I could have a look and see if I could rectify the problem myself.

The following morning I tried in vain to repair the vehicle. I couldn't reach anyone by telephone, so I rang a local mechanic who came out and finally got the lorry restarted at three o'clock that afternoon. It cost me more than £300 of my own money. I then set off for Liverpool.

My destination was Kirkby, which was where I had to meet the people at the warehouse. The lorry started to play up again. On hills it was reduced to crawling speed. I could not believe that I hadn't been pulled up by the police. I eventually got into Kirkby at 5.30 p.m. The warehouse had closed and the men I met up there said they had spoken to security at the warehouse and we would be able to park the vehicle in a compound until the morning. 'There is no way I am staying here until the morning waiting for this warehouse to open,' I said. 'I'm going to unhitch the trailer, leave it here, and get myself back to Essex.' They weren't too happy, but I wasn't giving them a choice.

I set off at about 8 p.m., and when I reached Birmingham, the lorry broke down again. I called the same mechanic out. He cleaned the fuel system, and once more I set off. Where the M1 and the M6 join, the vehicle broke down yet again. It was now the early hours of Saturday morning. I had been going since Thursday. I wasn't amused. I was £500 down, tired and pissed off. I thought: 'Fuck this.' I got out of the lorry and hitchhiked back to Essex.

I rang the people concerned that morning, told them where the lorry was, and went to bed. My money was never reimbursed and I was never paid anything for the journey. I was unhappy, to say the least.

A week or so later I heard on the news that Buster Edwards had hanged himself. He had been found by his brother Terry hanging from a metal beam in his lock-up shed near his flower stall at Waterloo station. An article in the *Sunday Mirror* stated that it was the fear of going back to prison that drove Buster to hang himself.

The article went on to say that Buster was involved with a gang who were van-dragging – stealing lorries and selling their contents. Buster's name came up after a lorry carrying stolen coffee beans was stopped by police in Kirkby, Liverpool. Three men were arrested. The beans had come from a wagon stolen in Dagenham, Essex, in June. The vehicle minus its trailer was found abandoned. I considered it a far-fetched coincidence that the police would descend on a stolen container five months after it had been stolen and that the vehicle, which was abandoned a hundred miles from the trailer, would be linked to it. Something kept telling me that I had been especially chosen to drive that lorry, and I should have been one of those arrested. It is only because I was late and I was adamant that I was going straight home that it hadn't happened. The fact that I never got paid for the job, or my expenses returned, reinforced my fears.

Again I was in turmoil. Common sense or paranoia – which one was talking? I had known Buster through the work I had done for James Fallon. I often saw him at Waterloo, and we became quite friendly. I regret if anything I did caused him to take his own life, as he was a very likeable person.

I was beginning to have serious doubts about the intentions of

Micky Pierce and Peter Clarke. The writing had been on the wall ever since my initial partnership with Clarke at Raquels. I couldn't work out exactly what they were after. It seemed quite obvious that, for whatever reason, they wanted me out of the way.

Chapter *Eight*

TONY TUCKER AND PAT TATE WERE BECOMING INCREASINGLY unpredictable. Their consumption of drugs was spiralling out of control. Both used huge amounts of steroids, and took cocaine, ecstasy and Special K, or ketamine. It's an anaesthetic that is used widely in the veterinary profession. It is exceedingly strong, and gives an out-of-body experience.

Tucker, once level-headed, was now often totally irrational. Tate was explosive. When they were together the mood was always boisterous and fun, but a single comment could alter it instantly. When they were together it seemed as if each was trying to live up to the expectations of the other. Tucker could be unusually abrupt and rude. Tate too became hostile. On their own, though, they were their old selves. Tucker was a very deep, private man. Tate was warm and friendly. The drugs were really messing up their heads – and their lives. I actually told Tucker this one night to his face, and he agreed it was true. Occasionally he would say he was going to give up the gear and start training again. He would disappear for a couple of weeks. Soon he would be back – and back on the gear.

But Tucker was no helpless drug addict. It was not the desire for drugs that affected him or Tate, it was the effect the chemicals had on their personalities that was the problem. When they were together they considered everyone to be a fool. They took liberties with people. You could say to them that what they were doing was wrong, and when they were apart they would agree, but the next time they were together, they would laugh at your remarks as though you were weak or not up to the competition in that league.

Tucker's reputation in Basildon was far greater than in London, where he wasn't a conspicuous player. The admiration being piled on them from the wannabes in Basildon was driving them on and on. They were careering out of control. I could see through the adoring disciples who gathered in the club. And I could see how easy it was to bask in their adoration.

Tate had recruited a stable of young girls. It was rumoured in the firm that he farmed these girls out to clients in London. Tucker had taken a 17-year-old mistress named Donna Garwood. She worked at a riding school near Basildon where he and his partner Anna stabled their horses. Anna was good for Tucker. When I first met him, he wouldn't have dreamed of getting involved with Donna. There was concern in the firm about the way Tucker spoke so openly in front of someone so young and impressionable.

Tucker, Tate and Craig Rolfe turned up at Raquels one evening with a man they introduced as Nipper, because of his size I guess. His real name was Steve Ellis. He was from Southend, and was a very likeable man. In time, I got to know him well. He was inoffensive and very funny. You couldn't help but like him. He was soon established on the scene. Everywhere the firm went, he was there. One weekend Tate, Tucker and Nipper went into a 7–Eleven store in Southend. Nipper threw a bread roll at Tate, who retaliated by throwing a cake at Nipper. They were all high-spirited and soon engaged in a food fight in the shop. The assistant kept telling them to stop, but they just got more and more carried away. Eventually the assistant said he was going to call the police. Tate ripped the phone out of the wall and told the man: 'You shouldn't say things like that.' They said they would pay for the damage, but as they were talking, the police turned up. Tucker and Tate walked off and Nipper was arrested. It was no big deal. In fact, everyone thought it was rather funny.

Shortly afterwards, Donna Garwood, Tucker's mistress, was trying to get in touch with him. She couldn't ring him at home in case Anna found out about their relationship, and so she rang Nipper to see if he knew where he was. When Donna asked Nipper if he had seen Tucker, true to form, he was sarcastic. 'He's probably at home giving his old woman one,' he said. Nipper hadn't said it maliciously. You could never get a straight answer out of him. He was always joking.

Donna told Tucker what Nipper had said when she finally contacted him, and made it sound as though Nipper was saying it with some venom. The next time I saw Tate and Tucker, they never mentioned the phone call. But they did say that Nipper had grassed them up to the police about the 7–Eleven incident. They said they weren't going to let him get away with it.

Usually friends were allowed into the club for nothing, but Tucker told me to make him pay, but make sure he was let in, because they wanted to get hold of him.

The following day Tucker and Craig Rolfe turned up at Nipper's house. Tucker stuck a loaded handgun into his temple and said he was going to kill him. He was threatened with a machete and they said they were going to hack off one of his hands and one of his feet. Then they looted Nipper's house. Rolfe plastered his excrement over everything that was left behind. Nipper fled. He was terrified.

On the Friday night, Tate and Rolfe came down to Raquels. We had a chat about everyday things. They said they were looking for Nipper. I said he wasn't in the club, but they wanted to check if any of his friends were there and so they had a walk around for about 15 minutes. Tate rang back later that night. He was obviously out of his head. He asked me if Nipper had turned up. I said no. I could hear him banging as if he was punching a wall. He was shouting, saying that he was going to kill Nipper. He said if he couldn't get hold of him, he would do his family. Nipper's sister, who was only 15 at the time, would be abducted, and they would cut her fingers off one by one until Nipper was man enough to show his face. There wasn't a lot I could say to Tate. I just said okay, I'd pass the message on, and put down the phone.

Mark Murray came to see me a couple of days later. He told me his partner, Bob, no longer wished to trade with him. Bob had already spoken to me. He could see the way things were going, and wisely quit. I said it was no concern of mine who he worked with, or who he worked for. Murray said it would not affect trade in Raquels, he just thought I should know and pass it on to whoever needed to know.

I was going to visit Reg Kray that week, and several times Murray had asked me if he could go too. I asked Reg and he said fine. Reg had previously met Murray's partner Bob, as he wanted to introduce dealers he knew to dealers who worked for the firm. I arranged to meet Murray at his home in Pitsea in the morning. Unknown to me, officers from police HQ in Chelmsford were keeping watch outside my house on the day I was due to visit Reg – as I wasn't doing anything untoward, I wasn't being particularly vigilant about my movements. They had chosen that day of all days to nick me.

I left my home about nine in the morning as I had to take my car to have new brake shoes fitted. I drove out of Basildon towards Southend to a garage, but the mechanic hadn't shown up. This made me late. I thought 'Sod Murray, I haven't got time to pick him up, I'll just have to make my own way there, and he can come another day.'

I drove back through Basildon towards the Dartford Tunnel on the A13. I got about ten miles out of Basildon, and every time I braked the discs screeched. I decided it would be too dodgy to continue my journey. I pulled into a service station and rang Mark. He said if I drove back to Basildon, he would meet me and we could go down to Maidstone together.

I turned around and drove back to Basildon. The police must have found all this very promising, as they must have thought that I was either picking up or dropping off a parcel. I parked my car at Murray's and we both got into his MG sports car and drove back the way I had come. Because of the confusion, Murray hadn't brought any gear for Reggie, which was just as well. When we indicated to join the M25, Mark said: 'Don't look back now, Bernie, there's an Old Bill car behind us.'

I looked in the mirror and saw a marked police car immediately behind us. It put on its blue lights and siren and pulled us onto the side of the road. We were on an elevated section so there was nowhere we could have gone, even if we had wanted to. They had obviously chosen this spot with care.

Two uniformed policemen got out and started asking us about road tax, ownership of the vehicle, and where we had been and where we were going. They asked to search the car. It was pretty basic stuff. I knew full well that they had not stopped us for a motoring offence. This was pre-planned. Seconds later two unmarked cars pulled up and detectives got out. To my surprise, they said they were arresting me for the theft of a vehicle. I tried to explain that the MG which Murray was driving was not my car. They said: 'No, we are arresting you for the theft of a Granada,' which was the car I had been driving earlier. It was registered in my name and not stolen.

They searched me, searched Murray and searched the car thoroughly, and then they said we would be put in separate police cars and taken to Brentwood police station.

Because of the searches visitors to prisoners undergo, I had left all my weapons at home, so I was not too concerned about the arrest. Murray was quite subdued when we got to Brentwood police station. On the other hand, I had the right hump. I was slagging the Old Bill off, telling them I had places to go. I didn't have time for their stupid games. I was quite surprised when we got to the police station and they apologised to Mark Murray and told him he could go – it was me they wanted.

These boys hadn't done their homework at all. They told me that a team of officers were at my home at that moment, searching it for drugs. I laughed and said: 'It's a fair cop. The paracetamol are in the cupboard above the sink.' I'd never dealt drugs, so I found the whole thing bizarre and pointless.

The alleged theft of my car had been engineered for the sole purpose of getting me to the police station to question me about the firm's drug distribution network. First the police had to put their paperwork in order and question me about the alleged stolen car. I had had my Granada for about 18 months. It was not stolen. What we all used to do was get a car on finance, make a few payments and then cease further payments. By the time the finance company had located you and repossessed the vehicle, it had been run into the ground and wasn't worth much anyway. I told the Old Bill the car wasn't stolen, I had just missed a few payments. It was, basically, the truth. They told me that my car had been picked up earlier by other officers and had been taken to a compound in Chelmsford where it would be handed back to the finance company.

What did surprise me was that the police did have paperwork concerning the purchase of the vehicle. Charlie Jones, Peter Clarke's sleeping partner, had stood surety for me when we had got the car on finance. I felt the Pierce–Clarke syndrome again. From the questions I was asked in relation to the vehicle, I knew these people had played a part in the run-up to my arrest.

Pierce had put up Clarke as a suitable partner when I took over from Vine. Jones, who ran the rival door firm, had not been mentioned, but he was part of the equation. Pierce had told me the stories about Vine which caused the trouble after I took over, and it was Pierce who asked me to take the lorry to Liverpool when the people had been arrested. The reason they gave me the gun should have sounded alarm bells, but I had put that to the back of my mind.

Once the police had legitimised my arrest by conducting a brief interview about the car, they got down to the real reason I had been pulled: they wanted an informal chat about drugs. I told them I didn't know anything. They gave me a long list of people in London and Essex I was associated with and I told them I just knew them through work. I was bailed to appear at Catford police station in south-east London for a minor deception charge for applying for a credit card in a different name, and bailed to appear at Brentwood for the allegation of theft concerning my car. I was then released.

When I got home I discovered those searching my house had left some paperwork for me. They had taken nine pieces of paper concerning my business, the registration document of my vehicle and a couple of bayonets and sheath knives.

I rang Murray and he was laughing at their stupidity. It should have been him they were tipping over, not me. I could tell from the police's reaction that they had found nothing. They were pissed off. When these people do pull you and find nothing, they don't think you're innocent, they just think you're a little bit cleverer than they imagined you were.

The following day I had to appear in Catford, south-east London. I had used a credit card which had been obtained in a false name. I wasn't going to mess about trying to box and cox my way out of that one. It was hardly worth it, as my later court case showed. I had obtained and used a credit card in a false name to the value of £1,000 and in return I had to pay £100 in compensation. Little wonder people turn to crime. It's all a question of what to say to the probation officer who has to prepare your report for the courts. Everyone was doing car and credit card fraud. It was a bit of extra cash. Nobody considered it a crime.

Drug dealers would open up bank accounts in false names and put in £500 or more a week for six to eight months. Once they had a good rating, they would apply for credit cards and perhaps a loan for a car. They would then withdraw everything and close the account. It wouldn't even be recorded as a crime, just a bad debt.

When I walked out of the cell where I was being held while they sorted out the paperwork for the case, I was surprised to see two detectives from Basildon. They said they had popped down to see me for a chat. I wasn't really in the mood for it. I'd done more chatting that week than Oprah Winfrey does in a year. They said they were just passing and were going to give me a lift back to Basildon, despite the fact that it was about 30 miles out of their way.

They wanted an off-the-record talk, but I insisted I had to go home first to sort out something urgent. I armed myself with a small dictaphone tape recorder while they waited for me. Then we drove to Church Road, a few streets away from my home. It was all very amicable. They said they wanted to discuss the events of the past few days. I had lost my car, had my home searched and spent the past two days in police stations. They were indicating that the police from HQ were turning the screw on me. As the discussion went on, it seemed to me that they were implying that come what may, Essex HQ had decided to nick me, whatever it took. I said: 'What are you trying to say, that if I am not caught fair and square doing something, the police from HQ at Chelmsford are going to fit me up?' They said yes, they may do.

For the benefit of the tape, I said, 'What, you can't be saying that they would fit me up?'

'It's a possibility,' one of them replied. 'Look, the Chelmsford police had plans which didn't come about. They wanted you for the people you knew, it didn't work out, so now they've got the hump.'

If I wasn't involved in the firm's crimes, they wanted me to tell them who was. I kept saying I didn't know what they were on about. They said I should assist them to keep HQ off my back. Eventually they said they were leaving, but they would keep in touch.

I went home. I had a valuable piece of ammunition: two police officers on a tape saying I was going to be fitted up. It was ammunition I hoped I would never have to use. I lodged the tape with a relative in case my home was searched.

The following day, Friday, 18 November 1994, I had arranged to visit Reg Kray. Tucker was meant to come with me this time. I rang his house and I rang his mobile, but I couldn't get hold of him. A person who wanted to install fruit machines and video games in pubs and clubs had promised Reg a percentage of the takings. Reg thought Tucker might be able to help him out. I didn't think Tucker would bother, so taking him on the visit wasn't that important. I set off to visit Reggie myself.

On the way home from Maidstone Prison I heard on the radio that a man had been found dead in a ditch in Basildon. I didn't think too much about it. When I got home, I continued to try and contact Tucker, but I couldn't get him. He was having his birthday party at a snooker hall in Dagenham that Sunday. If he didn't turn up at Raquels over the weekend, I would see him then and discuss Reggie's proposition.

That weekend a few of the doormen were telling me various

stories about what was happening with Nipper Ellis. They told me even Nipper's father had been threatened. Tate, they said, was going berserk. On the Sunday, I didn't fancy facing hours of listening to what they were going to do to Nipper. I'd had enough grief off the Old Bill all week. I rang Tucker's house and left a message on the answering machine saying I was too ill to go to the party. I later heard only 20 people turned up. Tucker's behaviour was being noticed by more people than myself. A year earlier there had probably been close to 200 people at his birthday party.

The next day, I was contacted again by the Basildon detectives. They said they needed to see me quite urgently. I armed myself with a tape recorder again. They picked me up, and we drove to Church Road. They wanted to know if I had heard anything at all about Pat Tate being shot. I said I hadn't.

They also asked me if Craig Rolfe had been up to anything in the past few days and if Tony Tucker drove a black Porsche. I said I didn't know about Rolfe and that Tucker had a BMW. They asked me if I knew anyone who had a black Porsche. I said I didn't. They said they knew I was lying as they had been watching me talking to a man in a black Porsche a few nights earlier. I wasn't being very helpful, so they said I could go and they would be back in touch.

These informal chats are engineered to break you down. Although the police cannot catch you getting up to anything, they want you to know that they are aware of your every move. By asking a seemingly trivial question, they are telling you that they are aware you are a witness or have been party to a particular incident. They want you to offer somebody up in order to save yourself.

I contacted Tucker and he was very keen to hear what the police had to say. He asked me to meet him as soon as possible. Tucker said that he and Rolfe had gone to Nipper's house – again he insisted it was because he had grassed them up over the 7–Eleven incident. Nipper had confronted Tucker and Rolfe with a pump-action shotgun, and they had made themselves scarce. He said they had been trying to get Nipper all week. He had also gone there on separate occasions with Tate.

Tucker said that on Sunday Tate had been at home getting ready for the birthday party. He was in the bathroom when somebody threw a brick through the window. Tate peered outside and Nipper opened fire from close range with a revolver.

Tate put his right arm up to shield his face. The round hit him in the wrist, travelled up his arm and smashed bones in his elbow. Nipper fled and Tate was taken to hospital. Tucker said: 'When Tate gets out, Nipper's going to die.'

This incident was not the firm's main problem. Kevin Whitaker, from Basildon, had been a friend of Craig Rolfe's for some time. Rolfe had introduced Whitaker to Tucker and they were starting to use him as a middleman and courier for drugs.

Whitaker had been involved in a £60,000 cannabis deal with a firm from Romford. It had gone wrong, and Tucker had lost out. It was just the type of deal I had warned him about getting involved with. Dealing with unknown people was a treacherous business. But you could never tell Tucker anything. He put pressure on Rolfe to resolve the matter because it was he who had put Whitaker up as being reliable.

As Whitaker was the go-between, the debt was down to him, and Tucker wanted to know how he was going to pay. Whitaker, who knew what was coming, had tried to avoid them. On the Thursday Rolfe had spent the day trying to get hold of him. Eventually he tracked him down at his parents' house and Whitaker agreed he would meet him to sort it out.

Tucker and Rolfe turned up in Tate's cream-coloured BMW. Whitaker blamed the firm from Romford for the loss of the cannabis, so Tucker and Rolfe said they would take him to the firm to confront the people. They were getting increasingly annoyed. It was dawning on them that they weren't going to get their money. They had hold of Whitaker, and they kept saying to him, 'Thieve our gear, would you? If you like drugs that much, have some more of ours.' They were forcing him to take cocaine and Special K. Like Vella's victims, Whitaker was becoming more and more terrified. He was pleading with them to let him go, but they were just laughing.

Whitaker was injected three times with huge amounts of drugs. Rolfe used a syringe and needle which Tucker had used for injecting steroids. Tucker said Whitaker passed out. He was out of his head on the gear they had forced him to take. They left Basildon and were travelling along the A127 towards Romford. Tucker said as they reached the Laindon/Dunton turn-off, Whitaker was slipping in and out of consciousness. They drove up the slip-road as there didn't seem much point in taking him to Romford. They turned left to go towards Laindon. Whitaker by now had completely lost consciousness. They pulled up at the Lower Dunton Road and told Whitaker to get out of the car, but they got no response. They got out and pulled Whitaker out, but he just collapsed on the side of the road. They drove off and looked back. Whitaker was motionless. Rolfe got out of the car and ran back to him. He stood over him and kept telling him to get up, but still there was no response.

'Fucking leave him,' said Tucker.

'You can't leave him here,' replied Rolfe. It was about six o'clock and everyone was coming out of work.

They drove the car back the short distance to where Whitaker lay. Tucker and Rolfe got out of the car, and they both put Whitaker back inside. They then drove back over the A127 to Dunton Road. Tucker said they looked at Whitaker, and they knew he was dead. They pulled him out of the car and he was put in the ditch.

I asked Tucker what he was going to do. He was laughing, but I knew he was concerned. He said the Old Bill were not treating it as murder. They would just think that Whitaker had taken a bit too much gear at someone's house and died. That person, not wanting a body in their home, would have taken him out and dumped him anyway. He said: 'When you had that trouble with Draper, I told you the best way to get rid of someone was to give them a bit of proper gear. We certainly won't be having any more trouble with Mr Whitaker.'

I told Tucker the questions the police had been asking. He did seem rather concerned that they had been linked to Whitaker so quickly. He kept telling me, and I think he was trying to convince himself, that the police could never prove that he and Rolfe had killed Whitaker.

Tucker was right. Detectives could find no evidence to support any murder claims. Whitaker was written off as a junkie who had overdosed. At the inquest, Coroner Dr Malcolm Weir called the death most inexplicable. Friends told how Whitaker made no secret of the fact he was heading for a rendezvous with Rolfe on the night he died. A message asking him to contact Rolfe was also logged on his radio pager. Rolfe was called as a witness at the inquest and asked to explain his contacts with Whitaker. He denied meeting Kevin, and said he only spoke to him on the phone to enquire about his baby son. Tucker also attended the inquest, but did not give evidence. An open verdict was recorded.

Tate was laid up in Basildon hospital after being shot. He had lost a lot of flesh from his upper arm but he seemed in good spirits. The firm was making sure of that. Despite being in a hospital bed under medication, Tate was supplied with a steady stream of drugs. It was quite clear that the other patients in the ward and the nurses were not happy. Each evening members of the firm gathered round his bed listening to blaring house music, taking drugs and generally having a party. Nobody dared object.

It was at Tate's bedside that I first met Darren Nicholls, a man Tate had met in prison and who considered himself to be a bit of a face in the drugs world. Darren had come to visit Tate, but I could see he was regretting it. Tate and Tucker didn't see him as anything other than someone they could use at a later date. They were slagging him off and taking the mickey out of him.

Although he was being humiliated and was seething with anger, he knew these were people he shouldn't upset. Nicholls listened in horror as Tucker bragged to Tate about the way he and Rolfe murdered Whitaker. Tate roared with laughter and said to Nicholls, 'He won't give us any more trouble, will he?' Nicholls smiled nervously, made his excuses and left.

Tate, like everyone else, suffered from paranoia. He had convinced himself that Nipper was coming back to finish him off, so he asked

Tucker to give him a firearm. He was at once supplied with a handgun. Within a couple of days a nurse discovered the gun while making up Tate's bed. She contacted the police and Tate was arrested. Because he was still out on licence for his six-year robbery sentence, he was automatically returned to prison for being in possession of a firearm – which broke his parole conditions.

Nipper remained off the scene. Fearing a reprisal attack, he had gone out and bought a handgun for £600 and a bullet-proof vest for £400. When Nipper was finally arrested for the shooting, the case against him was not pursued because the judge ruled that the gun that he had on him at the time of the arrest was not the gun that was used to shoot Tate. Nipper served seven and a half months in jail for illegally possessing a firearm. Even while in jail the death threats from the firm never ceased. Nipper said on one occasion two men came up to him in prison and told him a £10,000 contract had been put on him. A hitman even went to his father's door looking for him when he was released. Nipper eventually fled to the West Country where he now lives. It's unbelievable the amount of trouble a chance remark can cause.

I could see the writing was on the wall for the firm and for myself. The drugs and the violence were completely out of control. As soon as somebody put a foot wrong their loyalty was questioned, and once their loyalty had been questioned their popularity quickly diminished until they were deemed an enemy. Once deemed an enemy, they became the subject of some sort of violent attack. We were all waiting for our personal tragedies to happen.

On New Year's Eve we all went to a nightclub called Ad-Lib in Southend. Everyone was buying bottles of champagne at £80 each. At midnight, as everyone was cheering the New Year in, Mark Murray came over to me and shook hands. He said: 'I'm glad we met, Bernard. We will do a lot of business this year, we're really going to make a lot of money.' I smiled, and said: 'Of course.' I don't know what it was. I certainly wasn't sharing the firm's euphoria. I felt a sense of doom.

Chapter *Nine*

I WAS BECOMING INCREASINGLY PARANOID. I WAS CONVINCED that very soon I was going to kill somebody, or I was going to be killed myself.

Rumour, intrigue, accusations and counter accusations were creating a very unstable environment. The firm had a finger in every pie. As far as they were concerned, anyone or anything could be sorted. As our reputation grew, everyone wanted to be part of it. In one pub I drank in, the assistant manager used to take my money, give me my drink and twice as much in change, simply to be part of the firm in a small way. It was ludicrous. With this stupid glamour came the wannabes. They invented stories for the benefit of their friends. And these stories created concern, suspicion and further police attention.

Tucker was being blamed for shooting Tate by some of Tate's half a dozen or so girls, who were like a little fan club he used to have round him and go out with. They said if he hadn't carried out the shooting himself, he had arranged it. Tucker, they said, was jealous of Tate's friendship with Nipper. It was total nonsense. They even said Tucker stoked Tate's fear and paranoia after the shooting by giving him the gun to protect himself while he was in hospital.

Murray's dealers began to shun him. They could sense the danger. The firm was being linked to everything bad and unsavoury. Rumours about the murder of Whitaker were rife, although the police were only treating it as a suspicious death. The firm was also being linked to an attack on a man named Darren Kerr. Kerr had been in a telephone box in Purfleet when a car had pulled up. He had acid thrown in his face. Then he was bundled into the boot and dumped in Dagenham. Darren, who was 24, fit and handsome, suffered horrific injuries. He was blinded in one eye by the acid and the whole side of his face was a mass of angry red scars. His injuries were so bad he had to undergo surgery at the specialist burns unit at Billericay Hospital. Following the operation he was forced to wear a plastic face mask similar to those worn by ice-hockey goalkeepers.

While recovering in hospital he was paid another visit. A man turned up dressed as a clown. He had Dracula teeth, a clown's wig with a pink forehead and he was carrying a bunch of flowers. He asked the unsuspecting nurses where Darren Kerr was. The staff smiled at the clown and told him. He strolled in with his big red nose, shiny blue shellsuit top and trousers tucked into his socks. When he saw Darren he whipped away the plastic flowers to reveal a shotgun.

The clown opened fire and blasted a huge hole through the muscle and skin in Darren's shoulder. It missed his heart and lungs by inches. Darren staggered out of bed and saw the clown gunman walk calmly away. Nobody was laughing. Darren said later: 'I did not see him at first, because he had come in from the left, my blind side. I saw him late. He was aiming for my head. It was an instinctive reaction to twist away, and that's what saved my life.' People blamed Pat Tate for the shooting. If Tate did do it, he must have been a good shot – he was in Whitemoor Prison at the time. Darren did have links with underworld figures and he knew members of our firm quite well. But I don't think it was anyone in our firm who tried to murder him.

Debra was still urging me to go and see a doctor about my paranoia. She said if it made me feel better, she would come with me. I told her it was nonsense, but if it made her feel happier I would go, and she could come too. I went to my GP, Dr Denham. He asked me to describe what I thought was the matter with me. I told him in detail: feelings of being followed, of people talking about me. Even when I stood in front of a shop window, I had a feeling that I was going to be pushed into it. He asked Debra about my behaviour in general. She was rather more forthcoming. She told him I couldn't go anywhere without weapons and I was constantly suspicious of neighbours and friends.

Dr Denham told me that he would arrange for me to see a psychiatrist, Dr Murphy, at Basildon Hospital. In the meantime, I was prescribed Chlorpromazine, the trade name for Largactil. (Chlorpromazine was the first anti-psychotic drug to be marketed. It is used to suppress aggressive and abnormal behaviour, schizophrenia and other disorders where aggressive behaviour exists. It causes drowsiness, dizziness and muscle twitches.) Largactil is commonly known as 'liquid cosh', because it knocks you senseless. That night before I went to bed, I took three times the recommended dose, and for the first time in more than a year I slept through the night without waking. Previously I had suffered the recurring nightmare of being chased and stabbed to death. Whatever I thought of before I went to sleep, I always had the same dream. It wasn't a normal dream, either. Debra would tell me that I would actually fight in my sleep, it was so real. I might have appeared tough on the outside, but my mind was paying a terrible price.

Despite the medication, my paranoia did not diminish. A doorman named Ian, who had worked for me for about eight months, kept looking at me and laughing while he talked to someone else. Then he walked off. It kept preying on my mind and in the end I convinced myself that he had been talking about me. I went upstairs and attacked him. He couldn't understand why I was doing it. I wouldn't explain, I kept hitting him and hitting him, then I threw him out. When people tried to calm me down, I just got more violent. I was totally confused.

It was following this incident that I seriously considered for the first time getting out of the madness that surrounded me. But it's impossible just to walk away from that type of situation. Incidents follow incidents – each one leads to another – and with each incident you survive, the more prominent you become. Your piece of the action becomes larger. You climb the ladder in leaps and bounds, but the higher you go, the further you have to fall.

With everything I knew and everything I'd done, there was no possibility of just walking away from the firm.

In January 1995 Tucker gave Mark Murray the go-ahead to begin sorting out the gear in Club UK in south London. To make it pay, Murray would have to run a pretty slick operation. He would have to have enough dealers in there to meet the demand in order to reap the rewards his predecessors had earned.

Outsiders may have thought it was glamorous, but within the firm it was a different story. Nathaniel, one of Murray's dealers, was working at a club in Southend. The doormen's rent was being paid at the club, but the manager had spotted Nathaniel serving up (selling drugs). He told one of the doormen to grab Nathaniel and phone the police. The doorman got Nathaniel and locked him in the manager's office. The manager called the police and the doorman sat on Nathaniel until they arrived. He was found with 50 ecstasy tablets and a quantity of money. He was promptly arrested and charged. At his trial he was sentenced to 18 months' imprisonment.

Murray came to see me, and I said something should be done. What was the point of paying rent to the door firms if they offered no protection? They tried to say it was out of their hands because of the manager, but the doorman could easily have let Nathaniel 'escape'. The doorman was identified, and it was agreed that he would be attacked and stabbed in the carpark on his way to work. Murray wanted no part of it, and it was dropped as Nathaniel was one of his people. Little wonder he couldn't recruit anyone and those who worked for him were losing confidence.

Around the same time I was contacted by a freelance journalist. She told me that the newspaper she was working for had received a telephone call from someone who was saying that Raquels had people there openly selling drugs to anybody who would buy them. She knew I ran the door at Raquels, and she was warning me that someone might come to the club in order to get enough information to publish an exposé.

The next time I saw Tucker, I told him. But when I did the right thing, it was thrown back in my face. Tucker wanted to know why a journalist would warn me. I said I knew lots of journalists and they were just doing me a favour. Two years previously he would have accepted it for what it was, but now his vision was clouded by drugs and paranoia. Tucker told Murray not to tell me about Club UK, which was silly really, because it had been openly discussed, and we were all aware of what was going on. I had seen this scenario many times. Tucker was trying to make Murray feel like an important cog in the firm's machinery. In reality he was building him up in order to knock him down.

Without a partner, Murray found the going hard. He couldn't make Club UK work because he couldn't recruit enough dealers. He was selling approximately 500 ecstasy pills a night in Club UK, nowhere near the amount needed to reap any benefit. Needless to say Tucker demanded his rent, and Murray owed me £500 every week he was there. By the time he'd paid for his stock, there wasn't anything left. He was, simply, in debt.

Those on the outside looking in were impressed by the money floating round and the power we all had, but more and more people in the know were scared because of the excessive violence. Even some doormen refused to work with us. Most of them remembered Ian and Liam being beaten up – our own sort turned on for no real reason.

A friend of mine, Bill Edwards, asked me if I could arrange for him to work for Murray. I tried to advise him against it, but he said he needed the money and, despite my warnings, he went to work for Murray at Club UK. Tucker, still suspicious of me, knew Bill was a friend of mine, and arranged for one of the doormen down there, named Barry or Baz, to pull my friend for dealing. When Barry pulled him, Bill told him that he was working for the firm. Barry didn't take any notice. He hit him in the head several times with a knuckleduster. He said: 'You shouldn't have said you were working for the firm, it's grassing.' Bill came and told me what went on. He had several stitches in his head.

I rang Tucker and asked him why Bill had been beaten up. He

shrugged it off and said Barry didn't know who Bill was, and it was all a misunderstanding. I didn't believe it. I rang Bill and asked him if he wanted to do something about it. He said no, he wanted to forget it.

Tucker, it seemed, was also trying to send me messages. My best friend at that time was a bodybuilder from Barking in east London named Martin. He had worked the door for a number of years in the London clubs. He had recently come to Raquels by word-of-mouth via a friend. We got on really well. He didn't take any shit from anybody. He was always there when it mattered. As a doorman, he gave one hundred per cent. As a friend, you could not want better.

One evening we were working together in the Buzz Bar. It was very busy. Everyone appeared to be having a good time. It was all regular faces, no strangers, so we weren't expecting any problems. At about 9.30 two men came into the bar. One was short and stocky. His name was Barry Chart. The other was an Irishman named Frank Kennedy. He was about six foot tall and fairly well built. Chart had worked for me previously, but was now working as a doorman for a firm from Mile End, in east London.

Both were being quite sarcastic to the staff and customers. It wasn't too bad at first as they were fairly quiet. But the less we did, the louder they got. It was as if they were trying to see how far they could go. As I walked past, Chart said to me: 'All right, Bernie. Can you ask a doorman to come over?' It was a blatant insult. He was insinuating that I wasn't up to being a doorman. I grabbed hold of Chart and punched him in the face. Martin grabbed hold of Kennedy, and we led them to the double doors at the top of the stairs. As we were preparing to throw them out, I felt a sharp blow to the back of my head. Martin also was assaulted.

A fight broke out on the stairs. People we hadn't noticed previously jumped in. It was hard to say exactly what happened. I was trying to get people out of the building and defend myself at the same time. As faces appeared in the mêlée, I hit them. Somebody was holding on to my back and a man was trying to get up off the floor. I began to stamp on him. We were outnumbered. I produced a knife, and our attackers started to back off. As we moved forward they ran down the stairs and through the doors into the street. The only person left was Chart. He was lying on the floor unconscious, his face a mass of blood. Because of his size I couldn't pick him up, so I pulled him down the stairs by his arm. I left him in the street.

Somebody ran forward from the crowd and kicked him in the head. I don't know who it was. An ambulance turned up and took him away. As far as we were concerned, that was the end of the matter.

When we left work at about 11.20, we went over to the burger van to buy some tea before going our separate ways. The woman serving, Chris, told us that there were two vehicles full of youths driving around saying they were looking for us. We walked across the road and a Commer van and Fiesta car pulled up at the lights. A man in the van was shouting: 'You're going to die, O'Mahoney.'

The driver of the Fiesta joined in the shouting. We were outnumbered, but it was pointless running. We didn't know who these people were, or what their problem was. We assumed they were associates of Chart and Kennedy. I ran across the road and the man in the Fiesta tried to drive away, but he stalled the engine. A side window of his car was smashed, and I jumped onto the bonnet. The windscreen smashed and the men in the car jumped out and ran. We gave chase. The man in the van drove off and escaped, while the guys on foot were far too fast for us – they had fear on their side. We flagged down a passing cab and told the driver to follow the van. It went up a one-way street, and we encouraged the minicab to follow him. But the minicab driver had had enough. He slammed on his brakes, turned off the ignition, grabbed his keys and ran. The van disappeared into the distance.

Martin and I went back to our cars and drove home. There was nothing particularly unusual about this type of trouble. We thought we would hear no more about the matter.

A few days later, though, I was arrested by two of Basildon's finest and taken to Rayleigh police station for questioning. It was the age-old story. Two doormen from a rival firm had come to

Basildon to try and muscle in on our work. They had come unstuck, and had run bleating to the police for help. It was alleged that I had caused injuries to Chart's torso and broken his arm, his nose and cheekbone. The police said Chart was in such a state his family couldn't recognise him. I told the police it was Kennedy and Chart who had caused the trouble, and we had acted in self-defence.

During the interview, which was being taped, the two detectives produced a file. On the front in two-inch-high, thick felt-pen letters were the words 'Big, bad Bernie'. I said to one of the detectives: 'What the fuck is that meant to mean?' He said it was just a joke, following the reception their enquiries had met.

'I don't find it very funny, and I can't see how you can conduct a fair, unbiased investigation or speak to potential witnesses after writing something like that,' I said. 'It shows what frame of mind you're in. I don't wish to talk to you any more.' There was little they could say. The interview was concluded and I was bailed to re-appear at a police station for an identification parade.

I told the guy who ran the door firm from Mile End what had happened, and we were not going to forget it now that Chart and Kennedy had grassed us up. That night I received a phone call. I was told that Chart and Kennedy had not pressed charges, despite the police visiting them two or three times and encouraging them to do so. The people, therefore, who would be at the forthcoming ID parade would be the men in the Fiesta and the Commer van. We recruited witnesses in case there was a court case. I insisted that following the incident with Chart I went straight home from the club and was totally unaware of any trouble following that. The firm closed ranks and messages were sent out to those concerned. There wasn't going to be any court case.

The man in the Fiesta was named Chris Green, and the man driving the Commer van was Michael Ward, who occasionally called himself Williams. He alleged he had become involved because I punched his girlfriend while she tried to administer first aid to Barry Chart. It was total fantasy.

The very same night, Williams – or Ward – pulled up outside

Raquels and shouted: 'O'Mahoney, you're going to die. I'm going to shoot you.' I ran towards the van again, and he drove off. Rather typical. He wanted it all ways. He initially wanted to fight me. He lost, and then he chose to go to the police. Yet here he was again, trying to be a gangster. He had overstepped the mark and he had to learn his lesson. If he got away with it, every Tom, Dick and Harry would get ideas.

We found out Williams was staying in a place in Vange Hill Drive in Basildon. One evening after work another doorman and I went around there and banged on the door. Nobody answered. To wind him up, I wrote on the door in chalk: 'I have found you, Williams. See you soon, Bernie.' Then we went home.

A short time afterwards, I read on the front page of the local newspaper that there had been a fire at Williams's flat. A 25-year-old woman had jumped for her life from a second-floor window after a blaze ripped through the building. It was reported that she was recovering in Basildon Hospital having fractured her back and her wrists after jumping 20 feet. The blaze started in the hallway; there was no way she would have been able to get out. The woman was believed to be alone in her flat, with her Alsatian dog, which she threw from the bedroom window. It had survived the fall. Neighbours who were too scared to make their way down the smoke-filled stairway were led to safety by fire fighters. Fire investigation officers and forensic scientists were at the flat to find out what caused the blaze, believed to have been started deliberately.

Two detectives came to visit me. They said they were aware of the trouble I had had with Williams, and asked me if I knew about the fire and where I had been on that night. Obviously everybody thought I had started the fire. I gave them a suitable alibi and I heard no more. Williams moved back to Manchester, his native town.

There was still the matter of the damage to the car to deal with, however. The first ID parade took place shortly afterwards. None of the witnesses showed up, much to the dismay of the Basildon police. My solicitor wanted to know why, but the police couldn't explain it.

I was bailed to reappear for a second ID parade a week later. Obviously the witnesses, too, thought I was responsible for the fire.

There are two forms of ID parade. One is the traditional row of men, which the victim or witness looks up and down before indicating who he believes, if anyone, is the wrong-doer. The second form is where the suspect walks through a crowded area such as a train station or shopping centre. The witness then has to point him out to detectives. I opted for the latter, and it was arranged that I would walk through Basildon town centre, along a pre-selected stretch of the shopping mall where the witness would be with police. On the day of the ID parade, the town was deserted. My solicitor said it would be unfair for the ID parade to take place, so it was again aborted for a further week. Unknown to us, the witnesses had failed to appear again.

The police were getting agitated. They seemed to think the fire at Williams's flat was more than coincidental. The ID parade was put back to a later date so they could contact the witnesses and get them to attend. I don't know what it was, but I had a feeling that they would not be successful. The people who were screaming victim were the people who came after us in a van. They weren't innocent victims. Following the fire, they realised they were in deep and now they wanted out of it.

My solicitor indicated to the police that if they didn't attend on this third occasion, he would be applying for the matter to be dropped.

This was becoming more and more typical of our lives. As our reputation grew, so people either admired us, or wanted to pit themselves against the firm to get in on the action. Anyone who did get involved soon regretted it. The mood, from top to bottom, was getting uglier.

Chapter *Ten*

ON 27 FEBRUARY 1995 A NEW MANAGER, DAVE SIMMS, TOOK OVER at Raquels. He was from South Wales and admitted to me he had no experience whatsoever in running a rave/house-type dance club. He was purely a 'Sharon and Tracy' disco manager.

On his first night he tried a couple of textbook management course ploys to try and impose his authority. I told him in no uncertain terms that we were all there to make this work together, and I didn't want him coming in shouting and making a mess of things. He was taken aback. I told him he might be the manager, but he wasn't in charge. His big mistake was when he barged into the cloakroom where the doormen and their friends went for a break. He caught one of the doormen inhaling crack cocaine from a Coca-Cola can. Simms went berserk. I went into the office and told him he had no right to creep up on people. If the club ran smoothly, he should keep out of things. We had a big row – the first of many.

I only ever got on with three managers: Ralph Paris, Rod Chapman and Ian Blackwell. The others had little understanding of the area. They all used to say that they wanted better clientèle. I tried to explain to them that if your club was in Basildon, people on the east side would rather travel into Southend for a night out. And those on the west side would sooner travel into London. The only punters we attracted were the type of people who wouldn't get into those places, and in fact we'd done well to get the people we did. The average Raquels customer wouldn't be able to tell the difference between Liebfraumilch and Tizer.

I can't say for certain who tipped off the police, but I had only told four or five people about the tape recording I had of the officers who said I might be fitted up. But somebody did, and the officer they alleged was going to fit me up got to hear about it. He, quite naturally, was deeply upset that two fellow policemen would tell someone from the criminal world that someone was going to be dealt with in this way. I am not privy to what happened exactly, but I was told that there was an internal police enquiry about the matter.

John Hughes, a detective from Chelmsford HQ, came to see me. Before talking to me, he frisked me for any hidden tape recorders. He told me he'd got to hear about the tape. Somebody I was talking to was talking to the police. Hughes asked me about the contents of the tape, and I told him. He assured me it was nonsense. I have encountered many policemen in my life. I don't trust any of them. I did believe, though, that John Hughes had never had any intention of setting me up. He was a 100 per cent company man. However, the tape remained invaluable.

My appointment came around to see Dr Murphy, the psychiatrist at Basildon Hospital. I was uneasy about it. For some reason, I had imagined that Dr Murphy would be a man, but she wasn't. Before seeing Dr Murphy I was called into a side room, where I spoke at length to a Jamaican doctor about the feelings I was experiencing, and about my past from as far back as I could remember. I told him that I feared that I was going to kill or seriously injure somebody for a trivial matter. He took me seriously and wrote down most of what I said.

After a lengthy interview I was called in to see Dr Murphy. It may seem ludicrous, but I thought that secretly she was laughing at me and wasn't taking me seriously. I began to get annoyed. It was weird. I couldn't work out whether it was paranoia or that she was genuinely taking the piss. It was very confusing. Eventually she told me that there wasn't a great deal wrong with me. I just had a violent personality. I needed to go to group discussions, she said, to talk to other people. This would be the start of my treatment: 'Hi, my name's Bernie, and I feel like killing someone.'

I said: 'I don't think so, somehow.' She told me that was all that was available. The discussion deteriorated into an argument. In the end she said I would be sent to Southend Hospital for an EEG – a test to see if you have any sort of damage to your brain. I left the hospital feeling cheated. It had taken a lot for me to admit what I was really feeling, but I had just been told that there was nothing wrong with me. How many times have I read in newspapers of similar cases which turned to tragedy? The next time, I thought, I ought to go dressed as Lord Nelson. Perhaps then I would be taken seriously.

As well as my EEG, I was given an appointment to see Gary Ong, a community psychiatrist in Basildon. I think he, conversely, took me more seriously than my condition warranted. He asked me if I thought newsreaders on the TV were blaming me for the tragedies they were reporting. I left him feeling more confused than ever.

The EEG itself is rather unnerving. You have wires taped to your head, and various signals or currents are passed through. The whole process takes about an hour. I felt I was getting nowhere, so I went back to taking excessive doses of Chlorpromazine. I would be sitting there in a daze watching my limbs moving independently of me. In the morning I felt an unusual numb, wasted feeling, and I had mental blocks. It wasn't a good time for me – for both of me, in fact!

The firm's reputation, meanwhile, wasn't just growing in criminal circles. Nigel Benn's greatest moment in boxing was probably the night he fought Gerald McClellan, and it was Tucker who led Nigel into the ring. He did this for most of Nigel's fights. He was very proud to be his minder. That particular fight was awesome. Both boxers traded punches toe-to-toe. Few could have survived the punishment each meted out to the other. In the dramatic finale, McClellan slumped to the canvas, then lapsed into a coma. Benn had not escaped unscathed, either. He had fractured bones in his hand and cheek.

After the fight, Tucker returned to Basildon, and we all went out to a club in Southend. Mark Murray came with us. It was a memorable night. Tucker, still high after Nigel Benn's unbelievable win, was in a great mood. Drink and drugs flowed freely. Even a club manager from the area who was supposed to be unaware of what went on in nightclubs like Raquels was given two ecstasy tablets by Murray. He said he would try them later. Of course, all of the management and staff at Raquels were fully aware of what was going on there. You could not help but notice. They knew that it was the drug culture which was filling their club to capacity. Not only was it being filled to capacity, it was free from trouble – a first for this club. They were hardly going to root out the very thing that caused this new interest in the place. It's the same story all over the country with rave clubs: what else do people think kids do in a club for eight to ten hours where there's no alcohol on sale?

One evening, a man named Lee who dealt for Mark Murray came to Raquels with some other dealers and told me that they had been stopped by the police on their way into work. They said Mark had been taken to Basildon police station and they feared the police were going to search their flat in Laindon. Lee had a bag containing 250 ecstasy tablets there, but they were frightened to go and retrieve them in case the police arrived at the same time as they were at the flat. I told them they would have to go back quickly, as it would take the police some time to get there. I drove them to the flat and they went in and retrieved the drugs. We drove back to Raquels. I parked my car and went back to the club.

At the main door was a visiting senior executive. We exchanged pleasantries and shortly afterwards, Lee and the other dealers came to the door of the club. Lee told me that since getting out of the car, he had lost the bag. A frantic search began, the executive asked me what it was we were all looking for. I told him that somebody had lost some car keys and went upstairs. As Lee went to go into the club, the executive called him to one side and said: 'Are you looking for these?' He produced the bag containing the tablets. 'See me on your way out,' he said.

The executive never did say anything directly to me about the matter. But he did return the 250 ecstasy pills to Lee when he left. Dave Simms, the new manager, was visibly taken aback by events like this, and the many other instances of blind eyes being turned to the drugs trade in the club. In a vain attempt to reverse the trend, he booked The Pasadenas, a pop group who had enjoyed relative success in the charts. Another promoter of jungle music had been promised the premises for Saturday nights. In protest, the door staff walked out. We told Simms we were not going to work for that night, and that no other door firm would take our place. In short, the club would close on Saturdays.

But The Pasadenas were booked, and he said he had to honour the booking and we should see how it went. Everyone who came to the club that night was turned away from the door for whatever reason we could think of at the time.

A few weeks later, following the huge loss of custom on Saturday nights, it was agreed that the jungle promoter could start. It was an exercise to show Simms that although he was the manager, it was merely a title.

One Friday night in Raquels, I was standing at the bar in the diner upstairs talking to Tony Tucker and Craig Rolfe. Rod Chapman, the assistant manager, was also with us. One of the barmaids called Rod on the internal phone from downstairs and asked him to come down as she had a problem. Rod asked me to go with him to resolve whatever the difficulty was.

We went to the top bar near the main dancefloor area. A barmaid called us over and said there was an under-age girl in the club. She had refused to serve her, and the girl was getting stroppy. She pointed out a girl who looked about 18: she had collar-length straight black hair. I saw her walking off with a friend. She went upstairs to the diner area where we had been. I said to Rod: 'We'll go up and see if she has any ID.'

I called the girl over. She seemed distressed. I asked her if she had any ID. She said she hadn't as her purse had been stolen.

'I'm sorry, if you have no ID, you'll have to leave as the barmaid says she knows you and you are under age,' I said.

The girl became very irate. 'I had ID on the way in,' she said. 'Why are you asking for it now?'

'You may appear 18, but the barmaid says you aren't,' I said. 'Therefore you must show the ID or leave.'

'I have had my purse stolen,' she said. 'There is £300 in it. My dad's a policeman. I'm going to get him, and you'll all be in trouble.'

'Look, any story you tell me, I've already heard,' I replied. 'If you haven't any ID, you will have to leave.'

The girl became even more upset and began shouting: 'My dad's a policeman. I've had my purse stolen.'

'I'm sorry, you will have to leave,' I repeated. 'If your dad's a policeman, he will understand that if you haven't got ID we can't let you remain here.'

Eventually she went. To be honest, I couldn't have cared less if the girl was 17 or 18. I'd always judged people on the way they behaved. Most 17-year-old girls who came in the club were trying to act older than they were anyway, so they were well behaved. It was the 30-year-old men who behaved like 12-year-olds I objected to. If the barmaid hadn't said anything, I certainly wouldn't have.

At closing time, I was putting the chains on the fire doors and waiting for the staff to leave before going home myself. I heard shouting, and went to see what the problem was. At the front doors the barmaid who had had the row said she had had a fight with the girl, who had waited outside to have it out with her. I told her to wait inside the door until she'd gone. The barmaid said: 'Don't worry, she has already left.'

I went home and thought no more of it. It wasn't until a year later I found out the truth. Somebody who objected to the way the girl had been treated told me in confidence that what had really happened was that the barmaid had stolen the girl's purse from the toilets. The girl had her suspicions about who had taken it, and had challenged the barmaid to return it. The barmaid had then telephoned Rod to say that the girl was under age so that we would eject her, and the accusations would cease. The girl's name was Leah Betts. She was rightfully upset.

Leah had waited outside the club and, after a confrontation with the barmaid, had been assaulted. As a result of this incident, she was barred from coming into Raquels. Obviously I didn't know at the time that she had been a victim of this theft.

The third and final identification parade was set for 17 March, two days after my birthday. I didn't expect Williams or the Fiesta driver to attend.

Reg Kray asked me to go and visit him, just in case it went wrong for me. He wanted to wish me luck. I travelled down to Maidstone to see him and was very surprised to find that Freddie Foreman was in the visiting room with Reg. Fred is the top underworld heavyweight, in my opinion. He was jailed for disposing of the body of Jack 'The Hat' McVitie whom Reggie Kray and his brother Ron had murdered. He was unsuccessfully tried for the murder of Frank Mitchell, whom the Krays had sprung from prison and whose body was never found. Foreman was also blamed for the murder of Ginger Marks, who disappeared from a street in Bethnal Green, and he was jailed for nine years in 1990 for his part in the handling of part of a £7 million robbery from the Security Express headquarters in Shoreditch, east London. Freddie's reputation in the underworld cannot be matched. Some say the film *The Long Good Friday* is based on his life.

Reg introduced me to him. We shook hands and Fred introduced me to his wife who was visiting him. Fred said his daughter often went to clubs in London, and he would appreciate it if we would see her all right. I told Fred that if his daughter rang me, I would ensure she got into whichever club she was going to as a guest. You had to have respect for these people. Fred was a really nice fellow.

I went and sat down with Reg and he said he had come up with an idea for an advert. For his age Reg was very fit, and had a physique most young men would be very jealous of. He wanted me to contact any company which sold porridge. His idea was that they could use photographs of him weightlifting in an advert and use the caption, 'Look what 30 years of porridge has done for Reg Kray.' I must admit, I thought it was a very good idea, but I couldn't really see me touting it round, and I couldn't realistically see anyone taking it up. He was always coming up with schemes to try and raise cash.

When I got home, I rang Tucker and told him about Freddie Foreman's daughter, as she often visited one of the clubs Tucker ran. He said he would deal with it, but he didn't sound very convincing. Most villains would consider it an honour to do Freddie Foreman a favour. It was typical of Tucker. He had no regard for anyone, whatever their status. It took several calls to him before it was sorted out.

On the day of the ID parade I asked my brother Michael to come down to Basildon so that if any witnesses showed up, we could find out where they were staying. The idea was that he would wait outside the police station and follow any male who left there with police officers heading towards the town centre. Then he would follow them back to the police station and see which car they got into. By taking the car registration we could have it checked and find out their address.

The same morning a reporter rang me on my mobile phone. He told me that Ronnie Kray had died of a massive heart attack that morning at Wexham Park Hospital in Slough. He was 61 years of age. Two days earlier he had collapsed in his ward at Broadmoor Hospital. He had been taken to Heatherwood Hospital in Ascot, but had been transferred to Wexham after his condition had suddenly deteriorated. I was pleased that Ronnie had not died within the confines of Broadmoor.

Reg had said things weren't right when Ronnie was first admitted to hospital. He had applied to the authorities to visit his brother, but had been turned down. I tried ringing Maidstone to offer my condolences, but the prison had been inundated with calls and none was being accepted. I felt it best to leave Reg alone and sort out my ID parade problem first.

My brother and I went to Basildon. He took up a position by the police station while I went to meet my solicitor. We waited for some time, but the witnesses didn't show. The charges, we were told, would be dropped.

That evening I got a call from Reg. He seemed remarkably bright. Of course he was upset about his brother, but his anguish was a private matter. He was more concerned with Ron's funeral arrangements and ensuring there were no problems. He said David Courtney (the man who had tried to set me up to be stabbed) had offered the services of his door firm/security company to guard Ron's body at English's Funeral Directors in Bethnal Green, east London. I thought it rather odd. Courtney had never even met Ronnie, but some people would do anything for publicity, and it seemed Courtney wanted some. Reg asked me if I would go to the parlour to do a shift watching over Ron to ensure ghouls or publicity-seekers didn't pull a stunt. I said I would get in touch with Courtney and sort it out. I had no intention of doing so. Although I had a lot of respect for Ronnie and his brother, I thought this type of thing was for people who were doing it for some sort of sick glamour. I was later to be proved right.

A couple of days later, Reg asked me to visit him at Maidstone. He had been granted a special visit for 12 of his closest friends so they could have a meeting to discuss the funeral arrangements. It wouldn't take place within the confines of the normal visiting room. We were to be given a room to ourselves within the prison. I told Reg that I would be pleased to go and assist where I could.

At the prison I was searched. I was then taken by a woman prison officer to a wood-panelled room usually used for training seminars. Charlie Kray, the twins' elder brother, was there. Mad Frankie Fraser, a former fellow inmate and one-time member of the notorious south London-based Richardson gang, made famous for his use of gold pliers on his victims, was also there. Frank was a real character. He had recently been shot in the head outside Turnmills nightclub in London. When the police asked him who was responsible, he refused to answer questions. When they asked him who he was, he said, 'Tutankhamun.' He was referring to his bandaged head. Mummies don't speak.

Various other notorious criminals arrived in stretch limousines. Other people included prominent journalists and businessmen.

Reggie thought Ronnie's death might have been suspicious. However, he had spoken to the doctor who examined his brother and was now satisfied he had died of a massive heart attack following a blood transfusion needed because of a bleeding ulcer. Reggie said Ron was quite comfortable at the time he died.

Reg asked me about the possibility of doing a deal with the media – it was obvious that the funeral would attract a lot of attention, and there would be interest in exclusives. I said I would arrange it, no problem. I had talked to a national newspaper and a television company who were very interested in filming the church service, doing an interview with Reg and covering the funeral exclusively. They said the time was right to promote freedom for Reg now that his brother had died. I felt it was an opportunity that he should not miss.

The newspaper concerned asked me to ask Reg if they could have a photograph of Ronnie lying in state, as it were. Reg sounded offended and said no. I told him about the interest of the paper and the television company, but as with most things I had tried to do in the past, several other people had been given the same deal to sort out.

The media people who were keen to have the deal sealed would not wait for ever. Reg was not forthcoming and the idea was scrapped. Whatever deals Reg had, there wasn't even enough money left to pay for Ronnie's funeral. I believe to this day his expenses have still not been paid. As with the film *The Krays*, Reg in my opinion was badly advised.

Annie Allen, Geoff Allen's wife (the man I introduced to Vine for the bank job), telephoned me and suggested we attend Ronnie's funeral together. Alan Smith, a friend of mine from Edinburgh, also rang. He said he was meeting John Masterson and we could all meet up at the funeral parlour to travel together. Reggie had asked me to travel in the car behind him for Ronnie's funeral, and to remain with him throughout. However, Courtney had arranged for lots of doormen – strangers – to surround Reg, turning it into a circus. People who wanted to shake Reggie's hand were unnecessarily pushed back by these bouncers. I wanted no part of it. Annie Allen, Alan Smith, John Masterson, Tony Lambrianou (the man who had been convicted with Reg of killing Jack the Hat) and I all travelled together in a car to the funeral.

Ronnie had often talked to me about his funeral. He always said he wanted it to be a big event. He wanted horses pulling a carriage with his coffin on it. He got just what he wanted. The whole of the east end of London turned out to see his procession. I don't think there will be another funeral like it for a criminal. I don't think there had been one like it before. Ronnie's death wasn't just the end of his life. When they buried Ron, they were burying one of the last subscribers to honourable crime. You either get taken out from behind in cold blood these days, or by the police via a call to *Crimestoppers*. Ronnie's passing was the end of an era.

Chapter *Eleven*

WHEN I GOT HOME FROM RONNIE'S FUNERAL I WASHED AND changed and went straight in to work at the Buzz Bar with Martin. There had been a private party at Lennie McLean's pub The Guvners in the east end after the funeral for close family and friends. I had had quite a bit to drink then, and continued to drink while at work.

When I got home that night Debra, quite rightly, was annoyed because I hadn't been around all day and turned up drunk without getting in touch with her. We had a heated row and the next thing I knew there was a knock at the door. It was two police officers from Basildon. I wasn't in the mood for them and became quite abusive. They said they had had a complaint about a disturbance. I told them to go away and that there was no way they were getting into my house. They tried coming in the door, and I pushed them out. Debra was getting quite upset. She stepped outside to talk to them. Again they tried to enter the house, and I blocked their way.

'If you want to talk to them, then talk to them, but I'm going to bed,' I said to her. I slammed the door and went upstairs, but they continued to knock at the door. I went downstairs again.

'What's the problem?' I asked.

'We want to come in and talk to you.'

'Well, I don't want to talk to you,' I said, and slammed the door. If someone can't say what they want to say on the pavement, I know they're up to no good.

I had lots of weapons in the house, including a gun, and I began to panic. There were bayonets, knives, CS gas and ammonia hidden in various places. The gun was hidden in the ceiling in the kitchen.

I thought I had better get rid of it and the gas, because those were the only two things that I could not explain away. They'd searched my house three or four times before, and on those occasions I had told them that the reason I had the bayonets was because I collected First and Second World War memorabilia. The police had reluctantly given them back to me.

I looked out the window to see if the officers had gone, and it appeared they had. I removed the gun and took the gas from the cupboard near the front door. I took them upstairs into the bathroom and hid them in the skylight. I was unsure what to do. They probably weren't even going to question me about the gun. Knowing their procedure, I just had it in my head I had to get the weapons out of the house. Because it was me, I thought they weren't going to go away until they were happy.

I couldn't see Debra, either. I guessed she had gone with them or to her mother's. Ten minutes later her mother rang and said that Debra had called her from the police station. She was upset and she didn't want to go home. She was going to wait there until the police had spoken to me.

'I'm not going to speak to the police,' I said, and put the phone down.

I decided to hide the gas and the handgun in the garden. I rang a taxi, switched off all the lights and took the gun and the gas outside. I put them under a large plant pot. A few minutes later the taxi arrived. I said to the driver: 'Take me to Basildon police station.'

On our way, the driver remarked that two police cars had pulled out behind us. I had a feeling that this was far more sinister than it seemed, but I didn't have the gun on me and as far as I knew they had not seen me hide it. I felt quite confident.

As we arrived at the police station a police van swung in front of the taxi and another pulled up at the side. A marked police car pulled up immediately behind us. I got out of the car and officers in blue overalls with Koch machine-guns took up a position behind the van. They shouted at me: 'Put your hands in the air and kneel on the ground.'

RIGHT: Bernard O'Mahoney
with his wife Debra

BELOW: Bernard outside
Raquels on the last night
he worked there

Tony Tucker, Pat Tate and Bernard at Epping Country Club

Bernard and Tony Tucker at Tucker's birthday party

RIGHT: Mark Rothermel
and Bernard

BELOW: Mark Murray

ABOVE: Bernard with Dave Thomkins, taken while Thomkins was on the run for shooting Steve Woods

LEFT: Craig Rolfe

Bernard with Reggie Kray and Dave Courtney in Maidstone Prison

Bernard with Kate Kray, Charlie Kray and Tony Lambrianou

ABOVE: DCI Brian Storey, head of the enquiries into the death of Leah Betts and the Rettendon murders

LEFT: Steve Packman

ABOVE: Mick Steele

LEFT: Jack Whomes

I said: 'Fuck off, I'm paying the cab driver.'

'Put your hands in the air and kneel on the ground!'

'I've told you, I'm not a knocker,' I said. 'I'm paying the cab driver. Then I'll do what you want.'

'Don't put your hand in your pocket. Kneel on the ground!'

The police seemed more uptight and hyped up than they should have been. I didn't trust these people with truncheons, never mind guns, so I put my hands in the air and an officer ran up behind me and pulled my hands behind my back. He handcuffed me and pushed me to the ground. After searching me briefly by patting my pockets and clothing, he told me to get up.

'You don't understand. I've already told you I am not going anywhere until I've paid the cab driver,' I said. 'If you want, put your hand in my pocket, take the money out and give it to him.'

He refused, so I said I wasn't getting up. Eventually he relented and took the money out of my pocket. I turned my head. I could see the cab driver. He too was on the ground with a gun to his head. It was bizarre.

I was led into the police station where I was told that they had received information that I was in possession of a gun. 'Bollocks,' I told them. The police said I would be held while a search was conducted at my house. I was then taken into the charge room. An officer explained why I was being held. I was searched again. My shoes and personal belongings were removed and I was put in a cell. I really wasn't having a good day. I decided the best thing to do was to get my head down and have a sleep and see how things were in the morning. I found it hard to sleep, though. I knew the gun was there, and if they were determined, the bastards were going to find it.

They finally came to interview me at about three o'clock the following afternoon. Two detectives introduced themselves and they began to conduct a taped interview. They gave nothing away at first. They said: 'We would like to discuss some weapons we have found at your home.'

'If you tell me what you are talking about, I will explain,' I replied. The detectives told me they had searched my house. In the cupboard immediately behind the front door, they found a bayonet, approximately 18 inches long, in a sheath. They also found a baseball bat with the word 'Dentist' engraved on it. While searching the main bedroom they said they'd found an eight-inch knife in a sheath bound in blue tape. Finally, they said, at the edge of the lawn at the end of the path in the garden, they had found a small aerosol can and a leather holster which contained an automatic handgun. They had left the items 'in situ' to be photographed for the purpose of using them in evidence.

I told them there was nothing illegal about the weapons found in the house, which was true. There was nothing illegal about owning a baseball bat, either. I told them that the CS gas had been purchased while on a day-trip to France. It was for the protection of my wife who was at home most evenings alone with the children while I was at work.

As for the firearm, there were no bullets for it, I said. Whilst up north I had purchased it from a farmer on behalf of my brother, Michael, who is himself a farmer. My intention was to give it to him for use in killing vermin.

The police could only record what I said, they couldn't really contest it. During the interview it came to light that the two original officers who came to my home had gone away when I told them to, but parked down the street, switched off all their lights and kept watch without my knowing. They had then radioed for reinforcements and approximately 12 other officers – plain-clothed, armed and uniformed – had surrounded my house and kept it under surveillance. They had actually seen me putting the weapons in the garden. When I left, some followed me and others remained at my home.

The interview was concluded. I was told the items would be sent off for forensic tests and I was bailed to reappear at the police station in a few weeks' time. I got home at about six that evening. I had been due to visit Reggie that day. However, the police had been kind enough to ring the prison to tell him that I was otherwise engaged.

I sat in the house considering my position. If I couldn't get out of this, I would be convicted, lose my door licence and lose my job at Raquels. I began to wonder if that would be such a bad thing, really. I couldn't just walk away from the club. This was maybe the excuse that I was looking for. Then again, I had to provide for myself and my family. I really didn't know what I was going to do.

That evening I received a phone call from Peter Clarke. He told me he had seen a piece in the paper about me being arrested after going to Ronnie Kray's funeral. He asked me if the gun was the one he had given me. I said it was. He then asked if I had been charged with anything, and when I said no, he seemed quite surprised. 'Why is that, then?' he asked.

It was as if he was disappointed that I hadn't been charged. I had only been bailed to reappear at the police station, pending results. When you are caught with a gun, the police are unable to charge you with possession straight away, because it may prove later that the weapon is a replica, or it has a vital piece of the mechanism not working, such as the trigger or firing pin. This would not make it a firearm and the charge wouldn't stick. They have to have it confirmed that it's a working gun.

But I didn't tell Clarke this. He rang me the next day and told me he had a job which wanted doing in Birmingham, if I was interested. I asked him what it was, and he told me Jones, his partner, who ran a Basildon door firm, was selling a car to a man in the West Midlands. The man, an Asian, had arranged to meet Jones and he would have several thousand pounds in cash on him. The idea was that someone else would appear and rob him. The car would turn up later, and they would pretend to know nothing about it. He said it would be really easy. I said if it was so easy, why weren't they doing it themselves?

He said that they would be very busy, otherwise they would. I taped the conversation, because I had been suspicious of these people for some time. I told them I would give it some thought.

I rang the detective who had been named by other officers as the man who might fit me up. I told him that I had received a call from somebody who had asked me to commit a serious crime in the north of England. If information was received that I was up to no good in the next few days, they should ignore it. I was quite sure they would receive such information.

The detective asked me what it was all about. I told him briefly, without giving names and places. He told me I was being paranoid. I thought otherwise. The following day he rang me, and asked if we could meet. When we met he asked me to give my version of events. I told him that I believed Jones, Clarke and Pierce wanted me out of Raquels, or off the scene, at any cost. When I had been partners with Clarke at the club, he and Jones had held talks with the management behind my back. I told him about the trouble Pierce had stirred up between me and Vine; the numerous anonymous complaints that the licensing police and Basildon Council had received about me and other members of the door staff; the searches of my home and car for drugs; the accusation that my own car was stolen, backed by paperwork from Charlie Jones; the lorry-load of coffee beans to Liverpool and the men's arrest there; the fact they had given me the very gun I was now on bail for. I told the detective I thought Jones, Clarke or Pierce was an informant. By getting me arrested, they knew I would end up losing the Raquels door and then they could take over.

The detective would not say whether they were or were not. He said if I believed I had been fitted up with the gun, I should tell the truth. However, he said, if I named names, it could cause problems for me: not with the police, but other people. He said it was a matter for me to decide. However, he took on board what I was saying, particularly in view of the fact that I had a tape of one of them asking me to commit a robbery the day after I'd been released on bail. He couldn't help but admit that it did seem rather odd. He said he would keep abreast of the situation and I should tell him of any developments.

The very same evening, my telephone rang at home. Somebody asked if Jones was there. I would stake my life that it was the detective. I have asked him a thousand times to admit it was him, but he denies it. We agree to differ. However, I now knew my fears were not unfounded concerning Pierce, Clarke and Jones. They didn't have to go to these lengths. They weren't man enough to take it direct. If they had wanted it that badly, they could have had Raquels. They only had to ask.

Whatever the outcome, they weren't going to get it now. I had the tape from the police saying I was going to be fitted up. I had the tape of Clarke trying to lure me into committing a robbery. I also knew one, if not all three, were police informants. It was all good material to get me out of this mess.

Reg Kray got in touch. He said he had heard about what had happened, and he wanted to know if there was anything he could do. He said I should go down to Maidstone to see if anything could be done to sort the problem out. I wasn't really in the mood for it, but I felt sorry for Reg after losing his brother, and so I said I would go down to see him. I felt bad about not seeing him on the day after the funeral even though I had been locked up in Basildon police station and there was little I could have done about it.

The newspaper with which I had held talks regarding Ronnie's funeral asked me if Reg would be willing to give an interview about Ron's death and the funeral itself. He had snubbed their earlier offer and most of the best material had been given away to various other newspapers. I spoke to Reg on the phone before visiting him, and he agreed that he would do the interview. He wanted ten grand, but I told him that was impossible. In the end we agreed that he would do the interview and he would be paid according to the content.

I didn't like getting involved in his business. There were always too many advisers, and everything always ended in arguments. Reggie did the article and I felt it was the most sympathetic coverage he had ever had since being imprisoned. He too was pleased with it, and talks of setting up a deal with the paper for his first interview after he was freed were put in motion. It could have been quite lucrative. But his fan club were always advising him to do silly interviews with local papers. They were more interested in selling T-shirts with his picture on and making a bit of money on the way than getting him out of prison. I'd always been of the opinion that it was these people who were keeping him inside.

Once, they had organised a 'Free The Krays' march through London. Young children had gone on the march wearing T-shirts with pictures of Ron and Reg on the front; on the back they had printed 'The Krays On Tour', listing all the prisons they had been in during their 30-year sentence with dates. Little wonder those at the Home Office still considered them a threat. I'd always said they should have sat back and given just the occasional interview, talk the philosophical shit all government departments love to hear. Glorifying murder and events that straight people found abhorrent was not doing them any favours, but you couldn't tell them.

Reg was paid £3,000 for the interview, and I was given £1,000 for organising it. As usual, members of Reggie's fan club were up in arms, saying he should have been paid five-figure sums, which was nonsense. The most newsworthy points concerning his brother's death had been given in interviews with other papers for nothing weeks before this one appeared in print. I thought he had had a result.

He went into a rage on the phone, saying he should have been given more money. I was getting a bit sick of being criticised. If he had stuck with the original agreement about the exclusive rights for the funeral we would both have had a lot of money. But as usual people interfered. As far as I know this three grand was the best payment he had had out of the whole thing.

The row blew out of all proportion a few days later. The *News of the World* published an article. The headline read: 'Ghouls snorted coke off Ronnie Kray's coffin'. It was reported that people had snorted lines of cocaine and also that they set up an ouija board next to Ronnie's casket and tried to contact his spirit. Finally, they put a Sony Walkman on Ronnie's head and cackled with laughter, saying doesn't he look stupid with the headphones on? Reggie was outraged. Staff at the funeral parlour discovered tell-tale smudges on Ronnie's highly polished open coffin. They also found pieces of paper with letters written on them used for the ouija session. Reggie was reported as saying he wanted Dave Courtney to explain any lapse in the watertight security he had promised.

Reggie and the fan club spent most of the day ringing my house. As I knew several reporters, they wanted me to find out who was behind these acts against Ronnie and who had spoken to the paper. They were blaming everyone. I told Reg I would try to find out, but I didn't intend doing so. I was sick to death of this pettiness. I had been told what was going on at the funeral parlour at the time it was happening. That's the main reason I didn't want to get involved in watching over Ronnie. I knew people wouldn't be doing it out of respect and things were bound to happen. When I was told, I wasn't surprised. I even knew who was involved, but it wasn't my business. If you told Reggie the truth anyway, you would be met with counter claims and it would all just get messy. I had had it a thousand times with him and Ronnie.

Lorraine, a genuine friend of Reggie's, rang me up, very upset, saying she had been blamed, and for her benefit, I spoke to Reg and told him that I knew for certain that she was not involved. However, all Reggie did was round on me, saying why would I befriend Lorraine. I was meant to be his friend, not hers. I even rang the journalist who wrote the article and told him that Lorraine was being blamed. He also offered to help her. It was bizarre. Everyone knew who was responsible, but still Reg allowed the accusations to continue.

One avid fan of Reggie's was a man named Brad Allardyce. I had met him in Maidstone Prison where he too was serving a prison sentence. Recently he had been moved to Whitemoor Prison in Cambridgeshire where Pat Tate was also serving his sentence. Reg had asked me if Tate would look after Brad, as he was rather vulnerable. I was reluctant to ask Tate but I did so as a favour to Reg. Soon Tate and I were both regretting having anything to do with Allardyce.

Tate rang me a few times, asking who the fuck was this person I'd put on to him. He said that he was lining up something big for the firm from inside. He was going to finance a cannabis shipment from

Amsterdam using Nicholls, the man I had met at Tate's bedside, as the frontman. Tate said he was going to fund it using a syndicate's money. Allardyce, he said, was making him look like a fool. If the people he was hoping to get money from thought he mixed with the likes of Allardyce, it could blow the whole thing. All I could do was apologise.

Allardyce would ring or write to me. He seemed to think he was Reggie's right-hand man. In one letter, he wrote to me about an associate of Reg called Piper claiming he'd had Reg over on some deal: 'Gary Piper is in a lot of trouble, Bernie. He's used us and I will never let that go unpunished. Never. I'll bide my time, but when I get out, Bernie, he will be finished. Nobody crosses Reg without crossing me. I will make that cunt pay for what he's done. I am not stupid, Bernie, so I do not intend to end up back in prison down to him. But he will be sorry he ever crossed us. Reg means the world to me, Bernie. A lot of people think he has a lot of friends, but you and I know different. It's up to us to protect him. He is like a father to me, Bernie. I love him very much. Gary Piper is finished. Take it from me. Reg listens to me, Bernie, and he will always do as I ask. Because he knows I will only do what is best for him. Sometimes people take advantage of him. Well, that's all stopped now because I am his right-hand man. You're a good friend, Bernie, and Reg knows that. I've seen Pat Tate, he sends his very best to you.'

In another letter he sent me a visiting order and asked me to see him. He asked if I could bring some 'birds' – slang for doves, a type of ecstasy – and maybe some 'Mickey Duff', Cockney rhyming slang for cannabis ('puff'). He said he would get phone cards and start up his own 'food boat', prison slang for wheeling and dealing inside.

I don't know who this man thought he was. Censors who read the letter would hardly be fooled by somebody asking for birds and Mickey Duff. I'm surprised the police weren't kicking my door down at the same time the postman was at it. I really had to get away from these people. The wannabes were causing more trouble than the real villains.

Things happen in threes, they say. I'd been arrested for the gun,

I'd fallen out with Reg and everyone who knew him, and sure enough, disaster struck again.

Roger Mellin had never been in trouble in his life. His girlfriend Tracy had a disabled child. Roger was a really nice kid. He was young and impressionable. He had often asked about selling ecstasy for Murray in Raquels as he desperately needed money. I told him drug dealing is a mug's game and he ought to forget it. Murray, however, told Roger that he would pay him £50 a week just to store any excess drugs at his home. It sounded simple. They would be left there and picked up when required. Roger would have to do nothing for his £50. I told him he was mad. But Roger insisted he needed the money.

One morning Murray asked him if he would count out the pills for the various dealers. Roger didn't like the idea of them coming into his house, so he booked himself into a local hotel room. He sat on the bed and started sorting them out into different amounts. There was a knock at the door, and when he opened it police officers stormed into the room. On the bed were 1,500 ecstasy tablets, quantities of cocaine and quantities of amphetamine. Roger was well and truly nicked.

The police had been watching certain people and followed Roger to the hotel. When they had seen enough, they moved in. Roger was devastated. He knew he was going to serve a lengthy prison sentence despite the fact it was the first time he had ever been in trouble. It was a tragedy, really. He was a regular at Raquels. He had been lured into this nightmare for £50 a week. Somebody somewhere was determined to put our firm, which had become an insatiable monster, out of business.

Roger pleaded guilty at his trial. He never named those he was working for. For his loyalty, for £50, his girlfriend and her disabled child received nothing from the firm or Mark Murray. Roger was sentenced to five years' imprisonment. We used to say in Basildon that if you wanted loyalty, you should buy a dog.

*

When the dust had settled surrounding events at the funeral parlour with Ronnie Kray, Reg rang and asked if Debra and I would visit him. He was having an interview with Mary Riddell from the *Today* newspaper. He said he wanted us to be there. I didn't go because he asked me to, I went because I knew it would be the very last time I would see him. I didn't tell him – I didn't tell anyone except Debra. I had had enough. I wanted out. I asked Debra not to tell anyone for the time being. Things would have to be sorted. You can't just walk away from the situation I was in. When I went, I wanted it to be for good.

We started looking for a new home near Ipswich. We had found somebody who was interested in doing an exchange with us in a village called Great Blakenham. I made several trips there and it seemed to be just what we wanted. I didn't want my children growing up surrounded by people like my friends. I wanted them to have a future.

Mark Murray had been in Club UK for about seven or eight weeks now. He hadn't paid me one penny of the £500 a week I had been promised. Murray disputed the amount he owed me and Tucker, so I wrote a note detailing the money he owed me for introducing him to Tucker and the money he owed Tucker for the right to sell drugs in the clubs where our firm ran the doors. It included dates and the amount of drugs sold. It also carried a veiled threat that Murray should pay up or else. He had promised me £500 a week, and I expected it. If he didn't come down to the club on Friday to discuss how it was going to be sorted, I would be paying him a visit.

He came to the club and started making excuses. I told him I was going to America on holiday the following week. If I had not got the cash by the morning I was due to go I would be unable to travel and I wouldn't be very happy. I would come to look for him. He promised me it would be there.

I went to a travel agent's, and booked a holiday for my family. I needed to get away from everything to be able to think properly. I was getting sick of people like Murray. Tucker was feeding him, making him think he was something. Murray had started to believe it. He tried telling me he had no money because he was losing at Club UK. He had to pay for the pills that had been lost when Roger had been arrested. I said it wasn't my problem. The money had better be there.

He came to my house at six o'clock on the morning we were due to leave. Our flight left Gatwick Airport at 11 a.m. He couldn't really have left it any later. Nevertheless, he put the money up. I told him our arrangement was now cancelled. He shouldn't make promises he didn't know he could keep. As he had paid the £3,500 he owed, I was happy, and that would be the end of the matter.

We flew from Gatwick to Florida, where we rented a house not far from Disneyland. We spent a week there. It was glorious. We had our own swimming-pool at a luxury secluded home. We spent the day with the children in the theme parks and in the evening we would have barbecues beside the pool. We went on to Graceland in Memphis, then Los Angeles.

The holiday was just what I needed. In 17 days we spent £7,500, but that short break had put things into perspective. I couldn't continue the way things were. The gun, and the conviction that went with it, would give me my way out. It was depressing flying home from America. When we landed at Gatwick it was raining and grey. Dismal. It was just how I felt.

Back home it was business as usual. Two people, Gary Murray and Richard Hearn, had left separate messages on my answering machine. Both wanted to meet me to discuss a proposition. Gary Murray (no relation to Mark) was now selling the gear for the firm on Saturdays at the Jungle do because Mark Murray already had quite a lucrative job of serving up at a club in Southend on Saturdays. He also had Club UK to worry about. Gary Murray asked me if I would put Mark out and let him take control of Fridays also. I refused. 'It's none of my business. That arrangement can't be broken because money is owed by Mark,' I said.

Richard Hearn, who had worked as a dealer for Mark Murray, also asked me if he could take over from him. I told him to meet me at the club on Friday. I took him upstairs into a backroom and sent someone to get Mark Murray. When they were both in the room, I asked Hearn to repeat what he had asked me. He said it was all a misunderstanding, he didn't really want to take over from Mark. It was typical. Somebody wanted someone removed, but they wanted to do it behind a painted smile rather than confront the person direct. It wasn't my style. Hearn was thrown out of the club.

It seemed people were too scared to confront others involved with the firm. This fashion of disposing of them in other ways was becoming a bigger problem. Suspicion was on everybody. Nobody was left out. Some of the dealers even accused Tony Tucker of being an informant. He wasn't. The flavour of the month depended on which circle of people you were sitting with and at what particular time.

Three more of the firm's couriers were taken out by police as they were on their way from Basildon to make a drop at a London club. Nigel Coy, Richard Gilham and Jason Edwards were stopped by the police in Purfleet. Each had a bag tucked inside his boxer shorts containing 100 ecstasy pills. Nigel Coy admitted to the police he had made at least eight similar drops. Coy ran a hairdressing business called Coy Cuts, and when the police searched it they found another 168 pills. Coy was also in possession of amphetamine sulphate and admitted intending to supply. At his trial he was jailed for four years. Gilham and Edwards admitted possessing ecstasy with intent to supply. They were each jailed for three years.

Club UK was going badly for Mark Murray. Nobody wanted to do business with him. Roger had been arrested, so had Coy, Edwards and Gilham; Nathaniel and Lee, who had dropped the pills at Raquels when the management gave them back, had also been jailed for possession. Little wonder that Mark was forced to start dealing himself.

I went to a solicitor to discuss my prospects concerning the gun. He told me that as I had the tape and the names of those I thought had informed on me, I should call the police's bluff and threaten to expose the whole thing. Naturally the police would want none of it.

I was advised not to name those involved, but to threaten to do so. When it got to court, the police would refuse to name the informants and the case against me would be dismissed, which normally happens because the police won't name informants in court.

When I appeared at the Magistrates Court in Basildon to be committed to the Crown Court, my solicitor tried to get the case thrown out early and told the court the circumstances of how I came to be in possession of the gun. The prosecution would have none of it. So my solicitor wrote to the Crown Prosecution Service (CPS) about the 'alleged police informant' working with the Chelmsford Drug Squad – the people who had searched my house – in the hope that they would drop the case against me. The CPS would have none of it, either. They wrote: 'These allegations are totally unfounded and completely untrue.'

The police didn't want me bringing the fit-up tape up and they also didn't want me naming informants in court, but the CPS were preventing any deal going ahead. Another solution would have to be sought.

On 23 July I received a phone call late in the evening. I was told that a friend of mine and Tucker's, Francis Martin, the head doorman at Legends nightclub in the west end, had been shot. He was 36. He had been drinking with friends at the Frog & Nightgown in the Old Kent Road, and was shot at point-blank range moments after leaving. The gunman had been lying in wait outside. Nobody had any idea why it had happened. Friends of Francis chased after the gunman, but were forced to dive for cover as he turned and fired at them. He escaped in a red Ford Orion, driven by another man.

Francis was in a stable condition, but his injuries were serious. He had been shot in the back. Everyone was surprised that it had happened to him, as he was well liked and not involved in the drugs trade. These days, however, you didn't have to be involved in anything to qualify for being shot or wounded.

Tucker was quite upset about the shooting but we decided to stay away from the hospital, as we didn't know what the situation was.

Three weeks later, on 10 August, when we all thought he was on the road to recovery, Francis died of his injuries. It made me think more about my fate. Prison was on the horizon, but the way things were going, a grave could be round the corner.

Chapter *Twelve*

THERE WAS LITTLE SOLIDARITY IN THE FIRM NOW. THE VIOLENCE and the excessive use of cocaine had turned the meekest of men into explosive psychopaths.

People had turned to cocaine trying to reach the elusive high that had faded as their bodies had become used to the effects of ecstasy. Cocaine was associated with gangsters and villainy, and cocaine users were considered to be on a higher plane than those using ecstasy. It was a fashionable drug to be associated with.

If used over a prolonged period, cocaine destroys the septum, the structure which separates the nostrils. One member of the firm was able to put a bootlace up one nostril and bring it down the other, hold both ends and pull it up and down in a pulley-type motion – quite sick, really, but some people thought it was funny. Instead of one or two ecstasy pills per evening, some were consuming between eight and twelve. They were topping that up with lines of cocaine and amphetamine sulphate.

The atmosphere of evil was like a virus. It affected everyone. Dave Simms, the Raquels manager, disapproved, but his protests were silenced. In a bid to weaken us, he had cut staff numbers, saying the club could not afford the wages bill. The door had been cut so severely, there was now little security visible in the club. When there was an incident, those involved were put down with the intention that they remained so. This cocktail amounted to madness in its purest form.

The anger, frustration and hostility was also coming out in our work. On Saturdays there were only four of us working. One evening we were downstairs at the main door talking when we received a call on the internal telephone from the Buzz Bar. The barmaid told us there was a group of men in there causing trouble. I went to see what the problem was and found seven or eight soldiers, obviously home on weekend leave, drunk and making a general nuisance of themselves. I told them to leave, and one of them picked up a glass. I didn't say anything. I bent down and picked up a fire extinguisher which was by the toilet door. I swung the fire extinguisher and hit him with it. He was helped to his feet by his friends and they got him to the door. I threw the fire extinguisher. This time it smashed the double doors. They ran down the stairs and I went after them.

When we got out onto the street the other three doormen saw what was happening, and ran to assist me. One of the doormen, Jeff Balman, fell during the fight and was lying on the ground. We were greatly outnumbered so I ran into the club foyer and picked up a heavy piece of iron that I'd seen lying there. I ran into the street and went to hit the man who was standing over Jeff. I had the piece of metal in both hands, and swung it like a baseball bat. Jeff didn't see what I was doing, pushed the man off him and began to get up. The bar hit Jeff full on the side of the head and knocked him out cold. There was blood everywhere. The men saw what had happened and ran. We had trouble getting Jeff to regain consciousness. As we had always had a policy of not calling for ambulances, Jeff was put into a car and taken to hospital by another doorman. I told him to say he had not been working. At the hospital he was told to tell staff, and if need be the police, that he had been walking through Basildon and people had set upon him and tried to mug him. That way the trouble wouldn't be associated with the club and Jeff could put in for criminal compensation. He was diagnosed as suffering from concussion and detained. He needed 13 stitches in his head and was still receiving medical attention six months after the event for pains in his head and general dizziness.

We had no sympathy for Jeff. When he complained about his injuries, he was ridiculed. When he came into Raquels to get his wages, somebody told him that the management had got him some new safety equipment. We presented him with a child's plastic crash helmet from Toys 'R' Us. Jeff left the firm.

Two skinheads came into the Buzz Bar one Wednesday evening. One stood behind me, aping me, and laughing with his friend. I turned around and pushed him. I didn't mean to do it, but he fell backwards and his head hit the corner of a glass pillar, splitting it wide open. Martin heard the glass smash and ran from the other side of the bar with a bottle in his hand. The skinhead was on the floor, and Martin could not see the wound at the back of his head. He thought he had attacked me with a glass. Martin hit him a couple of times over the head with the bottle and we dragged him to the doors. He was thrown into one door, which smashed, cutting his upper arm. He was then beaten and thrown down the stairs. About half an hour later, people near the stairs began panicking. We looked down and the entrance was ablaze. The skinhead had returned and petrol-bombed the entrance to the bar. It was the only entrance, and all the people inside were screaming.

We told Rod Chapman to deal with the fire, and we ran out through the flames into the street. I saw the skinhead with a red petrol can in his hand. I had an Irish hurling stick in my hand. I ran across. He dropped the petrol can and said: 'It wasn't me, it wasn't me.' I hit him across the back with the stick. He fell to the ground. Martin had steel boots on, and he began stamping on him and kicking him in the head. He was begging us not to beat him any more. I hit him so hard across the back with the hurling stick it broke. He was unconscious. We picked the petrol can up and doused him in petrol. His friend, who had run a short distance away, was screaming, 'Please don't burn him, please don't burn him!' We told him to come to us, as we weren't going to do anything. He wouldn't. We emptied the remainder of the petrol over his unconscious friend and said we would burn him. His friend became hysterical. We walked back to the bar, where the fire had been put out. People said we had over-reacted, but there were 250 innocent people in the bar. If these people wanted to play with fire, they had to be prepared to take the consequences. You couldn't allow people to take liberties like that.

With the tension that was mounting within the firm, our actions were becoming more and more extreme. We couldn't justify everything that happened. David Arnell was probably the quietest doorman who worked with us. He wasn't a drug user. He was just surrounded by violence and acted accordingly. One evening three men, one a surgeon, were enjoying a night out at Raquels. Around 2 a.m., the surgeon, Dr Nwaoloko, left the club with his brother and waited for their friend outside. When their friend failed to appear Dr Nwaoloko asked me for permission to go back in, and I said go ahead. But Arnell stopped him going into the club, and an argument started. Dr Nwaoloko was pushed to the ground and kicked by Arnell several times. He lost consciousness briefly and suffered injuries to his forehead, jaw, cheek and neck. Arnell then went back into the club while Dr Nwaoloko was taken to his car by his brother. However, Arnell later went across the road and repeatedly smashed the doctor's head on his car bonnet. It was totally out of character for Dave.

I told him to plead not guilty and deny all knowledge of the attack. But when the police came he blurted out the truth, and pleaded guilty. He wasn't like us. I liked Dave. At his trial the prosecutor said Dr Nwaoloko now had a problem with his wrist resulting from the attack which prevented him doing his job as a surgeon. Because Dave had never been in trouble before in his life the judge said he would escape a prison sentence. Dave was ordered to pay £1,000 compensation and do 180 hours community service. He quit working that night, and has told me he will never work as a doorman again.

Tucker too was feeling vulnerable. When he used to come and see me on Friday nights to give me the invoices and the doormen's wages for the club, he would park at the top of the street in his black Porsche. I used to go up, open the door and get in. He would always have a handgun on the seat between his legs. He told me he had also applied for a firearms licence from Basildon police. He wanted to own a shotgun legally. There were plenty of arms around the firm, but as Tucker had no convictions, he might as well hold one or two legally which he could have at hand in his home without fear of being arrested. Because of his clean record, it was unlikely the police would refuse his application.

He had enjoyed a good roll in the past few months. The firm had been approached by a part-time drug dealer who had acquired £18,000-worth of cannabis to sell. Tucker told the dealer he had the right contacts and would sort out a sale for him. Tucker, Rolfe and the dealer travelled to Birmingham, where Tucker said his contact lived. While the dealer and Rolfe waited, Tucker disappeared with the cannabis. He turned up a couple of hours later and told them the police had busted them before they had got the money. He was lucky to have escaped. The dealer had to accept the excuse Tucker gave him or take him on. Losing 18 grand must have been a bitter pill to swallow, but it would have been less painful than calling Tucker a liar.

Everybody knew no one had been arrested. If that does occur on such a deal, the person who lost the drugs or claims to have been arrested has a duty to produce paperwork from those charged or from those who are bailed. Otherwise it is considered untrue. However, the dealer wasn't going to take Tucker on.

But Tucker knew he couldn't get away with these scams for ever. Hence the guns, which travelled with him everywhere he dared take them.

I was going backwards and forwards to Basildon Magistrates Court waiting to be committed to Crown Court on the matter of the gun and CS gas. The police were concerned that the CPS were not allowing me to bring the question of informants into the evidence. My solicitor told me that although it was the truth, it was going to be an uphill struggle. If somebody had offered to give me a gun and I accepted it, I was guilty. All other circumstances were mitigating at best, and did I really want to tell a judge about rival door firms involved in setting me up with guns etc? It was agreed that the best story to give the court would be the one I had initially given to the police: that I had purchased the gun on behalf of my brother, who was going to use it to shoot vermin on the farm where he worked. That story would not involve nightclubs and doormen. It was a fairly innocent affair.

The gas which had been bought to protect my wife, although illegal, was also a fairly innocent act. We all agreed that a lie was more believable than the truth.

I was told by the police that if I did not mention the fit-up tape and the fact the gun had been given to me by persons I claimed were informants then the seriousness of the charge would be played down in court. It would go through as I was telling it, a fairly harmless affair. I gave my word I wouldn't mention the tape and I wouldn't mention the informants. A deal was struck. It was better for all concerned. The prosecution despised me. I could tell by the way they looked at me and spoke about me. Court is like that. Very little of the truth comes out. Like life, they tell you, it's a game and you should play by the rules. It's true, I suppose, especially if you are in the team with all the star players. But it's a fucker when your side has all the disadvantages. What sort of game is it then?

At my final appearance at Basildon Magistrates Court, the magistrate ordered that I stand trial at Chelmsford Crown Court.

In October, Club UK in Wandsworth was raided by the police. The whole operation was captured on video film. There were more than 1,000 people in the club. Murray's dealers threw all their pills and powders on the floor in order to escape arrest. Murray lost 800 pills in total, pills he had not yet paid Tucker for. This was on top of the 468 he lost when Nigel Coy and the others had been busted, and the 1,500 when Roger Mellin had been busted. With this 800 he had lost 2,768 pills with a street value of £41,520. Murray was probably in debt to the tune of about 20 grand. Prison would have been salvation for him.

There are no financial advisers in the drugs world, and there are certainly no overdraft facilities. Tucker wanted his money, and he wanted it now. He came round to my house with Rolfe and asked me where Murray was. We all got into a car and went round to Murray's house. His girlfriend was there. Rolfe went in the front room and said: 'Where's Mark?' She said she didn't know. He asked if he had taken his phone with him. She said no, he had left it there. Rolfe picked it up and started making calls. Tucker was sitting on the settee with me. He was laughing. He said to her, 'Are you watching this programme?', pointing to the television. She said no. He ripped the plug from the wall, wrapped it round the telly and told Rolfe to go and load the stereo and the television into the car.

He then told Murray's girlfriend she was coming with us. She was very frightened, and said Mark would be home soon. He said: 'Don't worry about that, get in the car.' We all drove round to another friend's house. Fortunately Tucker had forgotten why, if he ever had a reason, he had taken Murray's girlfriend. I think he just did it to ensure she didn't warn Murray about the fact he was looking for him. Whatever, tired of waiting, we all went home.

That night Tucker and Rolfe returned to Murray's flat. He was back. Tucker pulled out a huge bowie knife, grabbed Murray by the neck and pressed the point into his throat. He said: 'I want my money, Murray. And for every week you owe me, you pay £500 on top. If I don't get it, you're dead.'

Pat Tate was due to be released from prison soon, and Tucker organised what he thought would be a huge party for his release. It was to be at a snooker hall in Dagenham. On Halloween, the day Tate came out, Tucker rang me and said he wanted me to go to the party with all the doormen. He and Tate had something they wanted to discuss with me which would be an earner for us all.

I rang him back that night and said I would be unable to go because I had to head up north. It was a lie. I was trying to get out of my situation, not get more involved. I wasn't the only one who felt like this: only 15 people attended Tate's coming-out party.

I did see him and Tucker that week. They, as well as everybody else, were talking about an article which had been in the local papers. Half a million pounds' worth of cannabis had been found in a farmer's pond near a place called Rettendon. It was believed that the 336 pounds of cannabis, wrapped in 53 different plastic parcels about the size of video tapes, had been dropped from a low-flying aircraft. Instead of landing in the field, it had landed in a pond, and the dealers were unable to find it. A farmer named Yan Haustrup found one parcel while cutting the hedges. He didn't know what it was, and threw it on a fire. He said he then found another piece near the pond, and contacted the police. Divers recovered the haul.

Tucker and Tate were saying the guy was a fucking idiot to throw it on the fire and then hand over £500,000-worth of gear to the Old Bill. Tate thought it would be worth looking to see if any of the shipment had been missed. But it was the drugs talking: he hadn't been straight since the day he got out. Rettendon to us was only a roundabout. There wasn't anything else there. There was just a church, a post office and probably 50 or so houses. We were hardly going to scour the fields after the police had crawled all over the place. Tate kept on about it. He couldn't believe that someone could be that straight and hand over anything of that much value to the police.

Tucker said he was going to find out who the drugs belonged to. He didn't like the idea of people trading on his manor if he wasn't getting a slice of the profit. He also knew that as the drugs had been lost, there would be a replacement shipment coming soon.

Word soon reached Tucker that the Rettendon drugs had been destined for a heavy firm from Canning Town in east London. He approached the people concerned and told them he was interested in purchasing any future shipments. They told him they were due to receive a replacement drop and they would keep him informed so a deal could be struck when it arrived. Tucker had a better idea: he was going to steal it.

The last time Tate was out of prison, the two of them had robbed a Canning Town cartel of £20,000-worth of cannabis and £250,000-worth of traveller's cheques. Canning Town is not the place to go around robbing people if you want to live to tell the tale.

Tate and Tucker called me and we met in the carpark at Basildon Hospital, outside the Accident and Emergency entrance – a place we often met. Tate said he wanted me to act as a back-up driver on a scam they were pulling off shortly. They were planning to intercept a large shipment of drugs at Rettendon. They had done this type of thing loads of times before, but they said this was different. This was the big one. I said I wouldn't be able to do it as I had noticed again the police were watching me.

I still felt something for these people. Before this nightmare we were now all in, they had been my friends. They were blind to any danger. Tate was driving Tucker on. I warned him to be careful, but as usual he just laughed and ridiculed my advice.

Tate's other get-rich-quick scheme was also under way at this time. He had approached shady car dealers, villains and dodgy businessmen to put up approximately £120,000 in cash for a shipment of cannabis from Amsterdam. Tate calculated that he would get up to £270,000 back on the investment. Darren Nicholls, the man I had met at Tate's bedside, was going to purchase the drugs and use what he called his 'suicide jockeys' to bring them into the country. These were the people, obviously desperate for money, who were prepared to drive cars laden with drugs from the Continent to England for between £6,000 and £8,000 a trip. The only risk lay with the 'jockeys'; it was reckoned two out of three cars got through Customs without being caught – more than enough profit to cover the occasional loss. Tate and Tucker were not even risking their own money; they felt they couldn't lose.

Mark Murray was having no such luck. In an effort to get his money back from Murray, Tucker insisted that Mark buy all of his stock directly from him. Murray had been deceiving Tucker for some time, buying weaker ecstasy pills for sale in the clubs. His reasoning was if you sold very strong ecstasy, a person would buy one and be out of their head for the whole night. That person would not need any additional pills. By selling weaker pills, the person would need three or more to get any sort of effect. However, Tucker's latest batch were a new type of ecstasy called Apples. They had been imported from Holland and were very strong. Murray had no choice but to buy them from Tucker at an inflated rate,

a) because Tucker said they were good and worth more, and b) because Murray owed him money and had little choice.

The pills caused a lot of people to be ill in Raquels. I was called up to the dancefloor one Friday evening. A youth had collapsed and his friends were concerned for him. I told them to pick him up and take him downstairs where we could assess the situation in the fresh air and light, away from the dark and crowded dancefloor. The kid was in a right state. I thought he was about 17 or 18. His eyes were rolling in his head. He was sweating and drifting in and out of consciousness. He got up and said to me, 'I want to go.' He walked out of the door and collapsed in the street. I told his friends to take him to hospital, but they were frightened his parents were going to find out he'd taken drugs. We led him over to a bench in the town centre and sat him down. A gang of youths were sitting nearby, watching.

I left him with his friends and went back to the club. I kept looking out of the doors to see if he was all right. I noticed his friends had left him. He was now lying across the bench. The group nearby always hung about the town and were trouble. I thought that they were going to rob him as he was unconscious. I went across to him and got him to his feet. He kept saying he was all right, and started to walk off. I saw him standing near the burger van and then walking towards the cab rank. I assumed he was getting into a taxi.

An hour or so later, the police arrived. They said a 15-year-old boy had been admitted to Basildon Hospital. It was thought he was suffering from a drugs overdose. As usual, the club denied all knowledge of it. The line was that these people took drugs while queuing up. We could search them, but we couldn't be held responsible for anything they did outside. As usual, it was bollocks.

Dave Simms had by now cut the door so dramatically that the club was virtually running itself. Nobody was searched going into the club and there weren't enough doormen to keep an eye on the activities of those inside, which is why we had to rely on somebody coming downstairs to tell us that there was a kid lying on the dancefloor unconscious.

On 6 November, Darren Nicholls went out to Stones Café in Amsterdam and purchased the cannabis shipment which had been funded by the money Tate had raised from the syndicate. It was smuggled into the country by the suicide jockeys and delivered to Tate a few days later. Tate and Tucker were ecstatic. They thought they were going to make a fortune. Tucker had just moved into Brynmount Lodge, a luxury bungalow complete with stables. He said he would be paying for it in cash. Tate was talking about reinvesting his cut, financing future shipments which would be brought in on lorries rather than cars. Their joy, however, was short lived. The cannabis turned out to be dud. Darren Nicholls was in great danger. They thought he had conned them.

On Friday, 10 November, it was business as usual at Raquels. I knew nearly everybody who came into the club, not by name: I knew the faces. They all said hello. As usual, nobody was searched. Mark Murray was plying his trade at the top bar. Because of the police successes against his dealers, he was serving up himself that night. Murray always stood near the steps at the top bar and asked people if they were sorted. He told them he had Apples, which were 'the bollocks'. Like many other people that night, a nervous teenager sidled up to Murray and asked if he 'could score'. He held the folded notes in his hand. Murray held the Apple ecstasy pills in his. They pretended to shake hands. It was the way all deals were done. Their hands touched, Murray taking the money, the teenager taking the pills. It was the type of deal that would be done a hundred times that night in the club. This time Leah Betts's fate was sealed. That deal was going to end her life, and change everybody else's.

Chapter *Thirteen*

IT WAS MONDAY MORNING, 13 NOVEMBER, AND I WAS FILLING MY car up with petrol at the garage, thinking about Christmas, of all things. It had been a bad year. I'd suffered enough grief to last me a lifetime: police raids, internal feuds within the firm – and I was on bail for possessing the gun. It couldn't get any worse. As I walked to the garage kiosk, I glanced at the news-stand. Every newspaper had a picture of a girl on the front page, and she looked familiar to me. Her eyes were closed, her mouth slack, agape, and there were tubes everywhere. I picked up a tabloid out of curiosity, and paid for the petrol. I looked at the picture. I was sure I had seen her before. I thought to myself, what a waste. I turned the page. There was a picture of Raquels. My heart sank. I knew this was going to cause us serious grief.

When I got home I sat on the stairs and put my head in my hands. I wasn't sure what to do. In the end I decided to ring Dave Simms, the general manager. The night before we'd had another row about staffing levels. Since his arrival he'd cut the door staff down from the original ten and the previous night we had only had four door staff on. Three were male, and the fourth was my wife Debra, whose job it was to search females who entered the club. Of the three men, two were in the Buzz Bar next door, which left me to police the whole of Raquels – the front door, the main dance hall and the dining area above. It was impossible.

At about 10.30 that night I closed the doors at the club because 400 people had entered. I told the promoters and Simms that no one else was getting in because we simply couldn't police the club. I was very abusive to him. He had cut the door to save money – and because he felt threatened by our firm. With a promise to review the situation, he left at about 11 p.m. Rod Chapman, the assistant manager, for whom I had a lot of respect, agreed with most of what I'd said. He was basically under the same constraints as me. He asked me to open the doors because if I didn't he'd get into a lot of trouble with head office. Out of sympathy for him, I agreed.

Around midnight a fight broke out behind the DJ stand, involving about fifteen people. Knives came out, ammonia was squirted and, because of the lack of doormen, it was very difficult to break up. I was furious that we'd been put in a position which was obviously dangerous. When you're outnumbered, you have to play for keeps. When somebody goes down they have to remain down. Inevitably, people get hurt. It's distasteful, but that's the nature of the business we were in.

At about a quarter to one, as we were dusting ourselves down after the fight, Janet Betts picked up the phone 15 miles away in the village of Latchingdon and dialled 999. Her stepdaughter Leah had just collapsed at home while celebrating her eighteenth birthday.

The first thing I said to Dave Simms when he answered the phone on that Monday was: 'Have you seen the papers today?'

'What do you mean?' he replied. I repeated the question. 'What's the problem, Bernie?' Simms asked.

'Some girl's collapsed after being in our club and she's in a coma.' I read him the text on the front page.

'There goes our four o'clock licence,' Simms muttered, which was a reference to Raquels being in the process of applying for an extension to their current two o'clock licence. That was all he seemed to be concerned about.

The next person I rang was Rod Chapman. He had already heard about it on the radio. I said to Rod, 'I'm sure I know that girl.'

'She is the one you ejected from the club when she claimed her purse had been stolen,' he replied. I knew I recognised her face. Then I started to wonder: if she had been allowed in the club, would the tragedy at her home ever have happened? Surely Leah would have just come into Raquels and got drunk like many others who celebrated their eighteenth birthday there. For some reason there had been no alcohol at her party. Would she have taken the ecstasy pill if there had been? If this, if that. I turned it over a thousand times in my mind. I thought, 'My God, what have we all done?' Rod really couldn't do anything, because he was answerable to Simms. I couldn't decide what to do and so I called my friend Martin. I told him what Dave Simms had said and we discussed what might or might not happen in the next few weeks. He suggested, and I agreed, that I contact Mark Murray, and we sit down and discuss our options.

In the event of an incident, Mark and I had devised a plan of action. Each Friday night when I saw him at the club we would name a different meeting place for the following week. If something happened beforehand that might endanger his operation, I could just ring him – or he could ring me – and say, for example, 'See you at five o'clock.' If the police were monitoring our calls they would have no idea what we were talking about or where we were going to meet. This particular week we'd arranged to meet at a pub called the Darby Digger in Wickford, approximately three miles from Mark's house and the same from mine. I rang Mark but his phone was switched off.

The first person to call me was the drugs squad officer, John Hughes. He asked me what was going down my end, and I said I'd only just heard what had happened. I enquired about the girl's condition and he said that Leah was going to die. She was only on the life support machine for the benefit of her family, but all avenues of hope were being explored.

I offered to see if I could – and I'm sure that I could have – get a similar pill to the one she had taken for doctors to analyse in the hope that, knowing the breakdown of the chemicals used, they could somehow help her. He told me that the police were already in possession of several of the pills from the same batch.

At this time everyone believed that the pills were contaminated, which I found hard to believe. The pill Leah had taken was one of the Apples Murray had been forced to buy from Tucker. Tucker had bought them from a source in Holland, and he claimed they were 100 per cent pure ecstasy; incredibly rare, incredibly strong, but not contaminated.

Policemen are remarkably like villains: they don't like talking on the telephone. Hughes suggested that we meet. He told me that in the meantime to expect a police raid on my home, because my name had come up continually on the hotline set up by the police hunting the pushers who had supplied Leah. Because of the interest he had taken in me, he knew that I wasn't a drug dealer.

I knew why I was being named. I was head of security at Raquels and I was part of the firm which controlled all of the drugs in the club and the area. It was fairly safe to assume that they would come for me at some stage. If anybody knew what went on in Raquels and that part of Essex, it was me.

Nobody else got in touch with me that Monday. I tried ringing Tucker, but he and Pat Tate were too busy trying to locate Darren Nicholls. Tate rang a man named Mick Steele, whom he had met in prison. Sixty kilos of the dud cannabis had been returned to him and he had dumped it in a lake at a quarry. But he hadn't reimbursed the syndicate or contacted Tucker or Tate to discuss the matter. Steele was a friend of Nicholls. Tate explained the situation and wanted Steele's opinion. Steele didn't believe Nicholls had deliberately given Tate dud cannabis, and agreed he would mediate to resolve the problem. Tate met Steele at the Carpenters Arms pub near Basildon, and said he would pay Steele £2,000 if he would 'chaperone' Nicholls on a trip back to Amsterdam to recover the syndicate's money. Rather foolishly, but with good intent, Mick Steele agreed.

The following day I was out of town. I had a court case in Birmingham to attend – various driving offences. I was banned for twelve months and fined £330. I was not bothered by such a trivial matter. I had far more important things to attend to. Driving back down from the court case I heard nothing but news of Leah Betts's condition and the police enquiry on the radio. Four addresses were raided that morning in Basildon. One of them was Pat Tate's flat, where Tucker's mistress, Donna Garwood, was living. A quantity of amphetamine was found, not a lot, just a bit of personal. But the fact that they'd raided Tate's flat spoke volumes.

Donna was a regular in the club; Tate was a member of the firm and had been out of prison for only two weeks. It seemed that the net was tightening. It was quite obvious that it was only a matter of time before the rest of us were raided. My big concern was that all the main players had run a mile, leaving me to face the music. So much for loyalty.

While those on the inside were trying to get out, there were people on the outside trying to get in. A man called Vic Peters appeared in the *Mirror*, his face hidden, obviously. His claim was that he had dealt kids pure poison. He also claimed he had sold ecstasy at Raquels, although I'd never heard of him. He claimed that the pills could be laced with rat poison, guitar wax or toilet cleaner and coated with hairspray. Peters said that whoever sold Leah that pill knew they were selling her poison. 'The pushers don't give a damn,' he added.

The man was a publicity-seeking idiot. He may have been in Raquels, but he'd certainly never sold ecstasy there. It's quite obvious drug dealers wouldn't sell pills coated with guitar wax or strychnine. They'd get rid of one or two, cause one or two deaths, and they'd be out of business.

He claimed that they deliberately laced tablets or capsules with deadly rubbish to maximise their profits and that none of the dealers cared if people died or suffered brain damage, because they had made a sale and they wouldn't see that person again anyway. He said he used to sell a hundred pills a night in Raquels. This is near enough impossible because what our firm used to do was recruit people who weren't actually willing to sell drugs. They would be told: 'Here's twenty pounds, you go into the club and see if you can buy ecstasy or any other drug off anyone. As soon as you find someone selling, buy it off them, come back to us and point them out; we'll take them to the fire exit, spin them, take all their money and take all their drugs.'

Our firm took half and the other half went to our recruit for his personal use. Either that or we paid him the money. Those drugs would more than likely be sold back to the firm's dealers who would benefit because a rival would have been taken out of the game. That was the way we'd keep rogue drug dealers out of Raquels and most other clubs kept them out of theirs. It was very difficult to see how this man was selling a hundred every Friday and had not come to our attention.

On Wednesday, 15 November, Mick Steele and Darren Nicholls travelled to Stones Café in Amsterdam in the hope of recovering Pat Tate's money.

I still hadn't located Mark Murray despite going to his house and leaving messages with everyone. I finally managed to speak to Tony Tucker, but he didn't want to talk to me. He said he'd got the hump over Donna Garwood, because she claimed she had been grassed up by a doorman, even though at that time no doorman had been spoken to by the police.

The pressure was on Tucker. If things went wrong in Amsterdam, his plans would be ruined. If he was arrested over the Betts incident, he would be finished. He could see his empire crumbling, and he was panicking. A menace fuelled by paranoia was growing. Everyone was putting their back against the wall and somebody else's name in the frame. Desperate people do desperate things, and I just knew this was the end, one way or another, for us all.

John Hughes and another detective called round on the same morning. They telephoned first and told me to meet them in a street at the back of my house where the garages were. I went round and sat in the back of the car. They told me my name had constantly been brought up for supplying Leah Betts, and they were surprised that my house hadn't been spun. They explained this away by saying the police investigating Leah's death were probably busy making a case against me. They were quite sure that the police would descend on me when they had all the evidence they needed. I wasn't surprised. Our reign at Raquels had won few friends. Everyone who had a grudge was now on the phone to *Crimestoppers*. True or false information – it did not matter. People knew it would cause me or the firm grief no matter what. The fact that I had never dealt drugs would not count.

As I moved to get out of the car, one of the detectives said: 'We have searched Murray's flat and this was in a drawer. Take it. Get rid of it.' He handed me a piece of paper, and as I walked away I was shaking.

It was the note I had written to Murray a few months before Leah had collapsed, urging him to pay me the money he owed so that I could go on holiday to America. It detailed the dates Murray and his dealers had worked in Raquels and Club UK in Wandsworth. It detailed the money Murray owed Tucker for the right to sell drugs on those dates and it detailed the £500 a week he owed me for 'introducing' him to Tucker. Underneath was a veiled threat, warning Murray he ought to pay as we were beginning to think he was mugging us off. The money Murray owed me wasn't illegal, but the other moneys mentioned were.

Here was the evidence that might have put Murray and Tucker in the dock for conspiracy to supply, but for reasons known only to the police, they were not going to bother to question us about the letter.

I thought they didn't want us being pulled because of the 'fit-up' tape I had. Perhaps they did not think it was worth arresting Murray and Tucker over two or three pills. They may have been biding their time, waiting to arrest them for something more serious. Things were best kept simple; they had two of Leah's friends. Involving members of the firm would have made things messy and undoubtedly more complicated. I gave Tucker the letter and he exploded. Murray, he said, should have disposed of it and he was going to pay if he got nicked.

That Wednesday was the first night the Buzz Bar had been open since Leah had collapsed. As usual Martin and I went into work at about eight-thirty, nine o'clock. There was an eerie atmosphere in there. It was as if everyone had their eyes on me – half looking for a reaction, I think. I felt like a condemned man. What made it even more strange was the fact that in the Buzz Bar there were four television screens. Every time there was a news item, images of Leah lying in bed with tubes coming out of her were coming up on these four screens. We had this dark room full of kids Leah's age, some on drugs, some not, loud music and pictures of Leah lying in hospital as a result of what went on in this very building. Strange, very strange, and unnerving, really.

There were the usual fools, who were coming up asking for my opinions on Leah. A couple of reporters were in there trying to buy drugs. So obvious: long raincoats, short, tidy hair, middle-class accents, and going up to people asking if they could 'score'. I was just glad to get out of work that night.

I got home around 11 o'clock and there was a telephone call from a local man who asked me if I had a problem with a person called Steve Packman. I'd never heard of Steve Packman in my life.

'Assure him I haven't,' I said.

'Is it all right if I give him your number?' the man asked.

I said, 'By all means,' and went to bed thinking that was the end of it.

About ten minutes later, there was another telephone call. I got out of bed, rather reluctantly, picked up the telephone and sat on the stairs. 'This is Steve Packman,' said the voice.

'I'm sorry, I don't know you,' I replied.

'I'm on police bail for the Leah thing. I've got to go back to the police station for supplying the pills which Leah took.'

'What has that got to do with me?' I asked.

'We have been told that you and the doormen have got a problem with me because of all the trouble at Raquels,' said Packman.

'No such thing,' I replied. He was very nervous and didn't seem to believe me, despite the fact that I'd never heard of him. He wanted us to meet so he could explain it all.

I'm always very wary of this sort of person, but they went with the game I was in and I thought I should meet him in case it was important.

'Can you come out now and meet?' he asked.

'Look, mate, it's fucking half eleven at night. I've just come in from work. I don't particularly want to get out of bed and go and meet you and listen to something which doesn't concern me,' I said. 'Ring me tomorrow, and if you wish I'll see you.'

I didn't have a very good sleep that night. The call played on my mind. The more I thought about it, the more convinced I was that someone was trying to set me up.

The following day, Debra and I were due to move. We'd bought a house in Saffron Walden. She'd gone over there to wait for the removal van and I took the children to school. I was driving home when I heard on the car radio that Leah had died in the early hours of the morning. Even though I knew two or three days prior to the event that she was going to die, I still felt saddened, particularly when I heard her family on the radio.

When I arrived Debra was at the front door, standing outside. 'Have you heard what's happened?' she asked. She had been very upset by what had happened to Leah. Debra had no idea of the firm's involvement. She had never been privy to the business side of things.

Around lunchtime Tony Tucker rang me. He was going mental. He was saying he wanted it sorted out and he wanted it sorted out today. There was too much police attention both on him and on the firm in general, he said. Now Leah had died, the shit was going to hit the fan. Tucker was stressed out because he feared the police attention from the Betts enquiry would unearth the dud cannabis deal with Nicholls and jeopardise the robbery he was planning at Rettendon. I explained to him about the phone call from Steve Packman, and I told him that I didn't really want to meet the guy because I didn't trust him.

'Look, if he's on fucking bail for it, he's the one who's going to be nicked, not us,' he said. 'If he's already in the frame, there's nothing we can do about it. It's not grassing. But I want the Old Bill off our backs. I don't need this now.'

Tate, Craig Rolfe and a few hangers-on had gone out to Ostend that day. They were to meet Mick Steele, who had managed to retrieve Tate's money from Stones Café in Amsterdam. Mick, who was no stranger to the drugs world, didn't mind sorting his two friends' problem out, but he wasn't prepared to carry large amounts of money into the country for them, in case he was stopped at customs. Tate and Rolfe had taken Donna Garwood, as well as two other teenage girls and a car dealer and his wife. The four of them each carried through a plastic carrier bag, one of which contained £30,000. The money was divided up in case Customs got lucky and stopped one person carrying the full £120,000. Mick was paid £2,000 for his trouble and he considered the matter closed.

I wasn't sure how I was going to get the Old Bill off our backs. It wasn't going to be easy. The world and his mother thought that we were responsible for Leah's death. People I had known for years had stopped speaking to me. Reporters were ringing Raquels and my house. They were saying to me, 'Is that Bernie?' Then asking, 'Look, Bernie, can you get hold of anything for us tonight?' It was just incredible. Everyone was convinced that either I or one of the other doorman had actually supplied Leah. I agreed with Tony Tucker: the spotlight had to be taken off us. But how we were going to do that, I just didn't know.

Not long after Tucker rang me, Steve Packman phoned again. He said he couldn't meet me that day because he had to work on his father's market stall near Fleet Street. He assured me that he'd meet me the following day. I still didn't trust him, but I said okay. I rang round a few people and asked about Packman, who he was and what he was up to. It seemed that a story was circulating in Basildon that on the Wednesday prior to Leah's collapse, Martin and I had confiscated 30 ecstasy tablets (Apples, the same type Leah had taken) from a drug dealer named Danny Smith in the Buzz Bar. After confiscating the drugs from Smith, it was alleged that somehow the drugs had found their way to Leah Betts.

The story was partially true. We had confiscated the Apples from Smith because we had found him selling them in there 'unauthorised'. He'd gone away and spoken to his main dealer, Gary Murray, who dealt on Saturdays. He had come into the Buzz Bar on that Wednesday night and said it was a misunderstanding. Smith was meant to meet someone outside to sell some pills, but it was cold so he came in to wait for them and we caught him handing the pills over.

I told him I couldn't care less about misunderstandings. He couldn't come in and sell pills when it suited him. 'If you don't like it, do something about it,' I said. At no time were any of those pills given to Steve Packman or Leah Betts.

The next day Tate and Rolfe were back from Ostend with the syndicate's £120,000. Still feeling mugged off by events, Tate and Tucker decided to teach Nicholls a lesson. A third of the cannabis that had been imported was of good quality. Tucker and Tate managed to salvage this from the haul. They sold it and pocketed £72,000. They also told all the members of the syndicate that Nicholls had not only delivered dud cannabis in an attempt to con them, he had also failed to reimburse them. Tate and Tucker were quietly confident that Nicholls would soon be dead, and they could keep the syndicate's money.

Tucker, now holding enough ready cash to convince any drug dealer he was a serious buyer, once more approached the Canning Town cartel who were waiting for the replacement drop at Rettendon. They told him it was due any day now, and he would be the first to know when it was available. Tate and Tucker knew that they weren't dealing with fools, so they decided to buy some firepower for the robbery. They approached a man named Micky Bowman from south London, and he agreed to supply them with a machine-gun, complete with silencer. They also recruited a minor player from the Canning Town cartel to find out what he could about the incoming shipment. They wanted him to tell them when, how, where and at what time the drop was going to be made.

They thought that they could buy anybody in the drugs world; they thought there was no loyalty, except to them. On this occasion they were wrong.

Tate and Tucker were concerned the police would raid their homes and find the syndicate's money. The police had, after all, already raided Tate's flat where Donna Garwood was living. The money was put into a Head sports bag and given to Tate's lifelong friend, John Marshall. Marshall was one of the few people Tate could trust to look after so much money.

The Thursday night after Leah's death, the Buzz Bar was empty. It's not usually busy midweek anyway, but that night it was deserted. A couple of people – ghouls, I call them – came in to look, then left. I spent most of the evening sitting down, trying to decide what to do about Steve Packman. People needed to know he was on bail for supplying Leah. I thought the only way to stop the witch-hunt against me would be if Packman was identified in a newspaper. That way everyone would know that a person had been arrested and he was not a member of our firm or in any way connected to us.

I rang Tony Tucker and started to explain. He didn't want to discuss it. 'Do what you think best, but get it sorted,' he snapped.

I spoke to a reporter I'd known for several years. He and every-body else was aware that people had been arrested and bailed, but nobody was quite sure who they were. Obviously they were keen to find out. He had told me that my name had been offered up to newspapers as the supplier, which I was obviously aware of because of the reporters coming into the club and ringing my house. I said: 'Look, I'm not involved in this shit.'

I told him about Packman and, although I didn't know at that stage where the meeting would be, I said I would ring to give him the details.

The following day was Friday, 17 November. There were more raids by Basildon police. During the previous four days there had been a total of 13 arrests. Everyone was becoming paranoid. The members of the firm were all too frightened to speak to each other on the telephone. No one was going out. It was a strange time. I'd have thought that rather than hide from each other, people would get together and confront the problem. But they were running scared.

Packman rang me and told me he was in London again and he had an appointment with his solicitor. As soon as he was finished we'd meet. I agreed, and arranged to meet him on a garage forecourt. I chose the location for two reasons. Firstly I feared he might be trying to set me up. This garage forecourt was always busy, so he couldn't say he was being threatened. Secondly we would be on the garage video camera so he couldn't later say he had been intimidated or anything else. I insisted we met there rather than in a pub or somewhere else where he could allege something that wasn't true.

I rang the reporter and told him where we were going to meet. I had reservations about the newspaper's involvement, because I was an obvious suspect. The newspaper man said that the conversation would have to be recorded. This was to alleviate my fears about being set up, but mainly because if Packman tried to sue them they could prove the meeting had taken place. They arranged to photograph him, and the tape would prove that the man I talked to was the man on bail.

I armed myself with a tape recorder to record anything that was said to me by the news people. I couldn't help but suspect I was probably being set up. Packman turned up about six o'clock. We shook hands, and the first thing he asked was if I had a problem with him. 'I've got no problem at all with you,' I said. We went into the shop.

He had long hair and was very, very nervous. I remember he kept touching his mouth and pushing his hair back. I think he was expecting me to assault him because he had heard these rumours. I tried to reassure him.

'Look, we didn't mean to cause you this trouble,' he said.

'What went on, then?' I asked.

He said that he knew Leah and her friend Sarah Cargill. They were planning Leah's forthcoming eighteenth birthday party which was going to be held at her father's house in Latchingdon. Leah and her friends wanted gear for the party. Leah wasn't allowed in Raquels and so she had approached a friend, Louise Yexley, who was unable to get anything, but she said she would ask her boyfriend Stephen Smith (the second person who was on bail). Smith and his friend, Steve Packman, were going up to Raquels that Friday, and Smith said they would try to get some ecstasy at the club.

Smith had made some amateurish efforts to obtain drugs for Leah's party. He had approached several people who told him they didn't know what he was on about. He told Packman that if he was approached by a dealer he should come and tell him. While Packman was standing at the top bar, he was approached by a man who asked him if he was sorted. He described the man as having long, curly shoulder-length hair and wearing a blue Schott bomber jacket. He was describing Mark Murray to me.

He said he returned to Stephen Smith, who gave him the money. He told me he then bought the pills which were later passed down the chain of friends. But he only told me this, he later said in court, because he thought that was what I wanted to hear. Packman told me he hadn't said this to the police. He'd told the police he was so drunk he couldn't even remember if he had been in the club.

I said he hadn't caused us any problem, that it was just one of those things. My parting words to him were: 'If I were you, take a bit of advice: keep your mouth shut.' We shook hands and he walked off into the night.

I went over to the reporters who were in a van and had been photographing Packman. I didn't think anything untoward had been said. I hadn't implicated the firm. The reporters had a photograph of the man who was on bail and who ultimately was going to be photographed when he appeared in court. It's just that they were getting there first.

Tony Tucker would be happy because the spotlight on the firm would be switched off as soon as Packman's picture appeared. Raquels would be happy because Leah hadn't been in the club. I was happy because the finger-pointing and gossip about me would stop. Or so I hoped.

I gave my copy of the tape to the reporters. I said I didn't want to see them again and walked off. I didn't ask for money for the story or the picture, and I wasn't offered any.

Two hours later I was at work at Raquels. It was the first night that the main club had been opened since Leah had collapsed. It was very eerie. There were teams of camera crews everywhere: Sky TV, LWT, the BBC. There were even a couple of foreign TV crews there. I felt as if they were all looking at me because my name had been bandied about so much in the past week. They were asking: 'How do these people get these drugs past security?' 'How do these people sell them unnoticed?' I felt like I was the centre of attention, as if I was on trial.

The police had gathered there to hand out leaflets which said that on Saturday, 11 November 1995, Leah Betts had collapsed during her eighteenth birthday party at home, having taken an ecstasy tablet which was obtained from a supplier in Raquels nightclub. Below this was the now famous picture of Leah lying stricken in a hospital bed. Below that were the words: 'She has since died. Do you know the identity of the supplier? Can you provide *Crimestoppers* with the name of this supplier? Your call is free, you do not have to give your name. You may receive a reward.'

People from everywhere were flocking to get these leaflets from the police. It seemed the queue for the leaflets was bigger than the queue for the club. Dave Simms had made himself scarce, like everyone else that week. He'd left Rod Chapman to man the telephones and answer the stream of questions from journalists. Rod had done a marvellous job, really. I felt quite sorry for him. He was inundated with reporters, cameramen, people trying to catch him out.

Simms was due back in that night, and I was quite keen to see him. We were told that all staff had to attend a meeting in the office prior to opening the doors of the club. The area manager, Colin Agar, was there. Basically we were told that we weren't to talk to the press. All questions were to be directed to the management. And we were to keep a low profile. There was to be strict searching. They had told us the day before that there would be extra door staff. We were even given brand new jackets (previously we hadn't worn a uniform), so we'd look a bit efficient, I suppose.

It was too little too late. Getting made up for the TV cameras wasn't going to change anything, particularly as the back of the jackets said Gold, from another club they ran. None of them fitted. In their haste to make us look efficient they also provided us with black T-shirts with 'Security' emblazoned across the front. The only problem was 'Security' was misspelt on some, and they read 'Securtiy'. Gold was going to be the new name for Raquels if it got its four o'clock licence. Quite ironic, really. There was to be no new club and no four o'clock licence. Not for some time, anyway.

When the management had finished telling us what we must and must not do, they were quite emphatic that there must be no violence. Incidents must be played down and handled discreetly. They asked if anyone had any questions.

'Has David Simms got anything to say?' I asked.

'What do you mean?'

'Well, have you got anything to say about last Saturday?' Simms obviously hadn't told the area manager about the fight. I was still very annoyed. 'Come on, then, tell us what happened last Saturday,' I said. 'Four door staff working 400 people in the club, people pulling knives out, ammonia and everything else. Now the door has nearly trebled to what it was last week. Why couldn't you have given me these people last week?'

'All I can say is that I apologise,' he said.

I was really furious. But, of course, no one person was to blame. I was asked to curb my language by the area manager. When I'd finished making my point, he said: 'One more thing, we'd like you to go in twos to Basildon police station because they want to interview you. Bernard, you go last.'

I started laughing. I said: 'Why have I got to go last? Does that mean that they're going to keep me the longest?'

He said, 'When you're called over, if you don't know anything, you can't say anything.'

I was expecting something like this from the police, but the more I thought about it, the more concerned I got. So I called my own meeting with the doormen downstairs. I said: 'Look, lads, no one's going over to the police station. This is a very, very serious matter and if the police want to question you, they'll either arrest you or ask you to be questioned, in which case you'll need a solicitor with you, or some sort of legal advice. I suggest we don't go over to the police station willy nilly and hope for the best.'

So I called down the area manager. 'Look, we are not going to the police. So ring them up and tell them.'

He rang them, and I believe the police said the interview was nothing formal, it wasn't to be a statement, or made under caution. I said if people wished to go, they could, but I wasn't going. I believe four went over. They were asked if they knew certain people, if they saw anything suspicious. Just general questions, basically.

Later on in the evening, we were warned to expect Mr and Mrs Betts, who were going to come down to the club and possibly walk around. I really didn't want this to happen. I thought it would create a terrible atmosphere in the club, and I didn't really want to face these people. Not that I had any personal guilt, it just didn't seem right.

We were told that if they did arrive we should be courteous and give them full access to the club. The doormen should not stay with them, but keep a discreet distance in case an idiot – and there always is one, especially in Raquels – should do anything silly or controversial.

Fortunately they didn't show up. But it was that night that I first set eyes on Superintendent (or, as I think he was then, Chief Inspector) Brian Storey, who was leading the Leah Betts investigation. He came through the main doors of Raquels after giving numerous interviews outside. He had a cup of coffee in his hand. The first thing I said to him was 'Where's mine?'

'You can have this one if you want,' he said.

'No, you're all right,' I said, and he walked off. I was quite surprised that he didn't want to question me. But, later on, as events unfolded, I got to know him more and more.

I would have thought the Leah Betts tragedy would have deterred our regular idiots from performing that night. But, as I said, Basildon is a very violent town. In full view of the television cameras and the police, a group of youths came to the doors and wanted to fight the doormen. They didn't give a particular reason – they never do. They were just abusive, using threatening words and behaviour, trying to make the news, I guess. I tried to calm them down but they wouldn't have it. All the doormen were saying, 'Watch it, Bernie, the Old Bill's here, the Old Bill's here, they're watching you.'

I've never been one to be too concerned about the police and so I hit a particularly mouthy one who seemed to be in some sort of authority. There was a scuffle and a doorman pulled me away. The guy I'd hit stood in the street, shouting. Fortunately for him, the police intervened. We didn't usually stand for that type of behaviour.

Several police officers approached him, and he ran. They chased him through the town and I believe he was arrested. From there on in the mood grew uglier.

Before long, there was a second fight outside. This time a man was nearly killed. Charlie Ayers, a 20-year-old, was attacked outside Raquels. He staggered to the nearby taxi rank where he collapsed in a pool of blood. He pleaded with two taxi drivers to take him to hospital but they refused. Charlie lost almost four pints of blood and nearly his life as well. He suffered a punctured lung and more than six stab wounds. He was rushed to Basildon's intensive care unit after police arrived at the taxi rank and called an ambulance. It was alleged in the local paper that taxi drivers had refused to take him because of the amount of blood he was losing and the mess it would have made in their cars. A man was arrested later that night and charged with grievous bodily harm with intent.

It was business as usual. Leah's death may have touched the nation, but it certainly wasn't touching the nutters in Raquels.

I waited all night at the club, expecting word from Mark Murray. I didn't expect him to turn up in person, but I did think somebody would come with a message, so we could meet. I also expected Tony Tucker to show his face, or for him to send some sort of message. Surely they were curious as to what was going on. But nobody came.

On Saturday, 18 November, the police were still making

themselves busy. I heard on the radio that there had been a raid in Brentwood. Nine hundred ecstasy tablets had been seized at a café. Two men had been arrested. I was losing count now of the number of people the police had arrested or pulled in for enquiries. I was just so concerned that they hadn't come to me. Not officially, anyway. But, as John Hughes told me, the only reason they hadn't was that they were probably building a case against me.

I didn't know what to do. I'd had it up to here with Raquels, and so had my family. If the firm had pulled together during the crisis, it would have made it so much easier, but I just couldn't reach anyone or see anyone or get to talk to anyone. Once you are in that situation, it's only a prison van, hearse or monumental tragedy that's going to get you out of it.

One of the doormen said jokingly to me that this would be a good time to make some money. He said: 'You're the head doorman, imagine how much money you'd get if you told the whole story about this place to a newspaper.'

'The way I feel now, I'd fucking do it,' I answered. 'I tell you what, I'll give it a lot of thought.'

I rang a reporter I'd known for some time, named Ian Cobain, on the *Daily Express*, and he expressed an interest. We agreed on £8,000, but I told him I'd only give him the ins and outs on the club. This didn't involve naming names, naturally. It related to the short-staffing and the dispute I'd had with the management. It was such a difficult decision to make, I called a meeting with the door staff and explained to them my predicament.

Whatever happened regarding the Leah Betts enquiry, common sense told me that the management would want to show that there had been changes, that is, changes in security. Matters were coming to a head. There was the dud cannabis saga, Tate and Tucker's plan to commit a robbery with a machine-gun, and the fact that when I appeared in court for the gun and the gas I would lose my door licence and as a consequence my job. Common sense told me we had reached the end of our reign.

Tucker had, without telling me, already consulted a solicitor about the letter the police had returned to me, despite the fact he hadn't been questioned. Murray had disappeared. It was plain to see it was now every man for himself. If I was put out of work, nobody was going to pay me any money, and nobody was going to look after my wife and children. So I said to them, 'I've made my decision and unless anybody objects I'm going to do this story.' No one objected. Everyone understood my position. I did my story with the paper and went into work that night.

It was very quiet, as I recall. All night long I just wanted to get out of there. I'd had enough of the place. I hated it, I loathed it. I was meant to stay until two o'clock. There was me, Martin, Debra and a couple of other doormen working. I didn't do anything at all that night. I just sat at the bar and had a drink. About 11 o'clock, I said to Martin, 'Fuck this, let's go.'

I went to find Maurice, the doorman from Bristol, whom I had a lot of faith in. I had first known about him from a previous manager of Raquels. He'd told me that his friend Maurice was in prison for breaking a man's arm during a road-rage incident and he was looking for work when he got out. I told him to bring Maurice up when he was released, and we'd sort him out. The evening he arrived in Basildon, he was given some money to tide him over and a job. We always looked after our own. He had worked for me ever since.

I said to Maurice, 'I want you to be head doorman. You will still be working for Tucker, but I'm going.' He said he would take the job and we shook hands. I went up to the office. I knew the manager would never agree to Martin, my best friend, running the door, because he was too much like me. Maurice was the sort of person the management would get on with. He was very professional. He wasn't a villain doorman.

I went to the office with Martin. 'I'm leaving,' I told Simms.

'What's the problem?' he asked.

'There ain't no problem. I don't like you, you don't like me, I'm leaving. See you later,' I said, and walked out.

I went downstairs to the main dancefloor area. I said goodbye to the barmaids, I said goodbye to Rod. I felt quite sad leaving him. I felt too much responsibility had been put upon him. When things went wrong he was the fall-guy, so saying goodbye was particularly difficult. I didn't really care about anyone else. The doormen had got their jobs, I'd remained loyal to them. I said to Martin and Debra, 'Let's get out of here.'

We walked out of the door together and the last five or so years were forgotten: goodbye Raquels. Leah's death, my meeting with Packman on the garage forecourt, my arguments with Tucker, the press getting on my case and the police hassling me. I had to get away from the intrigue. I was sick of the constant competition and life with a gun in my pocket 24 hours a day. Paranoid? I felt fucking quadraphonic. I had no idea how I was going to support my wife and children from here on in. The £8,000 payment from the newspaper would bail me out until I had something else sorted out. Any life had to be better than this, though.

I felt guilty about my close friend Martin. I knew his loyalty to me would be criticised. My leaving had to be a total departure. No occasional acquaintances from memory lane. If he had had children of his own, I was sure he would have understood my decision.

I felt good, I felt relieved. Fuck the firm, fuck the violence, fuck the police and fuck the grief. It all meant nothing now. It was all a thing of the past. Or so I thought.

Chapter *Fourteen*

THE NIGHT I WALKED OUT OF RAQUELS, WE DECIDED WE WOULD go clubbing to celebrate, so we drove over to a place in Southend named Ad-Lib. The people who hired Raquels out on a Friday also hired out this club. The music was much the same as they played at Raquels. We walked in the door and down three or four steps. Tucker and Tate were standing at the bottom with two girls. Tate smiled and put his arms around me. He patted my back, and said: 'It's great to see you, Bernie, how are you?' Tucker looked as if he had the hump.

'What's the matter?' I asked him. He shook hands with me, and said, 'Nothing.' Then he added: 'Can I have a word?'

We went out of earshot of the others, and he told me one of the doormen had grassed up his mistress, Donna Garwood. Donna was constantly causing problems. In Raquels she would come downstairs and say to me that such and such a man was giving her grief; such and such a man was staring at her. Tucker, she said, had told her if she had a problem in Raquels, I had to sort it out.

'What's the matter with her this time?' I said to Tucker.

He got annoyed and said one of the doormen grassed her up as she was in Tate's flat when the police found some whizz.

'That's bollocks, the police haven't even spoken to any doormen,' I said. He told me another doorman had confirmed it.

'Well, who's this other doorman then?' I asked. 'We'll go and see him.'

'I've got to go now,' he replied.

'Fair enough,' I said. 'Ring me up and we'll discuss what has been

175

said.' He walked out of the door. Tate turned round and put his arm round me again.

'Don't worry about him,' he said. 'Things are not going right, he's just got the hump.'

We shook hands, and Tate left to join Tucker. I waited a minute, and I thought, 'I'm going to clear this up.' I went outside. They were sitting in a blue Range Rover. It wasn't a vehicle they normally used. A few days earlier Tate, who had been out of his mind on drugs, had crashed Tucker's Porsche on his way home from Southend.

They had bought the Range Rover on credit, telling the garage proprietor they would pay off the full balance soon. Another item they were hoping the Rettendon robbery would pay for, no doubt.

I leant against the driver's door and said to Tucker: 'I'm telling you no doorman's grassed Donna up. Someone's just saying it to cause trouble. And as for this doorman who confirmed it, why don't we go round and see him tomorrow, and if you think he's lying we'll bash him.'

I gave Tucker my new mobile number, which was written on the back of a mobile hairdresser's business card, and said, 'Ring me then.' Tucker looked at the card, threw it on the dashboard, and said: 'Do I look like I need a fucking haircut?' I thought he was still being funny, but he laughed and said, 'Fair enough, we'll fucking bash him.' Then they drove off.

I don't know why I said what I'd said. I had just decided to walk out of Raquels. I had told myself I wanted nothing more to do with trouble. I suppose the habits of the past five years were proving hard to break. The conversation had put me in a lousy mood. I was sick of these wannabes trying to get in on the act and causing trouble. The others wanted to go to another club. I wasn't really in the mood, but as it was my last night, I agreed.

We went to Epping Country Club and then on to a club in the east end called the Powerhouse, but I couldn't enjoy myself. At 5 a.m. I shook hands with Martin and walked away. He is the best friend I have ever had. He is the most loyal friend I have ever had. Everything in this life has a price.

The following day I got a phone call. Somebody was telling me that Mark Murray's picture was on the front of the *News of the World*. Surely they had it wrong. I expected Steve Packman's picture to be in the paper, not Mark Murray's. I went out to buy a copy to see for myself. On the front page there was a photo of Murray and the heading: 'Revealed: man in ecstasy death quizzed'. The article said this was one of the men being quizzed by police investigating the death of tragic ecstasy victim Leah Betts. 'Jobless Mark Murray, 35, of Pitsea, Essex, was among six people held after Leah's death at her eighteenth birthday party last week. He faces further questioning after the *News of the World* handed cops a secret tape containing new evidence.'

The verbal undertaking I had received about the tape remaining confidential had been ignored. I knew now that the police had the tape. Turning the page, I read the headline '*News of the World* tape may trap Leah's killer'.

The article read: 'A secret *News of the World* tape could give police vital information in their hunt for the drug dealer whose ecstasy pill killed tragic Leah Betts. The cassette, recorded by an undercover reporter, may help cops piece together the youngster's movements before she took the fatal pill at her eighteenth birthday party last week.

'Last night detectives were set to quiz two men following evidence provided on the tape. The pair, Mark Murray and Steve Packman, are among six people already arrested over the lethal pill. Both were earlier released and bailed to reappear. Jobless Murray, of Pitsea, Essex, is a frequent visitor at Raquels nightclub in Basildon from where the £10 pill was supplied.

'Market trader Packman of nearby Laindon knew Leah when both attended Basildon colleges. Yesterday we handed our tape to Detective Constable Ian Shed, an officer on the case. He said: "This may be very helpful to us. Investigations are continuing into the chain of supply which ended in Leah's death. We want to find the main dealer."

'Leah, an A-level student, picked up the drug after finishing her

Saturday job at a local store. She took the pill as soon as she returned to her home in Latchingdon, Essex, where she had invited 20 friends to celebrate her birthday. She died after begging step-mum Janet, "Help me, Mum, help me."'

I hadn't seen or heard from Mark Murray since the night Leah's pill was purchased. I hadn't a clue, really, what was going on with him. I rang Tucker, but as usual he wasn't in or wasn't answering his phone, so I sent him a fax telling him I had quit Raquels the night before, and Maurice was taking over as head doorman. I said: 'There are no problems, it's safe, it's sorted.'

I heard nothing else all day. Nobody was talking to anybody that week. The following day, Monday, 20 November, Tucker rang. I wasn't in. He left a message on the answering machine. He was being abusive and threatening. He said I couldn't just walk out of Raquels and he wanted an explanation. He also said I was responsible for Murray being in the paper. He said: 'I thought only that other kid was going in. You shouldn't have put Murray in. I'm going to fucking do you.'

My problems are my own. Nothing will make me involve my wife and children. I knew what could happen. I didn't need to ask Kevin Whitaker, Nipper Ellis or his family. When the kids came out of school I booked them and Debra into a hotel just outside Basildon.

Darren Nicholls was in trouble, too. He had been getting a lot of grief from members of the syndicate who still believed he had not repaid their money. In desperation he approached Tate, pleading with him to come clean and admit he had been given the money back. Tucker, who was with Tate, told Nicholls that Tate wasn't in any position to pay anybody back for the time being. 'The fucking car dealers and their ponces can wait. When we pull off this job at Rettendon, they'll get their money back,' he said. Tate and Tucker were telling people they were relying on the Rettendon robbery to solve all their troubles. Tucker had to pay off his new Brynmount Lodge home, which was plunging him deeper into debt; he and Tate had made promises to pay the syndicate and the car dealer for the Range Rover. But in reality they had no intention of paying anybody. They never did, perhaps because nobody ever pressed them for money.

On the news on Essex Radio, Detective Chief Inspector Brian Storey confirmed that they had received a tape but he would not discuss the contents. He told the interviewer that he wished people would talk to the police instead of the newspapers. I think he was sending me a personal message via the BBC.

I was still owed a week's money as we were paid in arrears at Raquels. I rang Martin and Maurice and told them I would be down on Friday to collect it. Martin said: 'You had better ring me before you come, as I have heard that Tucker has got the hump.' I told him I didn't care, but I didn't want to involve him and so I agreed. We arranged to meet outside McDonald's (just around the corner from Raquels). Martin said he would have my money.

I tooled myself up. I put a huge combat knife in the back of my trousers, a bottle of squirt (industrial ammonia) in my pocket and went down to Basildon town centre to collect my money. Maurice and Martin met me outside McDonald's and advised me not to go round to the club.

'Tucker's there now with Tate, Rolfe and a few other people we haven't seen before,' said Martin. 'One of them's Micky Bowman.'

Bowman was the man who was supplying Tate and Tucker with the machine-gun. Even if he had delivered it that day, I didn't think Tate or Tucker would have the bottle to use it on me in the centre of Basildon.

'I don't give a fuck, I want my money,' I said. 'Tucker is doing this for the benefit of the management. He's making out he's got the hump with me to please Dave Simms, because Simms doesn't like me. Simms will always warm to people who turn against me. Tucker's got nothing to worry about, the door is his, Maurice is running it for him, it's safe.'

'Tucker's told me that he's holding your money and if you want it, you should get it yourself,' said Martin. 'But I wouldn't advise it – he's firmed up.'

I got really annoyed. I had been loyal to the doormen at Raquels.

Instead of backing me, they were all behind Tucker. Only Martin and Maurice were repaying that loyalty.

'I'll give you my wages, and get yours off Tucker,' Martin told me. 'You can go round if you really want to. You know I'm with you. But I wouldn't advise it.'

Martin needed the work, and Tucker knew he was loyal to me. I didn't want to cause him any unnecessary problems, so I agreed. He gave me his money and went back to the club. Tucker asked Martin if he had seen me.

'I know he's your mate, but we've got a problem with him,' he said.

'Well, I've given him my money. Now I need to get paid.' Tucker apologised and gave Martin my money. As far as I was concerned, that was the end of the matter. Everyone was happy. I was out of Raquels and out of that way of life. Tucker now had complete control of Raquels. There was no need for anyone to continue with a vendetta.

The following night, Saturday, 25 November, I was told that Tate and Rolfe went into the Buzz Bar, allegedly looking for me. I don't know what Tate's problem was. He and I had always got on well. I suppose he felt that because Tucker had the hump with me, he had to follow suit. It was always the way. Martin was in the Buzz Bar, and Tate asked him if he had seen me. 'Tell Bernie he can't hide forever,' he added. 'And when we see him, we are going to take lumps out of him.'

'He's my mate, I don't pass on messages like that,' Martin replied.

Tate should have learned from Nipper and Jason Draper that he couldn't go around making threats. If he was really looking for me, he knew where I lived. I was hardly going to try and hide forever. Nor was I going to give him forever to find me.

On Monday morning, 27 November, I appeared at Chelmsford Crown Court for possessing the gun and the CS gas. I pleaded guilty to the gas, but my barrister told me to enter a plea of not guilty for possessing a firearm. It turned out the gun which Clarke and Pierce had given me was a Rhoner model SM10 self-loading pistol. The lab report stated the pistol was designed to fire 8mm blank or tear-gas irritant cartridges so it could be used as a non-lethal self-defence weapon. However, it originally had a partial obstruction built into the bore of its barrel to prevent it from discharging a missile. This blockage had been removed at some point, and it was now possible for it to fire adapted cartridges. In short, it was a de-activated gun that had been turned into a weapon capable of firing bullets.

After discussion it was agreed I would plead guilty. The case was adjourned for two days, however. I was told that it would be beneficial for me if my wife and my brother attended the next hearing to give evidence to support the story I was going to give.

On 29 November I appeared again at Chelmsford Crown Court. A detective from Essex police was there. He spoke to the prosecution and together with my barrister they hammered out a deal. When my barrister returned, he told me that he didn't think I would be receiving a custodial sentence, so I need not worry. I would probably get a suspended prison sentence. Nobody wanted to make waves.

The judge came in and a statement from my brother Michael was read to the court. It said: 'I have worked as a farm-hand since leaving school. I cannot recall the exact date – however, approximately 18 months ago my elder brother Bernard came to see me at the farm. Bernard explained he had been socialising at a cattle market where he had met an old family friend. Our mother had worked for this man on his farm when we were young and we had maintained a close friendship ever since. Bernard said the man had sold him a vermin gat, which is local slang for a small handgun which is used for shooting rats etc. He had no use for it himself, but as it was offered cheaply, he had purchased it on my behalf. Assuming wrongly that I would want it, the handgun was, in short, useless. Nobody had ever seen anything like it. Even the calibre made it obsolete as you cannot purchase 8mm rounds. I told Bernard the old man had had him over and we all had a good laugh at Bernard's expense. I never saw the gun again, and it was only ever mentioned again when I was told Bernard had been arrested for possessing it.'

The prosecution didn't question my account. Nor did the police. The reason for possessing the gas – protection for my wife while she was at home alone – was also accepted without question. I was sentenced to six months' imprisonment which was suspended for twelve months. The threat of prison had been lifted. I now only had to deal with the threat from Tucker and the firm.

The police were still reaping the benefits of receiving a mine of information. On the same day I was in court, 15 addresses were raided in Basildon. Four men were charged with possessing drugs, including one who was also charged with theft. The police recovered 11 ecstasy tablets, half a kilo of amphetamine sulphate and herbal cannabis during the raids. They also unearthed a handgun, an electric stun gun, imitation firearms and a crossbow as well as child pornography and stolen property. A police spokesman said none of the addresses raided was directly linked to Leah Betts's death, but added that Essex police were fully prepared to respond when this type of information was supplied.

The following day, 30 November, I received a phone call from an Essex detective. He told me that I ought to watch my back as the police had received information that a firm was going to shoot me. He said Tucker was the man behind it, and I should take the threat seriously. I take all threats seriously, but life has to go on. I asked him if they had any other information, and he said no. A couple of people close to Tucker had called him. They said they had heard it being discussed. They were not prepared to give their names or any other details.

I guessed Tate and Tucker had been bragging about the machine-gun to people, like kids with a new toy, saying they were going to waste me. That was my problem. Their problem was that they were telling too many people about their business and their plans. I didn't expect a gold watch when I quit the firm. But I certainly didn't expect to be shot, either.

On 1 December 1995, the funeral of Leah Betts took place in Latchingdon. Her natural mother, Dorothy, had died four years previously, and Leah was to be buried with her at a cemetery in

Billericay. The Reverend Dr Don Gordon told hundreds of mourners that the teenager was not to blame. Rather, the guilt lay with a society that has allowed a creeping cancer of drug abuse to destroy many lives. Dr Gordon said that 'in the pursuit of materialism, profit and pleasure, many people had almost accepted drugs, and their dangerous effects, as a part of life. With it went a readiness to blame someone else for what was wrong. The truth is, we are all in part to blame.' There was a man who knew what he was talking about.

The service began with the coffin being carried into church accompanied by the hit single 'Wonderwall' by Oasis, Leah's favourite band. At the close, the Whitney Houston song 'I Will Always Love You' was played before the cortège left.

I sat in my car alone listening to the news bulletins about the funeral. You couldn't help but feel for her friends and family. I remembered kids in the club who had made jokes about her death. They sang the Jackson Five record, 'One bad apple doesn't spoil the whole bunch, girl.' But this was the reality. Joking about the death of an innocent girl in order to appear ruthless or hard seemed tragically sad and weak. No words, however admirable, from Paul Betts, Leah's father, or his wife Janet, Leah's stepmother, would stop this fashion. The danger they talked about gave this occupation an edge, making it more desirable, more daring, putting the user on a higher pedestal than their straight friends who didn't have the guts to try it. No officially run campaign could stop this fashion. Adults didn't realise that this culture was all about rebellion.

The next day I rang Tucker. 'I hear you want to speak to me,' I said.

'I've been told you put Murray in the paper.'

'I don't care what you've been told,' I said. 'You know it isn't true. I told you Packman was going in the paper, and you said you didn't give a fuck so long as the attention was taken off the firm.'

'Why didn't you tell me you were leaving Raquels when I saw you in Southend?' he asked.

'I had had enough of everything,' I explained. 'I admit I was wrong not to discuss it with you, but I just wanted to walk away. I told the manager that Maurice was taking my place, and the door was safe. You've not lost out. It is still your door. In fact, you have complete control now, instead of going down the middle with me.'

'But people are talking,' he said.

'I don't give a fuck about people,' I replied. 'Don't leave any more threats on my answering machine, I'm out of it.'

He said: 'I don't believe you, and I'm not leaving it.' The line went dead. I assumed he switched his mobile phone off.

Three days later, on 5 December, I was again contacted by a detective. He told me he had received information that the threats to shoot me were very real. Plans were being made for it to be carried out very soon. He also told me that DCI Brian Storey wanted to talk to me about the Leah Betts enquiry and in particular about the comments I had made in a newspaper about the way the club had been run.

'I've moved away from Basildon now, I don't need this shit,' I said. It was impressed upon me that I had no safe quarter. If I wanted to move away and start a new life, I could do without bad feeling from the police. I should do what they asked. It would be an informal chat. I could then go off and begin my new life, no strings attached. They also asked if Debra would be willing to talk. 'She has nothing she can tell you,' I said. 'She knows nothing.'

They said that every doorman would be spoken to, so it was in my interest to get it over and done with. I agreed that we would both attend South Woodham Ferrers police station the following day at about two o'clock. I insisted that it be an informal chat rather than any type of official interview, otherwise I would have to bring a solicitor. They agreed.

I was due to see a mutual friend of Tate and Nicholls the following day at two, in Great Blakenham, near Ipswich, where I was originally going to move. He was going to give me an update on what Tucker, Tate and Rolfe were up to. I wanted to know what they were planning for me, but there seemed little point now. The police were telling me exactly what the trio had in mind.

That afternoon it began to snow heavily. Soon everywhere was covered with a white blanket. That night Tate, who had only been out of prison for six weeks, was up to his old tricks. He was at home with his girlfriend, who called the London Pizza company in Wickford and asked for a pizza with different toppings on different sections. Roger Ryall, the manager, told the woman that they didn't do that type of pizza. Tate grabbed the phone and started swearing at him. The manager said later: 'I wasn't going to take that. So I said: "Get rid of that attitude, and I will send you a pizza."'

He obviously didn't know the type of man he was talking to. Tate became more irate and slammed the phone down. Half an hour later he turned up at the pizza shop, picked up the till and hurled it across the room at the manager. Fearing for his life, Ryall backed out of the office and pushed the panic button which was linked directly to the police.

It was his second mistake of the evening. Tate, fearing arrest and a return to prison, overreacted. He punched the manager in the face, grabbed him by the hair, and smashed his head into a glass plate on the draining board. Tate told him not to call the police, or he would come back and smash the place up and hurt his staff.

The panic button had already been activated, though, and officers arrived after Tate had left. When Tate was identified and the police told Ryall who he was and a bit of his history, he decided not to press charges after all. Tate's call was traced to his home, but he was not arrested. Only the firm could turn ordering a pizza into an orgy of violence.

Now I had spoken to Tucker myself, I wasn't too concerned about the rumours that were flying around. It was probably just wannabes stirring it up, gloating over the fact Tucker and I had fallen out. I thought that once I had spoken to the police, my purpose would have been served; nobody would have any further business with me. If Tucker and Tate really wanted me, they knew where to find me. They would calm down in time – after all, I'd done them no wrong. I could at last see light at the end of the tunnel. I felt that I was awakening from the nightmare.

Later that night Tucker, Tate and Rolfe went out into a field near Basildon to try out their machine-gun. They needed to test it as they had been told the Rettendon drop was being made very soon. They too thought their troubles were nearly over. The following day they had lunch at TGI Fridays at the Lakeside Shopping Centre. While they were eating, Tucker received the call he had been waiting for: the Rettendon drop was being made the next day, and the Canning Town cartel advised him to get the money organised. Everything, Tucker thought, was coming together. They just had to wait for the insider's call now, for the exact time and location of the drop.

Around the same time, Debra and I set off for South Woodham Ferrers police station. We were met at the door by four detectives. Two wished to speak to Debra. DCI Storey and another detective wanted to speak to me.

Debra knew nothing, and therefore could say nothing, so I said I had no objection to her talking to anybody. However, if, as they had said, this was an informal chat, I would only be prepared to talk to DCI Storey on his own. I think he knew the pressure I was under. He agreed that we should talk alone.

While I was being interviewed by the police, Tucker received a second telephone call. This time it was from his informant in the Canning Town cartel who was calling from a payphone near Great Blakenham. He told Tucker he wanted to meet him, Tate and Rolfe later that evening to show them where the drop was going to be made so they could rehearse the robbery at the scene. Moments later, the same caller telephoned Darren Nicholls from the same payphone. It's not known what was said but the call was logged on Darren's mobile phone.

Storey was well aware of the firm's involvement in just about everything. He knew what he could prove and he knew, despite knowing the facts, what was impossible to prove. Murray had been pulled and had been questioned, but nobody was going to give evidence against him. I assumed Storey knew nothing of the letter that had come from Murray's flat – he certainly didn't mention it to me. I could see his task was painful, but he knew at that time the only people he could realistically prosecute were Packman and Smith.

He asked me about the tape which had been given to him – against my wishes – by the journalist. What could I say? I could hardly deny I was the person on the tape. However, he understood my predicament. He had heard that Tucker had threatened to shoot me. These were serious people. He knew it wasn't an idle threat. He asked me if I would make a statement saying I was the person on the tape. I didn't have to implicate anyone. All I had to say was yes, that is me on the tape.

Storey added that there was always the possibility that if I refused I might be subpoenaed to court, although he made it clear he wasn't offering me an ultimatum; he was just being honest with me. I told him I understood my position. I couldn't put my family at risk for things I had done, but I wouldn't rule out the possibility of doing what he asked. I would give it some serious thought, discuss it with my family and speak to him again in a couple of weeks. I wanted the thing with Tucker sorted out first. I didn't believe Tucker was a threat to me, I told him. It was the wannabes around him who were stirring up the trouble. Storey told me that the information regarding the threats to have me shot was being treated seriously and that I should be careful.

The conversation lasted until about four o'clock. When I came out, Debra was waiting. She said they had only kept her for half an hour, and had asked about who was working on the night and other trivial matters, facts they already knew. I guess they had to speak to everyone who was in the building on the night the pill was bought. Procedure these days demands it.

Debra and I had arranged for her mother to look after the children. We left South Woodham Ferrers at about ten past four feeling a little better about everything. The snow was now quite heavy. It had settled and was perhaps three or four inches deep. We arrived at Debra's mother's house at about five o'clock and stayed for a cup of tea. Then we drove on to Wickford, where we had something to eat, before we headed towards the Rettendon turnpike, the main roundabout on the A130. By now it was about 6.30. It was a miserable night. The snow was still falling and it was pitch black.

Ironically, at around the same time, Tucker, Tate and Rolfe were travelling along the very same road to rehearse the robbery with a man they thought was their co-conspirator.

Chapter *Fifteen*

THE FOLLOWING MORNING I'D ARRANGED TO MEET MY BROTHER Paul in London. I travelled on the train, as I didn't fancy battling through traffic in the snow. At about eleven I rang home to see if there were any messages on the answering machine. There was one, a detective was asking me to contact him as soon as I got his message. It sounded urgent.

I rang him from King's Cross Station. 'We've found a Range Rover with three bodies inside,' he said. 'They've all been shot through the head. We think it's your mates.'

'What do you mean?' I asked.

'Do you recognise this registration – F424 NPE? I am sure it's them.' He told me he had seen them in the car before.

'I don't know what you're talking about,' I said. 'Tell me what's happened.' I was confused.

He repeated that they had found a Range Rover. Tucker, Tate and Rolfe were inside, but they had not been formally identified at that stage.

'Are they dead?' I asked.

'Very dead.'

I felt relief and sadness at the same time. Who? Why? I couldn't take in what was being said. I just couldn't believe that they were actually dead. One of them, maybe – but all three in one hit? It couldn't be right. It was some sort of sick joke.

Tucker, Tate, Rolfe. They'd all been warned, but they wouldn't listen. They should not have fucked with people in the game we were in. Any fool can pull a trigger – it doesn't take a hardman. They wouldn't listen, though. They thought nobody could touch them. I guess they were wrong.

The policeman wanted to know where I was. I said I would ring him later, and put the phone down. I rang Tony Tucker's mobile number. It rang and rang and rang. He wasn't going to answer. Unknown to me at that time, his phone was still in his hand. The police had not yet removed it from the body. Nor had they taken the body from the Range Rover.

I rang home. Debra wasn't in. I left a message on the machine saying I had been told that 'those three' had been found murdered. I told her not to answer the phone if it rang.

I walked around London in a daze. I really couldn't believe what I had been told. I even began to wonder if I had actually had the conversation.

Debra never got my message. She went straight to the school at 3.30 p.m. to pick up the children. She was met by two detectives. One walked across to her and asked: 'Are you Bernard's Debra?' When she said yes, he said: 'You and the children had better come with me.' They were put in an unmarked car. Nothing was said in front of the children, but Debra was told what had happened. The police feared a revenge attack of some sort might be carried out on me or my family, so they were going to keep them safe until I had been located. The police – and others – obviously thought that I was connected to the murders.

The police had also driven past my house to see if I was there. They saw that the front door was wide open, which caused them further concern. My home was in a rural location at the end of a half-mile-long driveway, surrounded by five acres of woodland. A couple of hundred yards away was the sea. It wasn't a place that could easily be found, but it was the ideal spot to attack somebody. They radioed the detectives on the case and told them what they had discovered. The area around my house was immediately cleared. Debra could not explain why the front door was open. She rang the house and recovered the messages from the answering machine. I had told her to meet me at Tilbury railway station in

Essex, which is by the docks, at about 8.30. It would be deserted at that time of night.

When I got off the train, there was no sign of Debra. I went to a phone box and rang her mother to see if she was there. I heard a loud tap on the window of the call box. A detective was standing there with Debra. 'You can guess what the problem is, Bernie,' said the detective. 'I hope you're not involved in this.'

I asked him what had happened. He told me that it was definitely Tucker, Tate and Rolfe who had been found shot through the head in their Range Rover on a deserted farm track at Rettendon. I was numb with shock. I had a bag with me. I opened it, and said: 'Do you want to search it?' I automatically assumed the police knew about the money Tate had left with John Marshall in the Head sports bag, and that's what they would have been looking for. Half of Essex knew Tate had given it to him, so the police must have known about it. To my surprise, he said no. He told Debra to get in one car and I was told to get into the back of another. Two detectives sat in the front.

The detective said to me again: 'I hope you're not involved in this, Bernie.'

'I'm not, I'm not. I'm telling you I'm not,' I said. 'We fell out. What we fell out over didn't warrant that. If you're thinking I'm involved, you've got it wrong.'

'A lot of people think it's you,' he said. 'You fell out with them. They threatened to shoot you. You didn't take the threat seriously. Next thing, they all turn up dead. What else are we meant to think?'

He told me the front door of my home was wide open. Had I left it that way? I said no. He said there was a possibility that someone was waiting for me at the house and suggested we both went there. He was armed. I said I would go in first. He wasn't going to argue.

I went in and called round all the rooms, but the place was deserted. The door wasn't damaged. She had never done it in her life before, but I guessed Debra mustn't have closed it properly when she left. It was just a coincidence. The detective told me that not only did the police think I was involved, but the firm also would think I was involved in the murders. He said it was something that I should give some careful consideration to. I kept telling him it had nothing to do with me. 'I am willing to go to a police station with you now,' I said. 'You can interview me or do what you want. I am not involved in their deaths.'

He put me in the car, left Debra in the house with the other detectives, and drove me down the road. He stopped and asked me who could have killed Tucker, Tate and Rolfe. There were so many reasons why they could have died – it's not as though they never upset anyone. I couldn't help him. I didn't want to help him.

'Your best bet is to go home and keep your head down,' he said. 'We'll be in touch.'

They left me in my house with Debra and the children. I still couldn't believe it. It was all over the news. I don't often drink at home except when I'm on a downer. But that night I drank till I could drink no more. I rang two members of the firm: both put the phone down on me. This couldn't be happening, just when I thought everything was going to be all right. I don't think I slept at all. Every face, every horror committed and witnessed, came to visit me that night.

The following day, all the newspapers carried the story. Tony Tucker's father, Ronald, collapsed and died when the news was broken to him. His wife was with him at the time. It must have been terrible for her. Her husband was only 63. To lose your son and your husband on the same day must have been agonising. It has always been the families that I have felt for, because they have no control over events. When you are involved, you're full of yourself, you forget about the feelings of your family.

There was a lot of speculation in the press. Some papers claimed the three had been murdered in revenge for the death of Leah Betts. They were calling it 'the Leah E-Wars'. The *Daily Express* reported that a gangland figure was in hiding after the execution of the three drug dealers. They said the gangster allegedly ordered their assassination after he was tipped off that they were planning to kill him. The man, who had links with the Krays, they said, was accused of revealing the trio's drug-dealing activities. It was nonsense, but it sounded remarkably familiar.

Some thought the three had been murdered in retaliation for the death of Kevin Whitaker, for which Tucker and Rolfe were to blame. Others said they had been murdered by the same gunman who had gone into Billericay Hospital dressed as a clown and shot Darren Kerr. Nipper Ellis returned from exile and appeared in *The Sun*. He claimed the three had been offered a chilling choice of how they died: 'a very reliable source' had told him that they were going to be given two options: they could be taken apart with an axe, starting with their fingers, moving on to their hands and then their legs; or they could opt for the quick way out: shot through the back of the head. They were told: 'Either way, you are going to get it. There's no escape.' Tucker and Tate, he said, messed their trousers first, then took their shots. Nipper confirmed the three were lured to the snow-covered farm track in Rettendon with the promise of another drugs deal.

'They had double-crossed too many people,' he told *The Sun*. 'They had made too many enemies. They often went to these meets, snatched the supplies and beat up the suppliers. But they did it once too often, and were set up themselves.' Nipper denied being responsible for the murders. He was a suspect because of his arrest for the earlier attempt on Tate's life. 'It wasn't me who did the shooting. But I'd love to shake the hand of the man who did it,' he said. 'He's my hero, and I will regret to my dying day that I could not take the credit for it.'

Everyone, it seemed, regardless of their views, wanted to be linked to this dramatic murder. My head was spinning. I thought that Nicholls might have set them up. They had ridiculed him at the hospital, stolen a third of the cannabis shipment and lied about being refunded their money. He certainly had a motive – but then so had I. The syndicate had a motive as did the countless people they had robbed and those they were planning to rob. Nearly everyone they had met had a motive, come to think of it.

The Range Rover had been covered with a tarpaulin, loaded onto a police lorry with the three bodies still inside, and taken to South Woodham Ferrers police station for examination. There was a tragic irony to this. Twenty-six years earlier, Brian Rolfe, then only two years older than his son Craig, had been found on Christmas Eve slumped over the steering wheel of his parked van in a lay-by near Basildon. He too had terrible head injuries. After police photographers had done their stuff, the van, with the body still in it, was loaded onto a transporter and taken to police headquarters at Chelmsford for detailed examination. So much for peace and goodwill to all men at Christmas.

When you're shocked, you do things you can't explain. I drove over to Rettendon. I didn't know exactly where they had been found. I stopped near a phone box at Rettendon Turnpike, which overlooks all the fields. Everything was covered with a blanket of snow. I looked out across the fields and thought about my friends. The men who died were not the people I had first met. The drug culture had turned them into unreasonable men. Drugs had given them courage to do things any rational man would have thought reckless. Wannabes had boosted their egos, reinforcing the belief they couldn't be touched. The rewards cemented the notion that they were right. Regardless of what had gone on, though, I couldn't help but feel sadness for Tate, Tucker, Rolfe and their loved ones.

The following day the police had completed all forensic tests at the site of the killing. I drove down there. To this day I can't believe they were so easily led to such a place. It is a long, unmade road, barely passable in a car. At the dead end is the gate where they died. I leant against the gate and again I was filled with sadness thinking about them.

There were half a dozen posies scattered in the snow. Notes from girls to Tate. One read: 'Prison did this to you.' Another spoke about his problem with drugs. Others said he was a wonderful man. People had also remembered Rolfe and Tucker. Messages were brief. Donna Garwood had left a posy with a note. She said she would love Tucker always. I thought it was really insensitive – hardly the type of thing Tucker's wife Anna would like to find at the spot where he died if she visited it. I tore it up and threw it in the bushes. I felt really sorry for Anna. Tucker had loved her dearly, but Tate and the drugs had messed his head up.

At the gate there was a sign which would have been facing them as they met their deaths. It read: 'Countryside premium scheme. Farming operations must still take place, so please take special care to avoid injury. The use of guns or any other activity which disturbs people or wildlife is not allowed on this land. Enjoy your visit.' Whoever did the shooting did not pay the sign much heed.

As soon as European Leisure, the owners of Raquels, heard what had happened, Tucker's firm was sacked from running security at the club. On 12 December, Charlie Jones, the man whom I believed had set me up with the gun, was given the contract to work there. Maurice, to whom I had given the club and considered a good friend, had agreed to stay there and work for Jones. I was really disappointed. He had no loyalty to me. How could he work for the very people who had caused me so many problems?

Two days later I was having a drink in Basildon with a friend. I couldn't get it out of my head that Jones had succeeded in getting Raquels. I went down to the Buzz Bar where two of his doormen were working. I began to get abusive and I was hit in the mouth. I pulled out a bowie knife and threatened them. They backed off. I told them it wasn't my door any more, but they were not having it, they had no right to be in there and they had better leave. They told me they agreed. I rang Jones. I told him what I thought of him, and that he would never be able to keep the club. That night his doormen walked out and they never came back. The very next day the doormen who had worked for me and Tucker were reinstated at the club. Jones had held it for two days.

Basildon District Council, who run the Registered Door Staff Scheme with the Basildon Police Licensing Unit, wrote to me and told me that I no longer met the criteria for registration because of the incident with the gun and the gas. To my mind this was unfair: the incident had not happened at my place of work, and was not relevant to my employment.

I was asked to attend a meeting. In an ironic twist Jones had also been asked to attend a meeting as he had been involved in an incident while working at a nightclub in Canvey Island. He had assaulted a customer and been convicted. He went into the meeting first and was somehow allowed to keep his licence.

On the face of it, I had had some CS gas in my home for the protection of my wife, and had purchased a gun for my brother for shooting vermin on his farm. But even if I'd been John the Baptist, they would have taken my licence from me. There were representatives from all political parties on the council as well as the police. They quizzed me about the Leah Betts incident. They also made it plain that they were aware of the Rettendon murders connection.

They wanted me to sit down and talk the philosophical shit that straight people love to hear. I wasn't going to play their game. I didn't need or want their licence, but this was personal.

One councillor said to me: 'Give me one good reason why I should unleash you on the public?' I told her that she was talking to me as if I was some sort of caged animal. I wasn't abusive, but I wasn't going to suck up to these people, either. I wanted to say my piece. They would not give me a decision there and then. They said they would ring me.

The following day, David Britt, the assistant chief environmental health officer who helped run the scheme, rang me. He was all apologetic, saying I had not been successful and my licence had been taken away. He said to me meekly: 'To be honest, Bernie, the reason you didn't get it is because you did not ingratiate yourself.' I told him in no uncertain terms that I wasn't going to suck up to him or anybody else. He could keep his licence. Sadly, they had managed to take it away from me long after the race had been run.

I then received a letter telling me I had been banned for at least seven years from working on the door or in any licensed premises in the Basildon District Council area. How they must have danced!

Four days before Christmas, the first of the three funerals took place. Twenty cars followed a horse-drawn carriage containing

Rolfe's coffin, which travelled from his mother's house in Pitsea to St Gabriel's Church. Seventy mourners attended the service at which Reverend Laurie Blaney said a few words prepared by Rolfe's partner, Diane Evans, and his mother Lorraine. After the funeral the procession of cars drove the short distance to Pitsea Cemetery. Wreaths were laid, including one from Diane and their six-year-old daughter, which said: 'You are not gone until you are forgotten. And we will never forget you.'

The following day the second funeral took place. Again, a horse-drawn carriage led a cortège of mourners as family and friends paid their last respects to Pat Tate. Relatives dabbed their eyes to hide their grief as they left St Gabriel's Church in Pitsea.

Family and friends had earlier gathered at Tate's Gordon Road house in Basildon before the coffin was taken to the church. Police directed traffic as a bell tolled for the 25-minute service in which Tate's brother gave a touching tribute. Four Daimler limousines carrying loved ones followed two others stacked with flowers. One floral tribute simply said 'Daddy'. Another card attached read: 'Thanks for the good times. I will never forget you. Your baby son, Jordan'. A large tribute made out of individually lettered floral wreaths spelled 'Brother'. A card said: 'You will always be in our thoughts and never forgotten in all our lives.' As the coffin was carried into the church by six pallbearers, one heart-shaped red-and-white tribute rested on top. Around 60 mourners sang 'All Things Bright And Beautiful' and recited the 23rd Psalm. Tate was laid in a grave next to Rolfe.

Later that afternoon Tucker was buried in Hornchurch. More than a hundred people attended. Most of them were doormen. I didn't go to any of the funerals. They weren't my friends at the end. I couldn't help feeling sad, regardless of our differences: these men were human. They had loved ones and children. Nobody, our victims included, should endure this misery.

The firm suspected that I was responsible for the murders, so it wouldn't have been wise to go even if I had wanted to. I have since visited Tate's and Rolfe's graves. All I can think of when I go there is what a terrible waste. I haven't been to visit Tucker's grave. I don't think I ever will. He was such a good friend in the beginning, I still cannot believe what he became.

After Tucker had taken over Raquels exclusively from me, his pal Nigel Benn had been booked to DJ there for a night. As the club wasn't attracting customers following the death of Leah Betts, Nigel had agreed that he would DJ there on 22 December, in the hope of bringing back the crowds. It was the night of Tucker's funeral. Benn, out of respect for his friend, agreed to honour the booking. He played to a packed house. But the success the club had previously enjoyed could never again be matched. Most who went there that night would never return. The promoters knew it.

They sent a letter to all of their members. In it, they said:

> We would like to inform you we will be closing our Friday nights at Raquels. This is due to the fact that despite our efforts to keep the night up and running, it has become apparent that the recent publicity surrounding Raquels has caused the club irreparable damage. We made the decision after careful deliberation to honour the contractual commitments to both the club and our DJs. For professional reasons, and also to be loyal to our members and to not let you down, we did have every intention to carry on. But after taking time out to consider things in general, we now feel that the night has run its course. It must not be forgotten that throughout the year that passed before recent events, we all had an excellent time in bringing to you a night which we felt was up there with the best in Essex. It was nice, though, to end the night on a high with the guest appearance of Nigel Benn to see it out in style. And thanks to all of you who came along to support it. He was simply gobsmacked with the reception he got from you lot. Well, as the saying goes, all good things must come to an end.

Rumours about me continued to circulate. Sandra Lea, the sister of my friend Dave, the Hollywood stuntman, rang me to say she had started work for a company in Basildon. Her supervisor was claiming he was a suspect in the Rettendon murders. He told her that I had gone into a café and 'done' a man. He was referring to Mick McCarthy, the man who had been paralysed after being gunned down while having breakfast. He told her that £10,000 had been put up to have me shot. Doormen from Bagleys (a nightclub in King's Cross, London) and Bass Brewery doormen were going to carry it out. There was no connection between me and these people. Members of our firm had been at Bagleys on the night a doorman named Dave Anderson had been murdered. I wasn't there, but this, I guess, was just another wannabe talking.

Mick McCarthy's shooting and Dave Anderson's murder were nothing whatsoever to do with me. It sounded a bit similar to the Leah Betts thing. Anything a bit sensational was going to attract idiots. This supervisor, I thought, was just trying to make himself sound sinister. He wanted Sandra to be impressed. These people were dangerous, though. I didn't want Tucker's friends thinking I was involved in the murders.

I was a prime suspect in the Rettendon killings. The police were making enquiries about my relationship with Tucker in particular. They had quizzed people at the club. Some time after their deaths I applied under the Data Protection Act to have information about me on police computers released. Although I have only been allowed to have a very brief summary, police thinking early on in the investigation was clear. Print-outs I received read: 'Associate of Tucker.' 'Associate of Tate.' 'Anonymous details: O'Mahoney as possible killer.' 'Used to be partner of Tucker.' 'Previous convictions: robbery, ABH, GBH and offensive weapons.' 'Anonymous messages and newspaper clippings received. All approved.' 'O'Mahoney as possible killer.'

The police were focusing their attention on me. The firm, despite the fact that I had been loyal to them, would not even acknowledge me. The atmosphere was extremely hostile. It was a very difficult time. Like my predecessor, David Vine, I was finding out that once you fall out of favour, regardless of whether you are guilty of anything or not, you are soon deemed unfit to associate with.

When Nigel Benn honoured his promise to perform at Raquels, it proved to be the club's swan-song. The following Friday it closed. Raquels had been open for over 30 years. In less than two, the firm's activities had closed it.

Chapter *Sixteen*

THE DAY AFTER THE BLOOD-SPATTERED BODIES WERE DISCOVERED in the Range Rover, the police charged Stephen Smith and Steve Packman with supplying the ecstasy that claimed Leah Betts's life. It made sense: the inquiry that sought to expose those at the most lucrative end of the supply chain was going nowhere; the police's most wanted now lay dead. In an ironic twist, the detectives who had been trying to gather evidence against Tucker now switched their efforts to gather evidence against his killer.

I felt like I was staggering from one nightmare to another. People were telling me the police had visited them and were asking why Tucker and I had fallen out. I was being told by policemen that the latest rumour in Basildon was that I had been shot in the head and dumped. It was unnerving to receive calls from detectives who wanted to know if I was still alive.

On the radio and in the press, Detective Superintendent Dibley, who initially led the investigation, warned of retribution for the killer from Tucker's closest associates. His words alarmed me. If the police considered me a suspect, so would Tucker's friends, and they, according to the police, were planning their own justice. Never one to avoid a situation, I decided that I would contact some of Tucker's friends and see how I was received. I telephoned about five people, but only one, named Mark, would speak to me. The others either put the telephone down or used lame excuses like, 'Sorry Bernie, can't talk, somebody's here.' Mark told me the police had raided his home. They had found a gram of cocaine and half an ounce of cannabis, but they were more interested in asking him about the murders. They asked him if Tucker or Tate owed me money or if there was more to my falling out with Tucker than I had claimed. Mark told them that he didn't know anything. On the one hand I had the police investigating me for a triple murder, and on the other the same officers urging me to become their star witness in the Leah Betts case. I didn't know which was worse – being a suspect or being asked to give evidence.

On 25 January, I had another meeting with DCI Storey, who wanted me to make a statement in relation to the conversation I had with Packman. I told him I couldn't decide what to do. He could see that I was struggling with the very thought of it, and so he told me to go away and think about it again before I made my decision. For two or three days I wrestled with my conscience, but I knew what I had to do; this nightmare had to end some time. I realised that if I wanted to shed the criminal make-up I had worn for so long, the only decision that I could make which would allow me to change my life would be to agree to co-operate with Storey's request to validate the tape.

I contacted him and we arranged to meet at a village police station. I will never forget sitting in that room, which overlooked a quaint row of shops. Below, people were going about their everyday business and I was sitting there watching them while I talked about the deaths of young people. I sat astride two worlds. I knew which one I wanted to inhabit. I consoled myself with the thought that I wasn't informing on anybody. I was merely saying, 'Yes, that's my voice on that tape.' I could hardly deny it. I looked up at Storey and said, 'All right, I'll do it.' I made the statement. I validated the tape. The door to my previous life was closed firmly behind me.

The police bent over backwards to help me from there on in. Personal security alarms were given to me and my family, electronic panic buttons were fitted in the house and armed police were briefed to attend if any of the devices was activated. The Leah Betts case had to have an end result: the whole country was talking about it. Even the Prime Minister had commented on the case in the House of Commons. I was going to be the principal witness against

Leah's teenage friend. It was obscene, like asking Hitler to sit on the jury of a war crimes trial, but they needed their pound of flesh. They needed their 'result', and they thought that I was the key to that result. I had to be looked after just in case I didn't turn up at court, for whatever reason.

In total contrast, the triple murder enquiry was, it seemed, being looked at almost reluctantly. The police arrested a man named Billy Jasper, an East End villain with all the right connections and a crack cocaine habit. Billy told the police that he was having a drink in a bar called Moreton's when his friend Jesse Gail came in. Jesse invited Billy to a nearby Mexican restaurant. While they were there, they were joined by a man named Paul. The conversation turned to Tony Tucker and Pat Tate and a drug deal that was going to happen in the near future. Jesse had been taking a keen interest in Tucker and Tate's business since they had robbed members of the Canning Town cartel he was associated with of £20,000-worth of cannabis and £250,000-worth of dodgy traveller's cheques. Jesse knew a man who was feeding Tucker and Tate information, but they were unaware it was a double cross: Tucker and Tate were being set up themselves. Billy claimed Paul said: 'Why can't we rob them?' And Jesse replied: 'We can't rob them because there will be comebacks.' Paul is then alleged to have said: 'We will take them out of the game, then,' before turning to Billy and asking, 'Do you want to earn five big ones [£5,000] to do a bit of driving?' Billy is said to have nodded and stuck his hand out: 'You've got yourself a driver.'

On the night the trio were murdered Billy told police he picked up a grey E-registered Uno Turbo from east London. He then drove to Palms bar on the A127 near Hornchurch, where he picked up Paul. He said Paul was carrying a Head sports bag which appeared to have a 'dead weight' in it. He got into the car and directed Billy to the Windmill Cab office at Upminster Bridge. Waiting outside was Jesse Gail. Paul got out of the car with the Head sports bag and disappeared with Jesse down the side of the building.

A few minutes later, Paul got back into the car with the sports bag and they drove off. Jesse got into his car and followed at a discreet distance before turning off moments before they reached Retten-don. Billy was directed to a lane where he dropped Paul off. Paul was wearing a blue tracksuit, a polo-neck top, white Reebok training shoes and surgical gloves. He told Billy that he was going to get four kilos of cocaine.

Paul returned 40 minutes later, carrying the Head sports bag and a rucksack. When he got into the car, he simply said: 'Let's go.' Then he phoned Jesse on his mobile and said, 'It's all sorted. I've got the parcel. See you in Moreton's bar.' Billy claims he was paid £5,000 for his services the following day. Billy alleges that he said to Paul: 'You cunt, you took them out of the game.' 'Don't ask questions,' Paul is said to have replied. The police, too, seemed to have adopted the same line; they didn't want to ask too many questions. They chose to disregard Billy's confession. Jesse Gail was killed some time later in a bizarre car accident. Tucker's firm claimed they were responsible.

The events going on around me were plunging me into a deep depression. On Tuesday, 13 February, I went for a drive. I needed to be alone. I needed to clear my head. I drove to Rettendon along the A130, which runs between Basildon and Chelmsford. At Rettendon I drove past the church and the post office before turning right into Workhouse Lane where Tucker, Tate and Rolfe had met their deaths. I was trying to make sense of it all. I was finding it hard to believe that it had really happened.

If Tate hadn't crashed Tucker's Porsche a few weeks earlier they wouldn't have bothered to buy the Range Rover. A Porsche could never have got down that track – it would have been far too low to cross such rough terrain. As I drove down I kept thinking: 'If Tate hadn't done this, if Tucker hadn't done that.' But neither Tate nor Tucker should carry the blame. Prison and drugs destroyed Pat Tate. Tony Tucker's behaviour precipitated our firm's demise. It was going to happen at some stage, we all knew that.

I stood by the gate where my friends had died. For some reason, I felt like shouting their names. I prayed to my father's God for their mothers and loved ones. I prayed the gunman would never be caught – even they wouldn't have wanted that; another life ruined, more children fatherless, more families devastated. I kicked the foot of the gatepost and realised that I had disturbed something. I bent down and there in the grass was a blue – live – shotgun cartridge. It was a new cartridge, but a film of rust had begun to form on the metal detonator's edge. It obviously hadn't been there long – a couple of months at the most.

Without thinking, I picked it up. As soon as I held it in my hand I knew that I had made a mistake. 'Why the fuck have I picked it up? My fingerprints will be on it now. If the police ever get hold of it, they'll draw their own conclusions.' I began to imagine all sorts of scenarios. I decided the best thing to do would be to 'lose it'. I walked up the track and threw the cartridge into an adjacent field beside a large oak tree.

When I got home I wrote down the fact that I had found the cartridge. I also told Debra. I couldn't convince myself that if it did ever become an issue, my explanation, supported only by Debra, would satisfy police suspicion. I decided to let it lie and see what happened. Two days later, on Thursday, 15 February, it was reported in *The Sun* that the police had swooped on Micky Bowman's home in south-east London. Ian Hepburn, writing in the paper, said, 'Marksmen from Scotland Yard's élite tactical firearms unit SO19 led the operation. Cops clad in steel helmets, visors and flak jackets surrounded the flat and took up positions with Heckler & Koch rapid-fire carbines, then the door was smashed down with a pneumatic battering ram. In Mick's flat they found a machine-gun. He was handcuffed and led from the building.'

Linking the find with Micky and the triple murder enquiry, the article went on to say that the police believed that the Rettendon killer had travelled with the trio in the Range Rover. When they had arrived at the murder scene they had got out of the vehicle and picked up the weapon, which was hidden nearby, while pretending to open the gate.

The article threw me into a total panic. If the police thought the weapon was hidden near the gate, they might know about the shotgun cartridge I had found at the very same spot. Why swoop on Micky Bowman? Somebody must have told them about him going to Raquels with Tate, Tucker and Rolfe when I fell out with them. Somebody must also have told them about him supplying the machine-gun. Did the gunman hide the cartridges near the gate with the weapon and then fail to pick one up during the murders? Had somebody watched me recover the cartridge? I decided that I had to tell the police what I'd found. I could not risk them finding out themselves and drawing their own conclusions.

I rang Ian Hepburn and told him what I had found. I asked him to contact the murder enquiry office and repeat what I had told him. I had never spoken to him before in my life, but he agreed. I wanted an impartial and plausible witness to be party to everything that could have happened from there on in.

Hepburn rang me back and said two detectives would meet us at a pub in South Woodham Ferrers called Marsh Farm. It is about two or three miles from the murder scene. When I arrived at the pub, two casually dressed men approached me and said, 'All right, Bernie. Don't worry, we're Old Bill.' They offered to buy me a drink, but I declined. There was no sign of Ian Hepburn, and they seemed to sense my concern. 'He's called. He's on his way,' they said. By the time police and journalist had got their act together it was dark, but we nevertheless all went down to the track where the murder had taken place.

They asked me to show them where I had found the cartridge and where I had thrown it. It was futile trying to look for it in the darkness as the area was overgrown. I was asked if I would sit in the detectives' car so they could ask me a few questions; I was asked dates and times I had been down the track, what car I had been driving, who I had been with and why. One of them took notes while the other asked the questions, reassuring me that it was just a formality. They said they would come back and look for the cartridge when it was light, and they would speak to me again at some stage.

On Friday, 1 March, I was asked to go to South Woodham Ferrers police station, where the incident room was based. Two detectives led me through the back into an interview room. In the corridor outside was a storeroom door, and on it a sign read: 'Risk of health hazard, Rettendon exhibits'. In that cupboard, behind that door, were my friends' clothing and personal effects, no doubt soaked in their blood. I don't know if I had been deliberately shown it for effect, or if it was a mere coincidence, but it made the whole horror story real.

The detectives asked me about my military career, adding that the gunman had executed the trio with ruthless efficiency. 'Someone who knew what they were doing, Bernie. An ex-military man, perhaps?' I said I knew what it looked like, but I had not murdered my friends. I had been in the army but I was hardly SAS material. I was told that I had to understand that a lot of people believed I was involved. 'Even if you didn't pull the trigger, Bernie, you had good reason to see the back of them. They were threatening to shoot you. Maybe it was a case of you or them? You could have done it out of fear.' All the time they were 'chatting' to me, I was aware that one of the detectives kept his gaze fixed firmly on my eyes, as if he was looking for a reaction.

When they had finished their 'chat', which had lasted for an hour and 45 minutes, they said they would need to see me again. I asked them if they had found the shotgun cartridge I had thrown into the field. They said that they'd only had a quick look, but it wasn't important as there was a game shooting area nearby and it could have come from there.

A live shotgun cartridge found at a place they believed a shotgun had been hidden prior to a triple shotgun murder being committed, unimportant? Perhaps like the letter in the Leah Betts case, it was unwanted evidence that might have produced answers to questions they would rather not have asked. They gave me their names and numbers on a piece of paper – 'Just in case you remember anything, Bernie' – and told me to go.

As we walked past the storeroom where my friends' possessions were, I felt myself reaching out to touch the door. Tucker's thick gold neck chain with a solid gold boxing glove on it, I knew, would be in there. He always wore it. I imagined it, caked in blood, and the police having to clean it before they returned it to his family. These morbid thoughts saddened me and made me feel deeply depressed. I found it hard to accept that I would never see them again. I was annoyed at myself for feeling sorry for them. Those three bastards would have murdered me at the drop of a hat. How on earth did we arrive at this?

The detectives couldn't resist a parting shot: 'Keep your head down Bernie, you know some people think you had a hand in this, and they aren't happy.' It wasn't a threat. I knew as well as they did it was a fact. Whether they actually cared about my well-being was another matter.

When I got outside, I had the urge to run, to get away from this bloody mess. I thought the detectives would be watching me from the police station windows, so I walked around the corner before running to a nearby gymnasium carpark where I had left my vehicle – I was still on the 12-month driving ban I'd picked up in Birmingham. I felt stupid. I felt hunted by the police and hunted by the people who, according to the police, were plotting my murder.

That night I decided to go to a nightclub in Southend where Tucker's friends still worked on the door. I put a handgun in the waistband of my trousers, covered it with my shirt and set off, feeling both angry and concerned. If they thought I was involved in the murder of their friends, they could turn up at my house at any time. I had to resolve this one way or the other.

They seemed surprised to see me when I walked up to the door, but I was waved through without having to pay. One of them said hello, and asked how I was. The others seemed unsure of what to say or do. Inside, the atmosphere was dire, the kind of ambience that would make an autopsy seem cheerful. At the bar, people moved away from me, a classic indicator that somebody had said something was going to happen around me. I wanted to straighten things out. I wasn't going to run. I hadn't done anything to these people.

I followed the head doorman, a close friend of Tucker's, into the toilets and told him to listen to me. I said the police had spoken to me about the murders, and I had also been told about the threats that had been made against me. I told him I wanted him and his friends to know that I had not killed Tucker, Tate or Rolfe. 'If people have got a problem with me, tell me so I can see them and sort it out,' I said. He assured me that he had no problem with me – but he couldn't speak for others. The atmosphere back in the club was very tense; it seemed to spread throughout the place. People began to leave. I finished my drink and walked out, expecting them to attack me on the street. They never came.

On Tuesday, 30 April, I arrived home to find a note had been put through my letterbox. It was from the two detectives who had 'chatted' to me before. The note said they wanted me to ring them urgently. All they would say when I phoned was that they wanted me to attend South Woodham Ferrers police station the following morning. They wouldn't say why, but they did say officers from another force would be there. Again I hid my car out of sight in the gymnasium carpark. I decided to tell these people that I was no longer prepared to be at their beck and call. I was sick of them and their questions. When I arrived I was introduced to two detectives from Leicester, who wanted to question me about the murder of taxi driver Danny Marlow. The case had been featured on *Crimewatch* and several people had rung in with information about my debt-collecting 'techniques'. When they had finished, the Rettendon detectives said to me: 'And there are just a few things we want to clear up with you.' I couldn't face any more of their questions. I told them that one murder enquiry a day was plenty for me.

The detectives from Leicester said they wanted to examine some paperwork concerning a debt I had tried to recover from Marlow. It was at my house, so I said they either looked at it now or never, as I was going out later. All this grief made me resent the fact that I had agreed to assist these people by giving evidence at the Leah Betts trial. I thought crossing that line would free me from a criminal lifestyle – being followed, being questioned, always on edge, always looking over your shoulder. I was wrong. I suppose the police thought that if I was being helpful in one area, I would open the floodgates. They were wrong.

I hated myself for talking to the police. I hated them thinking that they had me on their side. I sought solace in the fact that they despised me. Despising each other was all we seemed to have in common.

The police had heard whispers that Darren Nicholls and Mick Steele were somehow involved in the Rettendon murders. Instead of questioning them, they set up an elaborate sting to try and find out what, if anything, they had to do with it. Nicholls was put under surveillance and Steele started to receive menacing telephone calls. Two detectives posed as brothers Billy and John Mullock, who made a series of telephone calls to Steele from Belfast. They claimed they were both members of the IRA. The pair said they had given Pat Tate £40,000 towards the shipment of cannabis from Amsterdam. Tate, they said, had given the 'IRA's money' to Steele, who had failed to return it following the delivery of the dud cannabis. The Mullock brothers threatened Steele, telling him: 'The ceasefire is over. Make sure you check under your car for bombs.' In other calls they said: 'Don't fuck with us. We have A levels in whacking people. Give us our money back or you will be sorted out, just like Tate.' At one stage the Mullocks even offered to work with Steele importing drugs. Steele felt he had done no wrong, and therefore he had nothing to fear. He laughed off their threats, telling them they could 'go fuck themselves'.

Detectives used the same tactics to terrorise Pat Tate's girlfriend, Sarah Saunders. Sarah reported the threats she had received from the 'IRA brothers' to Basildon police. They just said they had traced the phone number to a well-known Republican bar in Belfast. The officers added to her growing fear by claiming the men had recently travelled to the mainland and detectives had unfortunately lost track of them. Billy and John kept asking Sarah what she knew about Tate's business dealings, but she was unable to help them.

Darren Nicholls, meanwhile, continued to use his 'suicide jockeys' to import cannabis. He had also become involved with two detectives. The boss of a company Nicholls worked for legitimately was friends with one of the officers. They all began to go clay-pigeon shooting together. Coincidentally, the 7.5 shotgun cartridges used to murder Tucker, Tate and Rolfe are the same types favoured by clay-pigeon shooters.

Nicholls soon began offering the officers information about those in the drugs world who displeased him, and before long he had become a registered informant. He was later to allege that within weeks the relationship between the three men took a rather sinister turn. Nicholls claims he told the two officers about the 60 kilos of dud cannabis he had dumped at the bottom of a lake in a quarry. They plotted together to blame two innocent men for putting it there, then convinced senior police officers to pay Nicholls a £400 reward for his 'public-spiritedness'. The trio went on a drinking binge with the money to celebrate. The officers arranged for Nicholls to sell drugs to customers and then for him to pass their names back so they could arrest them and gain promotion. They plotted to board a North Sea ferry and 'steal' £150,000 that was being taken abroad by a suicide jockey to purchase drugs. Drugs seized by other officers that were kept at the police station where the detectives were based went missing.

Nicholls said he didn't keep the detectives' favours for himself. When his wife was charged with motoring offences, he offered a £100 'bung' to one of the officers, and the charges against his wife were dismissed. The two detectives have always denied what Nicholls alleged, and neither has been convicted of any offence.

Nicholls was totally immersed both in the importation of drugs and the corruption that went with it. But unbeknown to him, both he and the detectives with whom he was associated were having their telephone calls and movements closely monitored. On 13 May, Nicholls was driving a Jaguar XJ6 along the A120 towards Braintree. His friend Colin Bridge was driving behind him in a Transit van containing cannabis with a street value of £25,000. The Regional Crime Squad and Customs stopped both vehicles. The drugs were discovered and Nicholls and Bridge were arrested. At the police station Nicholls was questioned about the importation of drugs, the alleged corrupt police officers and the Rettendon murders. He sat stony-faced and refused to comment.

On 17 May the police said they were going to charge him with the triple murder. Nicholls cracked. He said that he had been duped into taking the killers to the lane on the night of the murders. He thought they were going there to rehearse the robbery of an incoming shipment of cocaine.

When he learned he had been duped into being the getaway driver for a triple murder, he panicked. He told the police that is why he had become an informer; he wanted to put the killers behind bars. This was a blatant lie. In all the time Nicholls had dealt with the two detectives he claimed were corrupt, he had never offered any information whatsoever regarding the Rettendon killings. Now he was offering it five months later and from the confines of his police cell. The men Nicholls named as those who had committed the murders were his friends, Mick Steele and Jack Whomes. The detectives were delighted. Colin Bridge was released without charge and Nicholls became their star witness.

When asked why Steele, and in particular Whomes – who had not even met Tucker and Rolfe – would want to murder the men, Nicholls said it was because when Pat Tate was asked by 'Billy and John', the 'IRA' men, for their refund, he was insisting that Steele had their £40,000. The detectives pointed out to Nicholls that the IRA men were police officers and the calls were made *after* the murders. So Nicholls offered them a second motive. He claimed Steele was having an affair with Tate's girlfriend, Sarah Saunders. Steele didn't like the way Tate treated Saunders, so Steele and his lover decided to murder Tate. Saunders, the mother of Tate's child, could claim his life insurance into the bargain. No explanation was given as to why Tucker and Rolfe had to be murdered in this particular plot. Sarah Saunders denied any affair with Steele had ever taken place. Other statements were made by Nicholls, but the police refused to disclose them as they were deemed not to be in the public interest.

Throughout his time in police custody, detectives were keen to keep Nicholls sweet. They gave him a daily choice of takeaway meals – Kentucky Fried Chicken one day, Taco chips the next. In his cell they provided him with a colour TV, tables, chairs, a cabinet for his clothes and a multi-gym. He was even given a cup of hot chocolate before he went to bed at night. This for the man who had told them he had plotted with corrupt detectives to have two innocent men locked up for the dud cannabis he dumped.

Nicholls had difficulty remembering things concerning the murder. One officer spent more than 30 hours talking to Nicholls 'off-tape' in his luxury cell, with one interview lasting seven hours and 43 minutes. Even Nicholls's own solicitor agreed that this was an 'undesirable procedure'. After making numerous statements Nicholls decided that the dud cannabis that he had dumped was the motive behind the murders. He told detectives it was Steele who masterminded the importation of the cannabis. Nicholls had merely worked for him, travelling to Stones Café in Amsterdam to purchase the drugs before Steele brought them into the country in an inflatable boat. Whomes, he said, had met Steele when the boat had arrived back in England. Following the importation of the dud cannabis, Nicholls admitted it was he who had dumped it in the quarry and he who had travelled to Amsterdam with Steele to recover Tate's money.

These were hardly 'voluntary confessions' about himself and his crimes. These were facts Nicholls could not deny as he had used his credit card to pay for the trips. His telephone calls concerning his alleged illicit dealings with the detectives had been monitored.

The £400 reward he received for the dumped cannabis was a recorded fact, and satellite signals of calls to and from his own mobile phone were recorded by a transmitting station, which placed him at the murder scene at the relevant time.

For everything that couldn't be pinned on himself, Nicholls blamed Steele. He said Tate had fallen out with Steele, not him. 'Tate was telling people he hadn't received his money back from Steele and he was going to make Steele kneel down before shooting him.' This claim makes Steele very brave or very stupid, because according to Nicholls it was Steele who travelled in the Range Rover down a deserted lane with a dangerous man like Tate and two equally dangerous men, Tucker and Rolfe, who, Steele would have been aware, had already murdered their friend Kevin Whitaker.

Nicholls said Steele had told Tate a light aircraft was going to land a shipment of cocaine at Rettendon. Steele, Tucker, Tate and Rolfe were then going to rob it. The Rettendon robbery was the one Tucker and Tate had asked me to assist them with when we met at Basildon Hospital, so I should have been in the Range Rover with them that night. Nicholls did tell police there should have been a fourth man, but he said it was someone named Spindler.

But, according to Nicholls, there was no shipment. It was a baited hook and the trio took it. Nicholls said that at 5 p.m. on 6 December he met Whomes and Steele outside a motorbike shop at Marks Tey near Colchester. Nicholls got into Steele's Toyota and they set off towards Brentwood. Whomes followed the pair alone in another car. At about 6 p.m. they arrived at Thorndon Country Park. They parked their cars and Nicholls moved into Whomes's car, on which he was trying – unsuccessfully – to stick false number plates. Steele drove off in his Toyota and Whomes and Nicholls soon followed. At 6.15 p.m. the Toyota pulled into the carpark of the Halfway House pub on the busy A127. Steele parked and told Whomes and Nicholls to find a space where they could watch him, but couldn't be seen.

At 6.17 p.m. the Range Rover containing Tucker, Tate and Rolfe swept into the carpark and pulled up next to the Toyota. Whomes and Nicholls then drove off and headed down the A127 towards Chelmsford. At 6.30 p.m. Steele pulled into the Hungry Horse pub carpark at Rayleigh. Tucker, Tate and Rolfe had followed him there in the Range Rover. Steele climbed into the back of their vehicle with Tate, and the four headed off to Rettendon.

At 6.35 p.m. Nicholls dropped Whomes off at Workhouse Lane. Nicholls described Whomes as wearing overalls, new wellington boots and carrying a large canvas tool bag. Nicholls turned the car around and parked at the nearby Wheatsheaf pub carpark to await further instructions. At 6.47 p.m., the Range Rover turned into Workhouse Lane. Nicholls said the plan was to allow the Range Rover to drive into the open field under the pretence of showing Tucker, Tate and Rolfe where the aeroplane was going to land. Once the men were in the open with nowhere to run, they were going to be gunned down.

It was pitch black as the Range Rover edged its way down the track; the surrounding fields were bleached white as the snow continued to fall. The vehicle eventually pulled up in front of a locked gate. Nicholls said Steele thought they had blown it, as he was expecting the gate to the fields to be open. Steele got out of the back of the Range Rover just as Whomes, who had been lying in wait near the gate, emerged from the bushes. Through the open rear door Whomes fired the first shot into Rolfe's neck leaving a huge open wound. The second shot hit Tucker in the right side of the face near the cheek. Tate, in the back of the car, was then shot in the side of the chest, damaging his liver.

Rolfe hadn't suspected a thing; his hands remained on the steering wheel, his foot firmly on the brake. Tucker remained sitting upright in a relaxed position, his legs crossed, his mobile phone in his hand. Nicholls claimed Tate began to 'squeal like a baby'. He also smashed the rear passenger door window in a vain effort to escape. Whomes coolly reloaded, before shooting Rolfe behind the right ear, the blast exiting between his eyes, totally disfiguring him. Tucker was then shot in the right side of the face again, this time just above the jaw. The blast exited through the left side of his mouth. A third shot slammed into the back of his head, causing his skull to fracture so much a gaping fourth wound appeared above his right ear.

The pathologist later said that his head had 'exploded'. Steele and Whomes, according to Nicholls, had agreed upon a pact whereby both men would fire shots into the victims' bodies so one could not give evidence against the other. During the shooting, Steele's weapon is said to have fallen apart. He was said to have taken Whomes's pump-action shotgun and shouted, 'Give me some cartridges, give me some cartridges,' before shooting Tate through the head. Tate received a second shot to the head, but this only caused a superficial wound. When the weapons fell silent, the gun smoke cleared to reveal the carnage. Tucker, Tate and Rolfe were dead. Blood and tissue were sprayed on the windows and dashboard. Blood poured from their wounds. It was a gruesome scene.

Whomes is then said to have telephoned Nicholls on his mobile. He is alleged to have said: 'All right, Darren. Come and get us.' When Nicholls arrived back at the lane, Whomes climbed into the back of the car. He was wearing surgical gloves, and they were splattered with blood. Steele was delayed because he had to find all the pieces of his shotgun. He got into the front passenger seat, and Nicholls claims Steele said: 'That's sorted those fuckers out. They won't be threatening me again.' It was a similar phrase to the one that Tucker had used in front of Nicholls at Tate's bedside when he was discussing the fact that he and Rolfe had murdered Kevin Whitaker. It was at that moment Nicholls said he realised that somebody had been killed. He said that he was so shocked he nearly crashed into an oncoming car as he pulled out of the lane.

Steele began handing over pieces of the gun to Whomes, and repeatedly asked Nicholls if he was okay. Nicholls said Whomes laughed as he described Steele's gun falling apart during the shootings. Nicholls said: 'Mick told me that Jack was a cold-hearted bastard, because once Mick had got out of the Range Rover, Jack had leaned into the car and shot them all immediately. Then he reloaded without any emotion and shot them all again in the back of the head. He said it looked as if it meant nothing to Jack. Mick said he felt like the "angel of death". Then he said: "We have done the world a favour. Nobody will miss them."'

At approximately eight o'clock the following morning, farmer Peter Theobald and his friend Ken Jiggins scraped the ice and snow from their Land Rover and set off to feed their pheasants. Driving down Workhouse Lane, which was only 200 yards from the farm, they saw the Range Rover parked in front of a gate. They thought it might belong to poachers. Jiggins got out of the Land Rover and tapped on the window as he thought the occupants were asleep. He didn't think the vehicle had been there overnight as there was no ice or snow on the windows, unlike the Land Rover which had been parked only a few hundred yards away in identical conditions. There was no response, so Jiggins peered inside. He saw the blood-soaked bodies and rang 999 on Theobald's mobile phone. Within a short time, the quiet country lane was swarming with police as the investigations began.

Five months later, following Nicholls's statement, Whomes and Steele were charged with three counts of murder plus the importation of cannabis. The same week Whomes and Steele were charged, Pat Tate's friend John Marshall went missing. John was the man who was holding the syndicate's money for Tate in the Head sports bag. I knew John well; I often collected debts for him. He made his living in the motor trade but wasn't averse to the occasional drug deal. On the day he disappeared John had told his wife that he was going to Kent 'to do a bit of business'. He had £5,000 in cash with him and was carrying a Head sports bag; the police have never established what was in it. Throughout the week John's wife made various appeals for him to come home or at least get in touch. A week after he left home, his car was found in Roundhill Road, Sydenham, south London. A parking ticket had been slapped on the windscreen, indicating that the blue metallic Range Rover had been there for some time. John was under a bale of straw in the back of the motor; he had been shot once in the chest and once through the head. The £5,000 in cash was left in the glove compartment. The only thing missing was the Head sports bag. And so another blue Range Rover with a dead occupant was put on a police transporter. It was taken to Essex for the murder to be investigated there. Despite appeals from the police, neither the bag nor its contents has ever been recovered, and John's killer has not been brought to justice. Jack Whomes and Mick Steele certainly weren't responsible – they were in police custody at the time of the murder. Could it have been the syndicate recovering their money?

An empty Head sports bag was found in the Range Rover at Rettendon. The police considered it to be of no significance. It was never tested for traces of drugs or other evidence. The police have always denied there was any link between the murders. If there wasn't, why would Essex police investigate a murder committed in Kent or London?

On 24 February 1997, the second trial concerning Steve Packman and the death of Leah Betts got under way at Norwich Crown Court. The first trial had ended with the jury being unable to reach a verdict. The second trial yielded the same result, so the judge discharged the jury and a verdict of not guilty was entered. Detective Sergeant Derek Nickol had given evidence at the trial, during which he made a statement concerning Mark Murray. He said: 'We obviously had sufficient evidence to obtain a warrant to search his house and arrest him. No drugs were found in his house and he was subsequently not charged.' No mention was made of the letter the police had returned to me. I am sure Detective Sergeant Nickol wasn't aware of that fact, or he wouldn't have made such a statement. When questioned about me, the detective said: 'In the early stages of the Leah enquiry, there was information which led police to suspect Mr O'Mahoney might also have been involved in drug dealing at Raquels.' But he said: 'Further enquiries failed to reveal any evidence of that, and charges were never brought.' I was never officially interviewed as a suspect in the Leah Betts enquiry. What exactly the 'further enquiries' the detective referred to were, I shall never know.

When Mick Steele and Jack Whomes came to trial, there was a dispute about the number of shots fired at the victims. There was a dispute about whether or not a spent cartridge was missing from the murder scene and there was a dispute about the cartridges the police did recover. The officers disagreed on where one particular shotgun cartridge was found. Despite hundreds of photographs being taken, there is not one of a cartridge Detective Constable Bettis claims he recovered from the Range Rover's footwell. He said it might have accidentally been kicked into the position in which he found it. So, with police officers playing football with the evidence amongst the carnage, is it beyond comprehension that a live shotgun cartridge was dropped or mislaid by the killer and then overlooked by the police?

We shall never know where the one I found came from, because it was ignored by the police when it came to light. Was this because it bore my fingerprints, the principal witness in their high-profile forthcoming Leah Betts trial? This, despite the fact that I was a suspect in the Rettendon killings?

The Honourable Mr Justice Anthony Hidden told the jury at the Rettendon trial that they should treat with 'great caution' the evidence of Darren Nicholls. 'I need hardly stress the importance of Nicholls's evidence. So much hinges on what he said. Nicholls is a convicted criminal who was engaged in drug abuse and the importation of drugs into this country. You must bear in mind it was in his own interest to become a prosecution witness. Knowing he will have to come back to court for sentence, he hopes to get less time to serve.'

The jury deliberated for four and a half days, at the end of which Mick Steele and Jack Whomes were convicted of importing cannabis and murdering Tucker, Tate and Rolfe.

The news came on the radio as I was driving home. I couldn't believe what I was hearing. I pulled over and tuned in to another station. Surely I had misheard it. I couldn't believe that the jury had accepted what a man like Nicholls had said. The story he had told just was not right. Even though the dead men had once been my closest friends, I felt no anger and no desire for revenge against Steele and Whomes. Nobody can ever convince me that they are guilty. There are too many unanswered questions and too many obvious falsehoods.

Epilogue

MY STORY WILL NOT BE MUSIC TO THE EARS OF MANY. THE police asked me to tell the truth, but it could only be the 'required' truth. The whole truth was far too messy.

The misery, pain and death I have witnessed during the reign of our firm has left me in no doubt that I need to return to normality, whatever the cost. Images of my friends and associates who litter the graveyards and prisons of Essex, whose lives are ruined or lost, will haunt me forever.

I have left Essex in the hope my passage will be made easier. I will not be missed. Somebody will have filled my shoes and the posts left vacant by my friends. I am not a drug dealer, never have been. I was a vital cog in the machine that allowed the drug dealers to ply their trade. I know how they work, I know what they fear. I know that current efforts to combat the problem are failing. Far too much rubbish has been talked about drugs since the death of Leah Betts. 'Experts' say kids need educating, so they can make an informed choice. Then, in the next breath, they say nobody knows the long-term effects of ecstasy.

Thousands of young girls like Leah Betts go to nightclubs, but they are no longer pestered by a spotty kid for a dance around her handbag. They are pestered to experiment with speed, ecstasy or cocaine. Looking around the room, they see lots of others using drugs, they see chill-out areas, St John's Ambulance men, paramedics and, in some instances, doctors: all on standby for the benefit of those who have taken drugs. It gives the impression that taking drugs is a legitimate practice. The pressure to conform is immense. If the current attitude to the problem is maintained, tearful press conferences given by grieving parents will become so common they will no longer be newsworthy. And when dead kids are no longer news, we will all have reached rock bottom.

During Steve Packman's trial I was portrayed as a vicious thug with no morals. Packman said that I had threatened to 'burn down his house and break his legs'. His friend Stephen Smith said he was 'more scared of me than Mike Tyson'. It was not a pretty picture they painted, but little in the drugs world is pretty. There is no decency, and there are no morals; even the criminal code is redundant. That goes for everybody involved in it, including the police, who looked Leah's parents in the eye and promised to do all they could to bring to justice those responsible for ultimately causing their daughter's death. While the teenager lay stricken on her deathbed, they handed the main suspects a damning letter which could have led to them being prosecuted. I was the person who wrote that letter, I was the person to whom the police returned the letter. No questions were asked. I am the person they subpoenaed to court to play my part in their case. I told the truth, but it had to be their truth, nothing more, nothing less.

Listening to the police say they had no evidence against Mark Murray made me feel physically sick. Their words troubled me throughout the trial. They trouble me still. I have no doubt they would have gone on troubling me for ever. That is why I have to speak out.

The very same people are responsible for gathering the evidence that led to the conviction of Jack Whomes and Mick Steele, the two men who are said to have brutally murdered my friends. I do not believe they did, simply because I know much of the evidence which might have proved their innocence has been lost, or like the letter in the Leah Betts case, ignored. The defence in both cases didn't have the opportunity to consider the full facts. The police decided what they could and should not see. Whomes and Steele were not even told about the shotgun cartridge I had found.

I have no doubt I will be attacked for my revelations. They will have to justify their failings somehow. But I believe that the two men in jail are innocent.

Whatever consequences I suffer it will be a price worth paying. Following the judge's decision to discharge the jury and enter a verdict of not guilty, Steve Packman walked free from court, his name cleared, an innocent man. I had stated throughout the trial that he was not a drug dealer and shouldn't have been in the dock. There are others, however, who should have been. I had to smile when I heard the verdict. After enduring so much turmoil when trying to decide whether I should give up my way of life and tell the truth, the jurors good and true didn't believe me. Was this our man-made law at work, or was it justice? Probably the latter.

Mick Steele and Jack Whomes were convicted of importing cannabis and murdering Tucker, Tate and Rolfe. They were given three life sentences with a recommendation that they serve at least 15 years. Darren Nicholls walked free after serving 15 months for his one-man crime wave. No doubt this was yet another reward for his 'public-spiritedness'. I find it disturbing that the serious allegations concerning police corruption made by Nicholls were never proven. I have no doubt he was lying and the detectives are innocent, otherwise they would no longer be serving in the police force. Allegations concerning Steele and Whomes and the Rettendon murders made in the same breath were believed without question by the murder squad detectives, and this despite the fact Nicholls provided detectives with numerous motives for the murders and contradicted many of the details he gave. During the many interviews he had with the police, Nicholls clearly had trouble remembering the details of a night nobody could forget had they been present. Nicholls told detectives, 'I've fucked the story up again', 'I'm gonna say things wrong or remember them later', 'I'm hoping you'll remind me of things I can't remember' and 'I'll get it in the right order soon'. Nicholls is a self-confessed liar, a self-confessed drug smuggler and a man who admits he has previously set out to frame people for crimes they did not commit.

Mick Steele and Jack Whomes were led to the cells still protesting their innocence. Was this our man-made law at work or was it justice? Sadly, I think it was the former.

Detective Superintendent Ivan Dibley, who led the Rettendon murder enquiry before his retirement, said after the trial that he was convinced the cannabis which was dropped in the lake near Rettendon had something to do with the case. Pat Tate was still in prison when it was dropped and it didn't figure in Darren Nicholls's account of the murders. It does in mine. DS Dibley didn't explain why he was so convinced, and nobody bothered to ask him. I hope that now those questions will be asked, and the truth about what happened down that farm track that awful night will come out.

This book is dedicated to the victims of our reign,
to absent friends and loved ones

Leah Betts, *aged 18*
Andrea Bouzis, *aged 19*
Kevin Jones, *aged 20, all poisoned by ecstasy supplied by the firm*

Bernie Burns *(murdered – strangled)*
Danny Marlow *(murdered – hit and run)*
Kevin Whitaker *(murdered – drug overdose)*
Dave Anderson *(murdered – stabbed)*
Darren Pearman *(murdered – stabbed)*
Francis Martin *(murdered – shot)*
John Marshall *(murdered – shot)*
Tony Tucker *(murdered – shot)*
Pat Tate *(murdered – shot)*
Craig Rolfe *(murdered – shot)*
Chris Lombard *(murdered – shot)*

Jack Whomes
Mick Steele, *both serving life imprisonment*